THE SAN SABÁ MISSION
Spanish Pivot in Texas

THE SAN SABÁ MISSION
Spanish Pivot in Texas

By Robert S. Weddle

Drawings by Mary Nabers Prewit

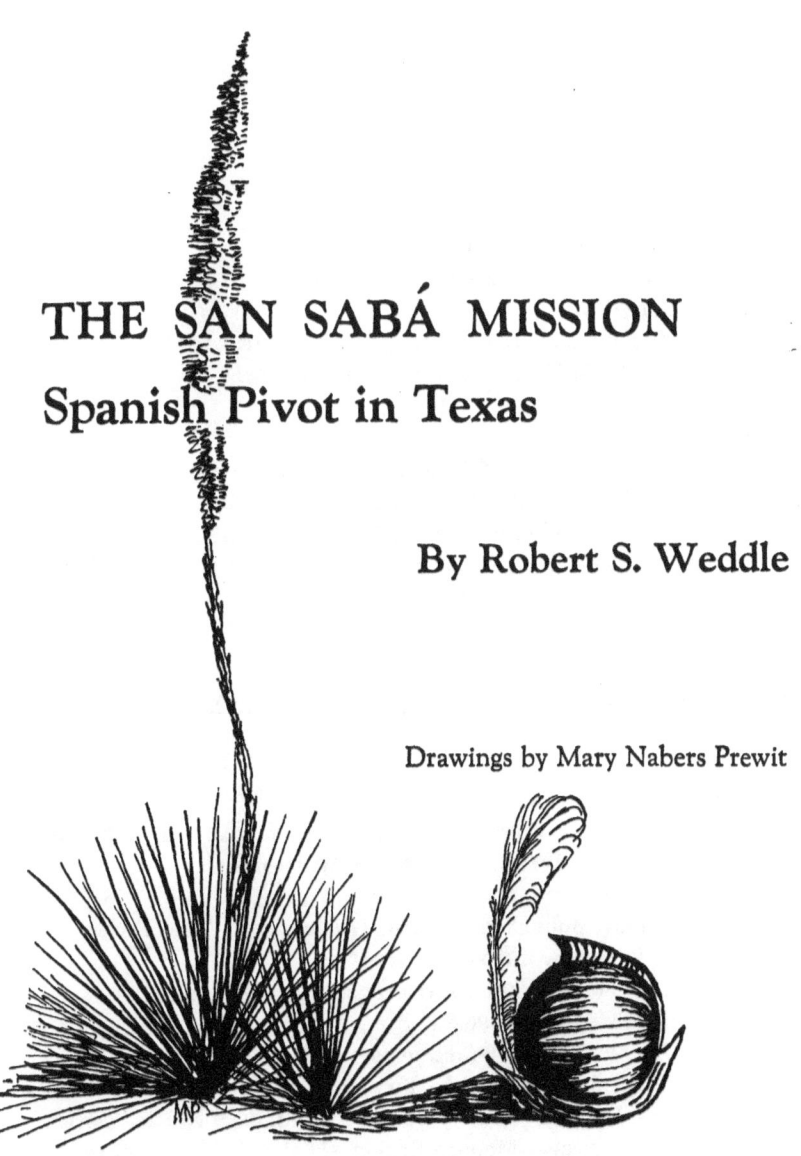

TEXAS A&M UNIVERSITY PRESS
College Station

Copyright © 1999 by Robert S. Weddle
Manufactured in the United States of America
All rights reserved
Originally published by University of Texas Press, 1964
First Texas A&M University Press edition, 1999

The paper used in this book meets the minimum requirements
of the American National Standard for Permanence
of Paper for Printed Library Materials, Z39.48-1984.
Binding materials have been chosen for durability.

Library of Congress Cataloging-in-Publication Data

Weddle, Robert S.
　　The San Sabá Mission : Spanish pivot in Texas / by Robert S.
Weddle. —1st Texas A&M University Press ed.
　　　p.　cm.
　　Originally published : Austin : University of Texas Press,
c1964. With new introd.
　　Includes bibliographical references (p.　) and index.
　　ISBN 13: 978-0-89096-911-3
　　ISBN 0-89096-911-6 (alk. paper)
　　1. San Sabá Mission—History.　2. Spaniards—Texas—Menard
Region—History—18th century.　3. Indians of North America—
Missions—Texas—Menard Region—History—18th century.　4. Land
settlement—Texas—History—18th century.　5. Texas—History—
To 1846.　6. Menard Region (Tex.)—History—18th century.　I. Title.
F394.S27W43　1999
976.4'68—dc21　　　　　　　　　　　　　　　　　　　　　　　99-38278
　　　　　　　　　　　　　　　　　　　　　　　　　　　　　　　CIP

*To Tim and Teresa
with fondest love*

Contents

Acknowledgments ix
Introduction to the New Edition xi

PART I: A PLAN CONCEIVED
    The Many Threads 3
    Instrument of Peace 17
    Winds of Change 25
    A Common Tie 30
    A Plan Evolved 36
    Pilgrims' Journey 42

PART II: LIFE OF THE MISSION
    A Mission Founded 53
    Storm Clouds 61
    Crown of Martyrdom 72
    Escape 79
    Scene of Death 85
    Frontier Terror 90

PART III: THE CHANGED FRONTIER
    Banner Borne by Pride 101
    The Great Mistrust 111
    Mission of Vengeance 118
    Aftermath of Failure 129

PART IV: THE RETREAT
    The New Commander 147
    New Apache Missions 156
    The Inspector General 167
    The Pivot 176

PART V: THE SPANISH LEGACY
    Forsaken Land 187
    Return to San Sabá 195

BIBLIOGRAPHY 213
INDEX 219

List of Maps

1. Spanish Texas in Eighteenth Century 4
2. Routes of Mendoza (1683–1684) and Bustillo y Ceballos (1732) 14
3. Region of San Sabá (Menard County, Texas) . . 74
4. Expeditions from San Sabá 152

Acknowledgments

This work does not represent an attempt to re-do that which has been done so capably by a number of eminent historians, but to build upon it. The author is indebted, therefore, to those listed in the Bibliography.

Many persons have helped, in many ways, and it is not possible to acknowledge all. Mrs. Clarence Wiseman of Menard, for invaluable assistance in translation, and my wife, Avis, for encouragement and forbearance, have earned special thanks. I am greatly indebted also to Mary Nabers Prewit of Pecos for the illustrations and to G. L. Rogers of Junction for preparing the maps.

Dr. Nettie Lee Benson of the Latin American Collection and Chester V. Kielman, archivist, University of Texas Library, and Mrs. Marie Berry of the San Antonio Public Library were especially helpful in the search for material. Dr. H. Bailey Carroll of the University of Texas Department of History helped bring the story into focus.

Often remembered with appreciation during the preparation of this work were Mrs. Eunice Gates, who taught me Spanish, and Dr. Ernest Wallace, who taught me Mexican history, both at Texas Technological College, and T. E. Anderson, who first challenged my interest in history at Bonham High School.

Acknowledgment is also due Mrs. Irene Marschall King and Hal Cunningham of Llano, W. E. Syers of Ingram, Miss Susan Miles of San Angelo, Hons C. Richards of Eagle Pass, and the Reverend Father Fidelis Albrecht, O.F.M., of Cincinnati, Ohio. The Menard friends who have loaned or given me material and contributed various forms of assistance include Mrs. John A. Powell, Clifford Rude, Perry Hartgraves, William F. Volkmann, W. C. Godfrey, Mrs. Kate Bradford, Mrs. Mary Alice Murray, W. M. Lewis, the late Levi Wilkerson and the late Mrs. Winnie Neel, and all the ladies of Menard Library Club, sponsor of Menard Public Library.

And certainly worthy of mention is the late Henry Reeve, whose untiring efforts for many years kept interest in the Spanish settlement at Menard alive and resulted in the organization of a Menard County Historical Society.

There are many others who have contributed in various ways. All are appreciated, though the space limitation demands that they go unrecognized.

Introduction to the New Edition

Two distinctly different personalities with divergent aims drove events of the San Sabá Mission episode that unfolded near present-day Menard, Texas, two and one-half centuries ago. On the one hand was Fray Alonso Giraldo de Terreros, president of the Mission Santa Cruz de San Sabá, who fervently desired the eastern Apaches' conversion and stood ready to receive the "crown of martyrdom" in the process. On the other was Colonel Diego Ortiz Parrilla, captain of Presidio de San Luis de las Amarillas, experienced in Indian warfare as in conflict with religious leaders for whose safety he was responsible.

On March 16, 1758—less than a year after the founding of Mission Santa Cruz de San Sabá—the mission president and another Franciscan friar, José de Santiesteban, won the crown of martyrdom, despite the colonel's best efforts to prevent it. The nascent mission, which never achieved its purpose, was destroyed by an attacking horde of two thousand enemies of the Apaches. Ortiz Parrilla was left to pick up the pieces. From these events arose the "Spanish pivot"—a turning point of the Spaniards' approach to the Great Plains.

For the Spaniards, the 1758 mission massacre signaled altered circumstances on New Spain's northern frontier. The attacking force comprised a native alliance that included elements of the plains Comanches, the Caddoan confederacies of eastern Texas and western Louisiana, and many tribes inhabiting the intervening territory. This Indian coalition, in combination with the failure of Ortiz Parrilla's military campaign to punish the offending natives, gave notice of change. At the Taovayas' (Wichita) fortified village on the Red River, he faced a superior Indian force, armed with French guns and mounted on stolen Spanish horses. Thereafter, the San Sabá garrison endured years of sacrifice to ransom Spanish pride. At last the presidio was abandoned with the realization that this was only an imaginary frontier, a lonely island in a sea of Indian hostility.

When my family and I arrived in Menard in 1956 as the new owners of the town's newspaper, the mission site was not known. The replica of the presidio, built as a Texas Centennial project and rapidly crumbling, was generally referred to as "the old mission," and it was not unusual to find mention of this early Spanish settlement as having been located at the town of San Saba, seventy miles away.

The San Sabá Mission: Spanish Pivot in Texas—whatever else might be said of it—has been a catalyst for change; but the active agents were those who struggled against meager resources and uncertain funding to carry on the quest for the mission site, which has now been found and proved archaeologically. At the presidio, an interpretive display has been added to increase understanding of this vital chapter of Texas' colonial past. A comprehensive plan for permanent preservation and interpretation of both sites has not yet materialized, but it now stands a better chance.

The year 1964 was a propitious time for the San Sabá story to be published. Two years previously the Texas Historical Survey Committee (now Texas Historical Commission) had launched the Official Texas Historical Marker Program, with former Texas Attorney General John Ben Shepperd as its driving force. Local survey committees soon were combing all 254 counties to identify historic sites for preservation and marking.

Shepperd's vision ranged far; he had the ability to take meager talents and encourage them to great contributions. It was at his invitation that I spoke in late 1964 to the Permian Basin Historical Society in Odessa. I may have mentioned in my presentation an idea being put forth by the Texas Old Missions and Forts Restoration Association (of which I was then president) for a mission trail patterned after California's. Shepperd, with his contacts inside the state government and across Texas, was to steer the plan toward creation of the present-day network of trails to guide motorists to varied points of interest, both natural and historical. It was he who involved me in several steps along the way: as a member of a committee convened by Governor John Connally to chart the course of the state's historical preservation efforts; in touring with the Texas Legislature's Forts and Missions Study Committee; and as a witness at that study committee's hearings. Several recommendations from both those committees were implemented, resulting in programs that are still functioning.

The study committee's report to the 60th Legislature recommended "that the State of Texas should begin a program of acquisition, development, and preservation of sites that are representative of the various phases and periods of Texas history." Multiple state agencies were to be involved. Some specific recommendations for funding were made, but San Sabá was not included. The replica of Presidio de San Luis de las Amarillas, completed in 1937, lay in ruins on a golf course, the road to the country club cutting through the compound. The site of Mission Santa Cruz de San Sabá, some distance down the San Saba River, remained unknown; it had been so since P. H. Hockensmith

Introduction

ran his plow through it in the 1880s or 1890s and turned up a human skull and pieces of old weaponry. The record flood of 1899 swept over the site, driving the Hockensmith family from their home. Half a century later, the Hockensmiths and the land they had tilled were all but forgotten.

In 1967 the State Building Commission, parent agency of Shepperd's Historical Survey Committee, contracted with Southern Methodist University for a study "to determine the reconstruction potential and present status" of the presidio and the location of the mission. The project was carried out by archaeologists Dessamae Lorraine and Kathleen Gilmore. Thus began the search that was to span almost three decades.

In 1972 the presidio was entered on the National Register of Historic Places. In response to a resolution passed by the 63rd Legislature in April, 1973, the Texas Parks and Wildlife Department made a feasibility report on "restoring and maintaining" the presidio and the mission. In part because the mission site was unknown and partly because the Spanish colonial period is represented in other state-owned sites, the report gave the matter a low priority.

The quest for the mission site, never an undertaking to be accomplished at a single stroke, has involved several institutions, as well as individuals of diverse talents, methods, and perspectives. The most comprehensive effort was conducted in 1990 for the Center for Historic Resources of Texas A&M University. It identified fourteen "potential" sites for the mission, including the Hockensmith place—now owned by Otis and Dionitia Lyckman—but failed to determine the mission site.

Mark Wolf and Kay Hindes took the search one step further. By means of aerial remote sensing, they located several promising anomalies, then enlisted the aid of Texas Tech archaeologist Grant Hall and his Archaeological Field School. Field testing during the summer of 1993 failed to locate the mission site. In early September, however, Hall, Hindes, and Mark and Kim Wolf returned to test another anomaly on the Lyckman property. Finding it freshly plowed, they were able to collect Spanish colonial pottery shards consistent with the eighteenth-century Spanish mission, as well as pieces of fired daub suggesting the chinking of log *jacales* remnants of the fire that destroyed the mission in 1758.

Two grants supported a ground-penetrating radar survey and (in January, 1994) further site investigation for unequivocal proof of the mission site. Another dig the following May disclosed additional posthole molds. Although the site is in a field that has been cultivated for more than a century, traces of shallow features such as wall trenches remained. Artifacts recovered—a religious medallion, glass and stone beads, nails, and fired musketballs—are consistent with other Spanish sites, as well as with proven aspects of the mission's history.

Hall returned to the site in May, 1997, with his Archaeological Field School. The south wall of the compound was established along the fence next to Ranch Road 2092. Indications of the chapel and traces of the north and west walls of the enclosure also were found. The graves of the two priests and other victims of the massacre have not been located. Further work at the site, needed to find the deeper features and determine the full extent of the mission complex, were to await additional funding.

As San Sabá was a turning point for the Spaniards, so was it for me. *The San Sabá Mission: Spanish Pivot in Texas*, first published thirty-five years ago, set my life on an entirely different course. When the opportunity to work in the archives of Spain came my way some years later, I was able to visit the ancestral village of Fray Alonso Giraldo de Terreros and his wealthy cousin, Pedro Romero de Terreros, who subsidized the San Sabá Mission. My companion for the bus trip from Seville was Edith Couturier, a fellow researcher in the Archive of the Indies, whose interest was Romero de Terreros and his philanthropies. At Cortegana (Huelva) in the Church of the Holy Savior, we viewed the baptismal records of both Fray Alonso, dated June 29, 1699, and Don Pedro, Count of Regla. On the front exterior wall we read a plaque that pays tribute to the native son of the parish and his martyrdom in the Apache mission on the San Saba River: "With his blood he sowed the seeds of religion and culture in Texas."

In 1999 a kinsman of the Franciscan friar and descendant of the count was serving as cultural affairs minister of the Spanish Embassy in Washington, D.C. In May, Juan Romero de Terreros and his wife, Carmen Fuente, and Dr. Couturier visited the rediscovered site of Mission Santa Cruz de San Sabá. The site was explained by Mark Wolf of San Antonio, himself a descendant of one of the Spanish soldiers on duty at the mission on the fateful day of March 16, 1758. The San Sabá Mission and its history still serves as a link between Spain and Texas.

PART I
A Plan Conceived

The Many Threads

In 1725 an aged Franciscan priest, veteran of the East Texas missions, looked with pain upon the ravages of the bellicose Apaches on mission settlements along the San Antonio River. Father Francisco Hidalgo was as much grieved by the behavior of his own people as by that of the Apaches. It was the practice of the Spaniards to answer these Indian raids with retaliation, taking captives and selling them as slaves. This policy had failed utterly to deter the Eastern (Lipan) Apaches from their attacks. Father Hidalgo believed that the answer was to establish missions for the Apaches. Effective Christianity, he knew, would change their ways, and he felt that making Christians of these Indians was entirely within the realm of possibility.

Father Hidalgo's sincerity is hardly open to question. He offered to go alone into the land of the Lipan Apaches to teach them the Gospel. But even though he was willing to risk his life for this cause, the authorities denied his request. A short time later this venerable old missionary, who had offered himself for martyrdom, died of natural causes. But he had sparked an idea that was to grow until the Mission Santa Cruz de San Sabá became a reality.[1] With each passing year it became increasingly apparent that the Spaniards must take measures to stop the Apache raids.

If the situation had changed by 1732, it was only for the worse. But that year brought developments which spoke of progress

[1] C. E. Castañeda, *Our Catholic Heritage in Texas*, III, 339–340.

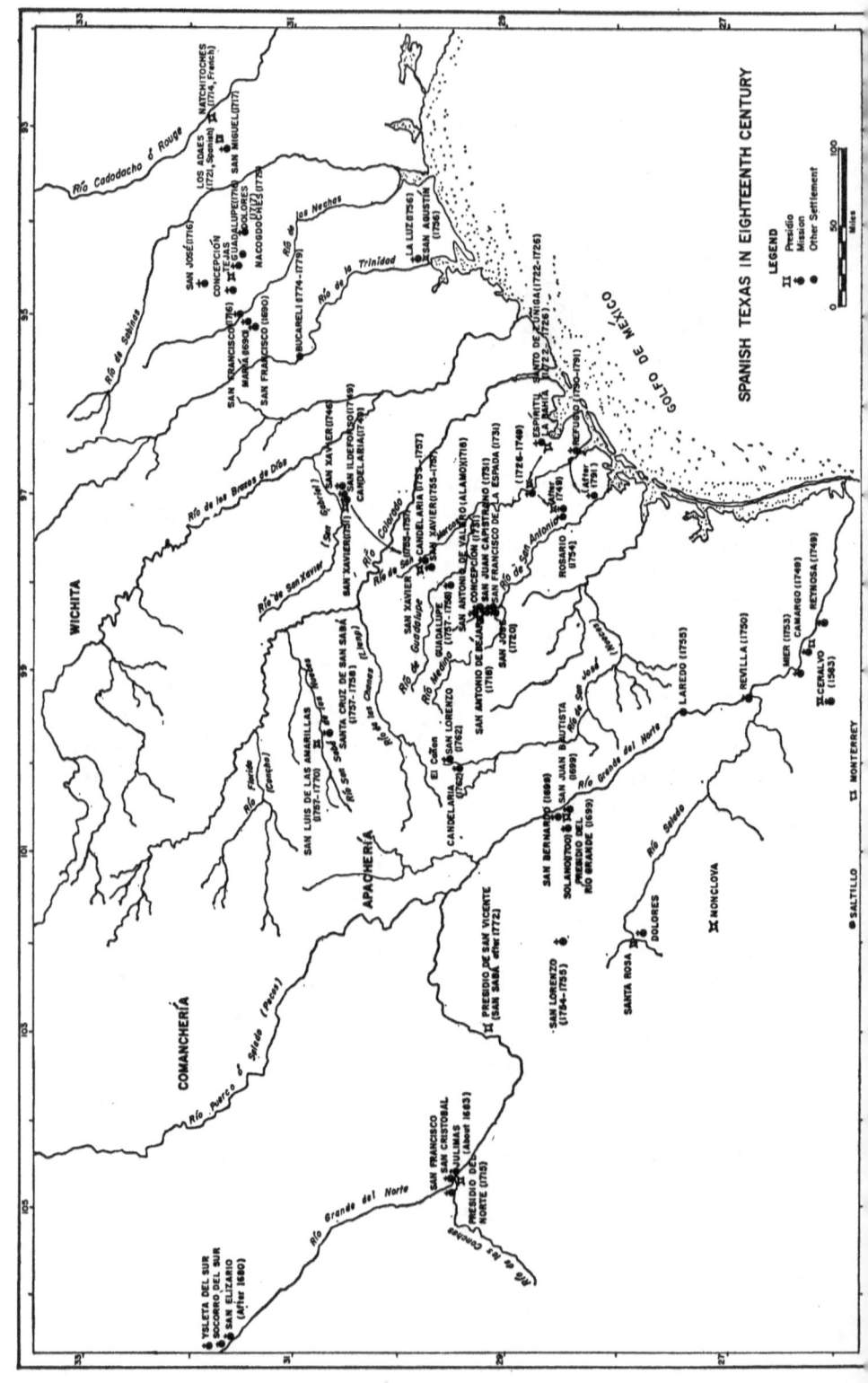

The Many Threads

toward dealing with the Apache menace. Though these developments appear superficially to have marked a trend in the opposite direction, they were important in the evolution of the San Sabá Mission. The year marked the first military campaign against the Apaches deep within their own territory. Incidental to the expedition was the discovery of the river on which the Mission was to be planted.

Trouble with the Apaches and the Franciscan missionaries' vision of ending the trouble by making them Christians were by no means the only considerations in establishment of the Mission. Spain's pride, her desire to expand her empire, and her attempts to defend the vast domain she already possessed were to be equally important.

It was two hundred forty years now since the Italian weaver's son whose rightful name was Christoforo Colombo had dropped anchor off Watling's Island in the Bahamas and claimed for Spain a whole new continent of indefinite proportions. During those two hundred forty years Spain had known glory such as she had never known before, and has never known since. She had gained the initial advantage of discovery, then moved out more swiftly and vigorously than did the French or the English to capitalize on it.

Columbus, through his discovery, had opened a veritable Pandora's box. Evils of lust and greed fluttered out. What started as a unilateral discovery quickly grew into a Hydra-headed contest. France and England wanted a share of the prize. Spain knew of no way to keep them from getting it. The question was, How much?

Now, in this year of 1732, the question still had no answer. The year by itself was to provide none. But like the first bud of springtime, or the first fluttering leaf in autumn, it spoke of the future.

If officials of New Spain in 1732 took a backward look at these two hundred forty years, they surely did so with pride, mingled with bitterness. Hernán Cortés, in conquering the Aztecs, 1519–1521, had found undreamed-of riches.

Shortly afterward occurred the nine-year trek across the wild land from southeastern Texas to the Pacific by Cabeza de Vaca. His secondhand stories of rich cities sent Francisco Vásquez de Coronado marching northward in 1540 with visions of winning for himself a prize to emulate that of Cortés. Although Coronado did not find his cities of gold, he did open the way into the upper valley of the Río Grande. Other *conquistadores* ventured north and founded settlements in New Mexico.

Hernando de Soto, meanwhile, had marched from Florida across the southern United States to eastern Texas in an expedition which speaks eloquently of the suffering and the hardship on which the Spanish conquest was built.

By 1574 some two hundred Spanish cities and towns were to be found in North America with a population of 160,000 Spaniards. Schools had been established for the Indians of México. While the Spaniards robbed the Indians of their independence and wealth, they offered them in return their Christian religion and a place in their society.[2]

England had watched with envy as Spain enriched herself with gold and silver from the New World. The English Sea Dogs began to raid the gold-laden galleons, seizing enormous plunder. The Spanish Armada struck back at the English fleet but was severely beaten. A storm completed the destruction of the Armada.

Spain had lost her mastery of the seas. Pirates began intercepting the stream of treasure flowing from the West. As a result of the defeat of the Armada, Spain's American empire would know definite limitations. The continent was too vast, the frontier too long, to be held by a declining nation.

Both English and French now had established claims to the New World and were seeking to establish colonies.

The French moved down the middle of the continent, claiming by right of original exploration all the territory from Hudson's Bay to the Gulf and west to the Rocky Mountains. René Robert Cavelier, Sieur de La Salle, sailed down the Mississippi to the Gulf and claimed its valley for his king.

While the English colonists battled the forest, the Indians, and the French to gain a toehold on the Eastern seaboard, the French pressed upon the boundaries of New Spain. After a voyage to France, La Salle returned to the New World in 1685, bent on founding a colony at the mouth of the Mississippi. Through error his ships sailed past the delta and landed on the Texas coast.

From this first French penetration of Texas sprang new Spanish interest. It was the same kind of interest which, three quarters

[2] James Truslow Adams, *The Epic of America*, p. 19.

The Many Threads 7

of a century later, brought the Spaniards to the San Sabá River to found a presidio and a mission.

Spanish missionary activity among the Indians of the Southwest started with Friar Juan Padilla, who accompanied Coronado's expedition and remained in the wilderness to convert the savages. He died a martyr to the cause of Christianity. Priests accompanied other expeditions up the Río Grande, and a string of mission settlements arose in New Mexico.

In 1680 the Indians of the upper Río Grande Valley of New Mexico revolted against the Spaniards and drove them from the province. The refugees settled on Texas soil in the vicinity of present El Paso. Missions soon were established here also. These were the first Texas missions, though they were apart from what generally is considered as the Texas mission movement.

To these settlements in 1683 came Texas Indians of the Jumano tribe, asking the Spaniards to found a mission in the Texas hinterlands. Captain Juan Domínguez de Mendoza led an expedition, accompanied by Friar Nicolás López. He marched from the Río Grande into the Edwards Plateau region and made camp at a place called San Clemente. It was believed for years that the site of San Clemente was on the Colorado River fifteen miles southeast of Ballinger, but a recent study offers the South Llano River a few miles southwest of Junction as being more likely.[3] Both locations are in the same general region as the San Sabá Mission, established seventy-three years later.

Mendoza and Father López returned to El Paso six months from the start of their journey, full of enthusiasm for a mission in the region they had visited. Then they went on to Mexico City to attempt to persuade the viceroy, the Marqués de la Laguna, whom they told of having seen a French flag among the Indians on the Pecos.[4] For the first time the argument of a French threat was being used to induce the Viceroy to authorize a new mission at a particular site in Texas. The argument was to be heard many times again.

[3] See J. W. Williams, "New Conclusions on the Route of Mendoza, 1683–84," in *West Texas Historical Association Year Book*, Vol. 38 (October, 1962), pp. 111–134.
[4] Paul Horgan, *Great River: The Rio Grande in North American History*, pp. 300–301.

But the Viceroy already had knowledge of the movements of the French. From a French corsair captured off the coast of Yucatán, he had learned of La Salle's plan to establish a colony on the Gulf. The threat was developing in eastern Texas, not western. And it mattered not that La Salle reached Texas shores through error; the fact was that his colony was designed not only as a means of controlling the Mississippi Valley and the northern Gulf shore, but also as a base of attack upon Spanish treasure fleets and México itself.

Between 1685 and 1689 the Spaniards searched by land and sea for La Salle's colony. In 1689 a land expedition led by Captain Alonso de León, accompanied by Father Damian Massanet, found Fort Saint Louis. Already its threat had been removed by disease and the murderous Karankawa Indians.

Prompted by fear of further French encroachment, the viceregal government of New Spain approved a plan for establishing a settlement among the Tejas Indians (Hasinai Confederacy). The first East Texas mission, San Francisco de los Tejas, was founded in the spring of 1690 in what is now Houston County, near the town of Weches. A second, called Santísimo Nombre de María, was built a few months later.

The new missions were beset by many problems. Fear of the French abated, and, as Spain needed to conserve her resources where possible, she abandoned the missions in August, 1693.

Below the Río Grande the French were temporarily forgotten, though the Texas Indians were not. In 1682—the year La Salle first sailed down the Mississippi—steps had been taken by the Franciscan order to send trained specialists into the mission field, beginning a movement which was to reach out to the banks of the San Sabá River.

Established that year in México was the Colegio de la Santa Cruz (Holy Cross) de Querétaro, where Franciscans who wished to spread the faith among the Indians of New Spain could prepare themselves for this Herculean task. Two other mission colleges were founded from the first one: Nuestra Señora de Guadalupe de Zacatecas and San Fernando de Méjico. Priests from all three seminaries helped to carry the missionary effort into Texas.[5] The time to start was nigh.

The pleasant forgetting of the French ended abruptly when the

[5] Castañeda, *Our Catholic Heritage*, III, 18–21.

The Many Threads

French trader, Louis Juchereau de Saint Denis, appeared suddenly at the Spanish settlement of San Juan Bautista on the Río Grande (near present Eagle Pass, at Villa de Guerrero, Coahuila). Having established a settlement on the Red River at Natchitoches, Louisiana, in 1714, Saint Denis had crossed Texas to seek a trade agreement with the Spaniards. His appearance and his proposal for trade so alarmed the Viceroy that he ordered an expedition to East Texas to build new settlements as a barrier to westward movement by the French.

The Mission San Francisco de los Neches was established a few miles from old San Francisco de los Tejas. Missions Nuestra Señora de los Dolores, Nuestra Señora de la Purísima Concepción, and San José de los Nazonis were founded in eastern Texas. San Miguel de los Linares was located east of the Sabine in Louisiana, just eight leagues from the French settlement of Natchitoches.

Unlike the first East Texas missions, these looked like a serious attempt to colonize the region. There was a big difference also in the attitude of the French. The first time the Spaniards had found the French threat already abated, but now the French were well established and stood in threatening posture on the threshold of Spanish territory. There could be no turning back for the Spaniards.

Some five thousand Indians lived near the new missions. The task of the Spanish priests and soldiers was to convert them and win their allegiance so they might be used in any future conflict with the French. Such a conflict was a very real possibility.

In 1718 a Frenchman named Bienville founded New Orleans. That same year the viceroy of New Spain in Mexico City recognized the need to extend the occupation of Texas and to strengthen the missions already in existence. The missions were far from any base of supplies, unconnected by any line of forts or settlements with the frontier presidios of northern México. To remedy this, Mission San Antonio de Valero and Presidio de San Antonio de Béjar were founded on the San Antonio River. Thus the beginning of the present city of San Antonio was made.

Amid continual rumors of French hostility and aggressive aims, a small band of Frenchmen attacked a Spanish lay brother and a soldier in June, 1719, at Mission San Miguel, east of the Sabine. The inhabitants of the eastern Spanish settlements panicked and soon withdrew to San Antonio, leaving the missions abandoned until 1721.[6]

Founding of Mission San Antonio de Valero was followed, meantime, by establishment of Mission San José de Aguayo. Several years later three of the East Texas missions were removed from their original sites and re-established at San Antonio. The Villa de San Fernando grew near the missions and the presidio.

Near Mission San Miguel de Linares, Presidio de Los Adaes was established in 1721–1722, in the vicinity of present Robeline, Louisiana. This was the Spanish capital of Texas until the seat of government was moved to San Antonio in 1772.

Meanwhile, a new force appeared on the Texas frontier: the sanguinary and cannibalistic Apaches, impelled southward by their enemies, the Comanches. The Tejas tribes, which the Spaniards had early befriended, were enemies of the Eastern, or Lipan, Apaches, as were most other tribes. The Apaches were resentful, and probably fearful, of this new alliance between the Tejas and the Spaniards, and consequently began a deadly harassment of Spanish settlements. The Spaniards, with little knowledge of the intertribal feelings of the Texas Indians, then sought peace with the Apaches and heard proposals to establish missions for them.

But standing between two hostile Indian tribes could only lead to disaster; the Spaniards were caught in the longstanding enmities among the various Indian tribes. Thus their effort to colonize Texas moved toward a climax, which was the massacre at the Mission San Sabá.

Pushing inevitably toward this climax was a chain of events which had begun with the early settlement of New Mexico, bringing into play a threat which paled the French to insignificance. Since the coming of the Spaniards to the New World, great cultural changes had taken place in the native populations. These changes stemmed from the Spaniards themselves, for the Spaniards had brought horses.

The impact of the horse on the lives of Indians of the Southwest and on colonization and civilization of the American continent is incalculable. Before the coming of the horse, these Indians had

---

[6] Horgan, *Great River*, pp. 336–337.

The Many Threads

trudged on foot for centuries, but with the horse they rapidly advanced their capabilities for hunting and warfare.

In 1598 Don Juan de Oñate had brought to New Mexico several thousand animals, including three hundred mares and colts. A few years later, after the establishment of the capital of the province at Santa Fé and after the conquest of the Pueblo Indians, the Spaniards developed trade with natives living to the north and the east. Indians were employed to care for horses in the Spanish settlements, and soon these Indians were returning to their native haunts with both horses and horsemanship.[7] With the horse the red man was able to hold back the white, but he also hastened the doom of his own civilization.

To compete in hunting and warfare, Indians without horses had to obtain them by raiding Spanish settlements or other Indian tribes.

The horse, which did so much to make possible the Spanish conquest of the New World, also worked to limit Spain's expansion. With the new capabilities in the hands of the Indians, both the Spaniards and the French were to encounter a formidable enemy. The Indians' new implements—horses stolen from the Spaniards and firearms provided by the French—mixed with the Spaniards' naiveté in Indian affairs, were the prime ingredients of the San Sabá massacre.

Competition for the bison intensified as the Indians became more adept in hunting. Because of the increased mobility of the Indians, the South Plains hunting ground became a coveted prize for the warlike tribes. Early in the eighteenth century a decisive conflict arose between the Eastern Apaches, the earlier inhabitants of the Texas Plains, and the Comanches. The Comanches, who previously had inhabited the mountain regions of Colorado and Wyoming, pushed southward to drive the Apaches from their native land.

The Wichita tribes, now obtaining French firearms as well as Spanish horses, also pressed against the Eastern Apaches, becoming more belligerent in their war of long standing. Indeed all the neighbors of the Apaches had become their enemies. The Comanches encroached upon them from the north, the Spaniards

---

[7] W. W. Newcomb, Jr., *The Indians of Texas*, p. 86; see Newcomb, Chapter 4, for an account of the Plains Indians' transition "From Foot to Horse."

from the south, the Wichitas and other tribes from the east. The Apaches were caught in a three-way squeeze. Their backs were to the wall in the struggle to hold their own land against many aggressors.

Provoked by the Spaniards' founding of missions for their enemies, the Apaches moved southward to sweep through Bandera Pass and raid San Antonio, or across the Río Grande to attack Spanish settlements in northern México, always stealing as many horses as they could.

During this time the Franciscan priests at San Antonio, growing weary of Apache depredations, proposed missions for this wily tribe. Father Francisco Hidalgo, one of the original nineteen missionaries who had come from Spain to found the missionary College of Querétaro, came forth in 1725 with his proposal to end the Apache raids with the Christian Gospel. But his plan was not approved.

The three East Texas missions were moved to San Antonio in 1731. During that same year fifteen Canary Island families were brought to San Antonio to further the colonization effort of New Spain. These events seemed to arouse the ire of the bellicose Apaches even more, for they attacked with renewed vigor. They drove off the livestock, harassed the mission Indians, and killed many settlers, often mutilating the bodies of their victims.

After Father Hidalgo, other missionaries of San Antonio were equally appalled at the soldiers' practice of making slaves of Apache captives and of vindicating one killing with another. Three successive presidents of the San Antonio missions pressed for a change in policy which would end the brutality on both sides. Each proposed missions among the Apaches, to stop their raids and to make Christians of them.

But such a radical change required time.

The settlement along the San Antonio River, thanks to the Apaches, rubbed elbows with disaster on several occasions. Possibly it was saved from annihilation only because the Apaches, too, were hard-pressed and could not afford to lose a large number of warriors. They still had only bows and arrows, while the Spaniards had firearms.

Nevertheless, they kept the settlers at San Antonio on edge; the military leaders at Presidio de San Antonio de Béjar insisted that the Indians must be punished. The first punitive expedition

The Many Threads

of note came in 1732, portending the change that was to influence the founding of the San Sabá Mission. Before the end of 1745 the Spaniards made two more expeditions, pursuing the Apaches into their own land. At least two of these expeditions reached the San Sabá River near the future site of the Apache mission.

In this significant year of 1732 the governor of Texas, Don Juan Antonio Bustillo y Ceballos, led 157 Spaniards and 60 mission Indians in a raid on the Apaches on the San Sabá, probably near the eastern edge of present Menard County. The priest who accompanied the force was Father Gabriel Vergara, president of the San Antonio missions, who had succeeded Father Hidalgo as the chief advocate of missions among the Apaches.

Bustillo's force, with fifty pack loads of supplies and nine hundred horses and mules, trekked many miles out of its way to the San Xavier (San Gabriel) River, near the locations where the San Xavier missions later were established. Bustillo had been informed he could pick up a reinforcement of Tejas Indians on the San Xavier, but the Indians did not come, possibly because they had been discouraged by the French.

Early on the morning of Tuesday, December 5, Bustillo came to the San Sabá River. He is credited with its discovery, though it is quite likely that Mendoza had crossed the stream in 1684. On learning that the Indians called the river Las Nueces, he named it El Río San Sabá de las Nueces, honoring the holy abbot, Saint Sabbás, whose special day it was.[8] The force continued up the river until scouts reported an Apache village had been sighted.

At dawn on December 9, after creeping up on the Apache camp during the night, Bustillo, with one hundred handpicked men, attacked. Having received absolution from Father Vergara, the force charged across the San Sabá River to meet seven hundred warriors of four Apache tribes.

The Apaches, defending themselves in their own land, fought

[8] C. W. Hackett and Charmion Shelby (trans.), *Pichardo's Treatise on the Limits of Louisiana and Texas*, II, 98–99. Saint Sabbás, a native of Cappadocia, in Asia Minor, lived from 439 to 532 and was abbot of the monastery near Jerusalem that now bears his name, say Hackett and Shelby in a footnote, citing *The Catholic Encyclopedia*, XIII, 286. Thus it appears that Z. T. Fulmore (*The History and Geography of Texas as Told in County Names*, p. 25) is in error in his thesis that the River was named for Holy Saturday (*San Sábado*), though Bustillo's battle with the Apaches was fought on Saturday.

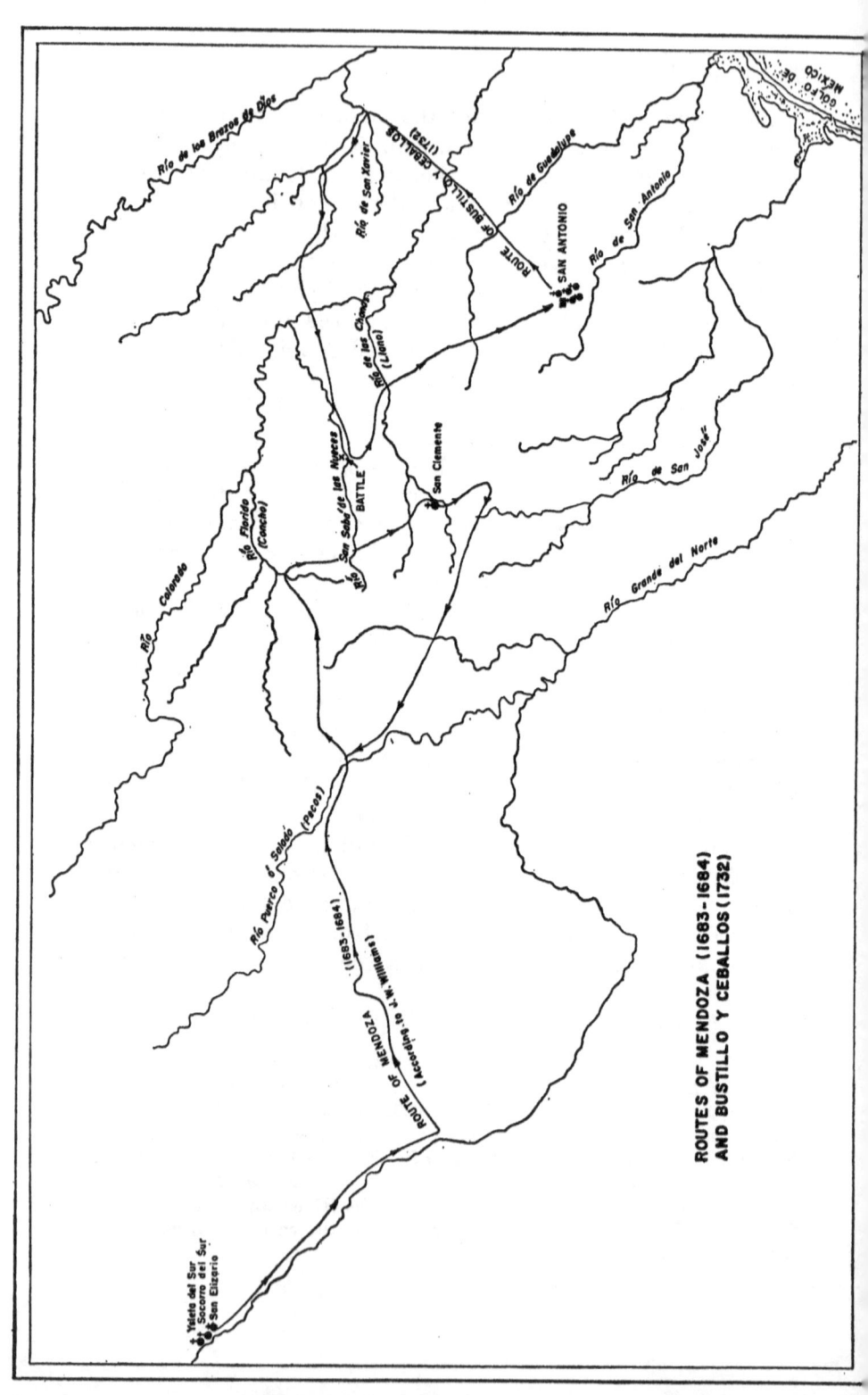

The Many Threads

hard. They waited for the Spaniards to fire, then closed in before their attackers could reload their muskets. But still the Indians' bows and arrows were no match for firearms. After a four-hour battle, they withdrew to the hills, leaving behind a large number of dead.

Bonilla says two hundred Indians were slain, but the exact number of Indian casualties could not be determined; as the Apaches fell, their fellow warriors dragged their bodies into the swollen river. Seven Spaniards fell wounded, and one of them died a few days later. The Spaniards took thirty Indian women and children prisoners and captured seven hundred horses and one hundred mule loads of pelts and other plunder.[9]

Following this campaign numerous citizens of San Antonio, headed by Father Vergara, again pressed for a change in policy toward the Indians, hoping to reach a settlement with them. The peace effort was successful for only a short time because the advantages of such an arrangement were not yet apparent to the Apaches, who soon manifested their animosity anew.

The Apaches raided San Antonio relentlessly from 1736 to 1739, killing several soldiers and settlers. Captain José de Urrutia of Presidio de San Antonio de Béjar pushed for the new campaign against the Indians. In the winter of 1739 his force marched from San Antonio for the San Sabá.

The expedition had met strong opposition from Father Benito Fernández de Santa Ana, Father Vergara's successor as president of the San Antonio missions, and as the advocate of a change in policy toward the Apaches. But the priest failed to stop the expedition.

Urrutia's men discovered Bandera Pass, through which the Apaches made their forays. After crossing the pass, they pressed on directly to the San Sabá River country, where they surprised an Indian camp and seized a large number of captives. Urrutia apparently took the shortest possible route to the place where the town of Menard now stands, near the ruins of Presidio de San Luis de las Amarillas, and returned the same way.

Father Santa Ana and the other missionaries of San Antonio were incensed at the continued enslavement of Apache captives,

---

[9] Castañeda, *Our Catholic Heritage*, III, 39–41; Antonio Bonilla, "A brief compendium of the history of Texas, 1772," translated by Elizabeth H. West in *Southwestern Historical Quarterly*, Vol. 8, p. 41.

but the military ignored them. Toribio de Urrutia, who had succeeded his father as captain of Presidio de San Antonio de Béjar on his death in 1740, moved against the Apaches in 1745. Father Santa Ana went along on this expedition, which also may have reached the San Sabá, though the exact location of the battle is unknown. The Spaniards surprised a village of Lipans and Natages and, with many warriors away, they rounded up a large number of captives. Says Dunn, "Indeed there is reason to suspect that this was little more than a slave-hunting expedition." [10]

Father Santa Ana's bitterness against such punitive expeditions cut deep into his soul. While the padres mourned the bloodshed, however, these campaigns served a more constructive purpose. The Spaniards were becoming familiar with the unsettled area northwest of San Antonio, and their new knowledge was to be a factor in winning establishment of Mission Santa Cruz de San Sabá.[11]

[10] W. E. Dunn, "Apache Relations in Texas, 1718–1750," *SWHQ*, Vol. 14, pp. 251–252.

[11] Name of the mission frequently is given erroneously as "San Sabá de la Santa Cruz." The name is "Santa Cruz de San Sabá," as verified by letters of Father Alonso Giraldo de Terreros in A.M.S.F. Both the river and the general locality of the Mission and the Presidio were called San Sabá (note accent), not to be confused with the present town and county of San Saba. I use the Spanish accent throughout to make this distinction.

Instrument of Peace

Lord, make me an instrument of Your peace.
Where there is hatred, let me sow love;
where there is injury, pardon; where there is
doubt, faith; where there is despair, hope;
where there is darkness, light; and where
there is sadness, joy.

O Divine Master, grant that I may not so much seek
to be consoled as to console; to be understood
as to understand; to be loved as to love; for
it is in giving that we receive; it is in pardoning that we are pardoned; and it is in dying
that we are born to eternal life.

Saint Francis of Assisi

In seeking to understand, rather than to be understood, Father Benito Fernández de Santa Ana understood much. In seeking to love, rather than to be loved, he found within himself the capacity, even, to love the vengeful Apaches. By his own choosing, he was an instrument of peace and not of war; he sought to be a brother of the savage, and not his conqueror, to bring to the Indian the blessings of his own religious faith, and not to slaughter him or to make him a captive slave.

Though years of official procrastination intervened, the Mission Santa Cruz de San Sabá and the Presidio de San Luis de las Amarillas finally came into being, the products of the love and the understanding of Father Santa Ana, the son of Saint Francis.

Because the vision of mortal man is finite, however, this new mission led not to peace but to more bloodshed and strife.

After Father Hidalgo's demise Father Vergara had become the chief sponsor of a conciliatory policy toward the Apaches. He had witnessed the slaughter of the Indians by Bustillo's men—to whom he had given absolution—and he now urged that the prisoners taken on the San Sabá River be employed as instruments for making a peace treaty.

He believed that the Apaches were the major deterrent to the unqualified success of the missions; if they could be subdued with missions, the missions could have peace. The distrust of the Apaches themselves doomed his good intentions to failure.

As a result of Father Vergara's efforts, the Apaches entered into a brief period of peaceful trading with the San Antonio settlers. But in March, 1733, two soldiers were slain a short distance from the fort by a band of Apaches, who stripped the flesh from the bones of their victims. The peaceful intentions of Father Vergara, like those of Father Hidalgo before him, went for naught.

Following Captain José de Urrutia's campaign in 1739, Father Santa Ana urged that military expeditions against the Apaches be stopped. "Neither God nor King gains anything," he vowed, "while the hatred of the Indians is increased, and the peace of the province . . . is becoming more disturbed. . . . Since the purpose [of plundering and taking captives] is so vile, so is the outcome." [1]

Unlike the military men from Presidio de San Antonio de Béjar, Father Santa Ana sought to understand the Apaches. He also sought to understand the attitude of the soldiers and the viceroy, Conde de Revilla Gigedo. Consequently he was able to present to the Viceroy in 1743 a petition that seemed to make sense. But the mills of government grind slowly—

His study of the Apaches told him that their old enemies, the Comanches, were pressing hard against them; perhaps they would welcome the Spaniards as allies. His knowledge of the Viceroy's problems told him that the activities of the French as they moved westward up the Río Cadodacho, which the Frenchmen called "Red," were being viewed apprehensively by the government of New Spain.

[1] C. E. Castañeda, *Our Catholic Heritage*, III, 41–43. This work is the principal source on the steps leading up to the founding of the San Sabá Mission treated in this chapter.

He sagely pointed out to the Viceroy that not a single Spanish settlement was to be found north of a line from San Juan Bautista on the Río Grande to San Antonio to Los Adaes, east of the Sabine. This vast region could be taken by either the French or the English, and the Spaniards stood in danger of being left with only a little triangle along the Gulf of Mexico. It was important, said Father Santa Ana, that the region to the northwest of San Antonio be explored and occupied by the Spaniards.

And here, at least, the Viceroy surely conceded the logic of the priest's reasoning. Shortly after he received Father Santa Ana's petition, the French and the English were fighting again over their colonial claims, in a conflict known as King George's War. Sooner or later, one of these powers would overcome the other, and circumstance favored the English.

Father Santa Ana's understanding of the military problem led him to point out to the Viceroy that a presidio in Apache country would relieve the garrison at San Antonio of continued attacks. The mineral resources of the new region would become available for the enrichment of the Spanish treasury, he suggested.

He did not forget another consideration that to him was of prime importance: the large number of souls to be saved.

This appeal was made in 1743. In 1745, when San Antonio verged on destruction by the vengeful Apaches, now enraged by Urrutia's enslavement of many of their people, Father Santa Ana's friendly policy saved the settlement.

During the siege an Apache captive from the missions fled to his people and informed the chief, whose daughter was held hostage by Father Santa Ana, that the captives were being treated kindly, and that the Spaniards wished to be friends with the Apaches. With this information the chief called off the attack. The first peace gesture from the Apaches followed.

Soon the Apaches came regularly to solicit the friendship of the Spaniards, these overtures undoubtedly prompted by their fear of the advancing Comanches as well as by Father Santa Ana's kindness. Apache chiefs and officials of the settlement together attended a "love feast" at San Antonio, November 28, 1749. Even Captain Urrutia, the veteran campaigner against the Indians, now proclaimed that the former enemy was sincere in its bid for peace. He released the Apache captives, and the peace treaty was consummated. The San Sabá Mission moved a little closer to reality.

Father Benito Fernández de Santa Ana had succeeded in sowing love where there had been hatred, pardon where there had been injury, faith where there had been doubt. And now, as a result, hope blossomed out of despair, and light out of darkness, though much darkness remained.

While Father Santa Ana served as the instrument of peace, the role of Father Mariano de los Dolores y Viana was that of the fiery brand. When Father Santa Ana was president of the Querétaran missions at San Antonio, Father Dolores was minister of Mission San Antonio de Valero. Though the two looked toward the same goal, they differed on the means of reaching it.

After the "love feast" the Apaches came to San Antonio in large bands. They proposed to camp there until a mission was founded for them. But the missions of San Antonio were not prepared to take them in, and establishing new missions elsewhere would be time-consuming. The missionaries feared the Apaches would not be disposed to wait; they might, in the meantime, make other alliances, and these would not be to the best interest of the Spaniards.

Father Dolores favored a mission for the Apaches on the Guadalupe. Father Santa Ana's plan called for missions on the Pedernales, and for moving the garrison of Presidio de San Antonio de Béjar to that location. The Viceroy's advisers referred the matter to the council of Villa de San Fernando (San Antonio).

Father Santa Ana's illness then forced his permanent retirement as president of the San Antonio missions. Father Dolores, named as his successor, presented a case to the San Fernando council, discrediting the Pedernales plan. But his argument defeated itself. The council opposed not only removal of the garrison from San Antonio but any plan whatever for founding a mission for the Apaches. If these Indians were interested in mission life, they said, let them come to San Antonio.

Both Father Dolores' Guadalupe plan and Father Santa Ana's Pedernales plan were the losers. The San Sabá Mission was shoved farther away. But Father Dolores refused to be defeated so easily.

The council, he informed Captain Urrutia, was refusing to face the facts; and the facts were that the Apaches had given repeated

Instrument of Peace

and unmistakable proof of their sincerity. They now brought their wares regularly to San Antonio to trade, and for more than a year they had committed no depredations. Many had lived voluntarily in the missions at San Antonio while waiting for a mission of their own. Some had even received the sacrament of baptism. As a token of good faith, a chief had returned six horses stolen by his braves from the San Xavier missions.

Father Dolores invited Captain Urrutia to conduct his own investigation. The captain did so, and had to admit the validity of the priest's argument. But conflicting reports continued to fall on the ears of the already distrustful officials in México. They floundered in the wallows of indecision.

Father Dolores was undaunted. He turned in June, 1751, to Governor Jacinto de Barrios y Jáuregui. In short, he asked the governor either to request the Viceroy's approval for missions in the Apaches' own country or to go himself to the Apaches and tell them they need harbor no hopes for such missions.

Governor Barrios held that the government of New Spain owed the Apaches nothing. They were, to his mind, fickle and treacherous. He recalled, for example, the 1749 murder of Father Francisco Xavier Silva, and the four soldiers and four civilians who accompanied him, between San Antonio and the Río Grande. Only the Apaches' fear of the Comanches, he maintained, drove them to seek the friendship of the Spaniards. What they really wanted was to have the guns of the Spanish soldiers on their side in the war with their enemies, the Comanches.

But Father Dolores had achieved a milepost. His letter to Barrios, and the Governor's written reply, went on to the Viceroy, who passed it to a subordinate for study. This lesser official suggested that the captain at San Antonio and Governor Barrios be asked to study the various proposals for Apache missions, to report on the feasibility of such a project, and to recommend suitable sites. The keystone had fallen into place.

There are three generally accepted reasons for placing the presidio and mission on the San Sabá River at this particular time.[2] Most often considered to be the primary reason is the desire of the Franciscan missionaries to spread Christianity among the Apaches, thereby ending depredations by this savage

[2] See W. E. Dunn, "Apache Relations in Texas," *SWHQ*, Vol. 14, pp. 198–274.

tribe. It is doubtful, however, that this reason merits the significance usually attached to it.

The padres, in attempting to influence the Viceroy to establish the mission, pointed to the large portion of Texas without a single Spanish settlement and warned that the French or the English might eventually claim this region if the Spaniards did not. Though the missionary aims of the priests were the moving force, the desire to extend the empire probably was the real reason the Viceroy eventually acceded to their urging. Already Spanish officials foresaw the possibility that the English might drive the French from the New World, then push on into Spanish territory.

The third reason usually given for the San Sabá project is the mistaken belief that valuable mineral deposits lay in the hills along the San Sabá River, though surely this reason did not merit serious consideration.

Pushing back the frontier and extending Spanish dominion appear to have been the primary goals. The San Sabá project was a significant part of an extensive movement by Spain to secure her hold in the New World. It is significant in history because it propelled the Spaniards into a new situation and hence marked their pivot in Texas. It is ironic that neither the English nor the French invaders, whom the Spaniards had feared, were chiefly responsible for the pivot, but invaders of another kind—the Plains Indians.

Undoubtedly Father Dolores, in his zeal for an Apache mission, received invaluable aid from the French themselves. In 1739 the Mallet brothers, with a party of eight or nine men, had made their way first to the Platte River and then to Santa Fé. They had succeeded in breaking through Comanche country and the Spanish frontier. They returned to New Orleans with the impression that the people of New Mexico were willing to trade, and that the Comanches were not an insurmountable barrier.

Thus encouraged, the French Governor Bienville sent a party led by Fabre de la Bruyère to open trade with Santa Fé by way of the Arkansas River. The band did not reach its destination, but a French post was established on the Missouri. About 1746 the French traders entered into a treaty with the Comanches and the Jumanos (probably Wichitas), and the trail to New Mexico was made safe. From 1748 to 1750 forty-five Frenchmen were reported among the Comanches near Taos. In 1752 Chapuis and Feuilli from Fort Chartres came to Santa Fé and brazenly proposed to open a regular trade route between Illinois and New Mexico.

The Spaniards were not alarmed at first. They permitted the Mallet party to return unimpeded. But when the French tide showed signs of becoming a flood the attitude changed. Fearing the consequences of a French-Comanche alliance, they sent the intruders as prisoners to México, and thence to Spain for trial.[3]

While establishment of an Apache mission in Texas met delays, a mission for the Texas Apaches was founded in México. The founder was Father Alonso Giraldo de Terreros, then president of the missions on the Río Grande, who was fated to die, a martyr to the cause of Christianizing the Apaches, at the Mission Santa Cruz de San Sabá. Father Terreros founded the Mission San Lorenzo near San Fernando de Austria in Coahuila, December 21, 1754. This mission was short-lived. Soon Father Terreros was called elsewhere; his successors were unable to hold the enthusiasm of the neophytes. The Mission came to an unhappy end October 4, 1755, when the Indians revolted, burned the buildings, and deserted.

In the eyes of some, this failure of a mission for the Apaches in Coahuila strengthened the argument for placing one in their own country. Dunn says it "led logically to the establishment on the San Sabá River."[4] But Father Santa Ana and Father Dolores had done the spadework, without suspecting that their efforts would be responsible for placing in the history of the Spanish missions in Texas a new chapter of tragedy.

The Apaches' quest for missions, in every case, was to endure only as long as it suited their convenience. And in every case this was just long enough to get the Spaniards into trouble.

This effect gave rise to bitterness on the part of the Spaniards, who branded the Apaches as faithless and despicable. It is doubtful that the Apaches understood the full implications of asking the Spaniards to establish missions among them; they surely did

[3] Castañeda, *Our Catholic Heritage*, IV, 57–58.
[4] W. E. Dunn, "Missionary Activity Among the Eastern Apaches," *SWHQ*, Vol. 15, p. 200.

not comprehend that they were committing themselves to an agreement which the Spaniards considered to be most binding.

In the Apache mind the request for missions probably was looked upon simply as the step, the gesture of friendship, necessary for forming an alliance with the Spaniards. With the Comanches and the Wichitas pressing on them from the north and east, and the Spaniards from the south, the Apaches realized the time had come for them to choose sides. They chose the Spaniards. That they did so with reservations seems hardly surprising, for the Spaniards were the intruders in the Apaches' land.

The Spaniards' bitterness against the Apaches is reflected by Morfi, who says that, had the Spaniards not "befriended" the Apaches, the missions founded for the Indian nations of the north might have been successful. In Morfi's view the Apaches had from time immemorial made themselves despicable to all those around them, hated by all the tribes for their cruelty.[5] When the white man, who had suffered but little of their total savagery, allied himself with the Apaches, the Indian nations of the north could take this bond only as an act of hostility.

But now, to the country where the Spanish soldiers once had gone to kill and capture the Apaches, they returned to explore and to look for mission sites.

[5] Juan Agustín Morfi, *History of Texas, 1736-1779* (translated by C. E. Castañeda), II, 376.

Winds of Change

From Mexico City to San Antonio in April, 1752, came orders for exploration of Apache country. This was a year of tragedy for the Spanish settlements in Texas, and it was the following year before the orders could be executed. In June, 1753, Lieutenant Juan Galván of Presidio de San Antonio de Béjar mounted an expedition to explore the land of the Apache, known as Apachería.

Father Mariano de los Dolores had gone to the badly troubled missions on the San Xavier (San Gabriel) River. The problems which plagued these missions made it inadvisable for him to go on the expedition. He sent Father Miguel de Aranda of Mission Concepción instead.

With only a few men from Presidio de Béjar, Galván and Father Aranda explored the Pedernales River country, then the Llano River region, without finding a desirable location. Then on the San Sabá Galván found what he was looking for: an abundance of water and an alluvial plain with good arable land. Beneath a horseshoe bluff that rises on one side of the river, Galván erected a large wooden cross to mark the chosen site for the proposed missions and for the presidio where he himself was to serve.

The Galván party found a number of Apaches at the River, and the Indians gave them a hearty welcome. Soon other Indians gathered. Each kissed the hand of the missionary, vowing to join the mission when it was established. A religious service was held at the foot of the cross, and the Indians took part.

A convincing report came out of the Galván expedition. Though the military officer signed it, there is some speculation that the real author was Father Aranda, working under the supervision of Father Dolores. It told of indications of rich mineral deposits in the hills along the San Sabá and of the likelihood that a substantial number of Apaches would come to the future mission. The report recommended that a large garrison be stationed at the new location, to keep the Apaches in line and to ward off attacks by Comanches. New Mexico was not far distant, the report continued, and communication with this province should be greatly facilitated by the new mission; but this was an unfortunate, though understandable, mix-up in geography.

With the Apaches reduced to mission life, the report set out, the soldiers stationed at San Antonio no longer would be needed there. These soldiers, plus a few from each of the other presidios, could be used to man the new presidio on the San Sabá.[1]

When the report reached Mexico City, Father Santa Ana was consulted. He gave the San Sabá plan his support. Yet the Viceroy's staff was not satisfied. The objections of Governor Barrios still haunted the practical-minded officials. They ordered Don Pedro de Rábago y Terán, former governor of Coahuila and now the new commander of Presidio de San Xavier, to investigate further.

The orders reached Rábago y Terán at San Xavier November 30, 1754. He went to San Antonio and left from there December 23, accompanied by Father José López and twenty-five men. The route varied slightly from that taken by Galván, with the direction generally the same. Rábago's men, after observing mass on Christmas morning, ran into a snowstorm. But they marched on, and, as they explored the Pedernales and Llano regions, their findings paralleled those of Galván.

The morning of December 30 dawned cold and still, with a thick layer of frost glistening on the countryside. The caravan angled more to the northwest, passing between two towering hills, which they called "Puerto de Baluartes," and soon came upon the San Sabá River near present Menard. They made camp near the cross erected by Galván, and Rábago named the site Paso de la Santa Cruz (Holy Cross Ford).

On the return trip the Rábago expedition met two bands of Apaches, both of which received the news of the proposed mission happily and promised to enter it when it was established. This

---

[1] C. E. Castañeda, *Our Catholic Heritage*, III, 360–363.

encouragement was rewarded with liberal gifts—in which the Indians were interested indeed—and the Spaniards and the Apaches parted amid vows of everlasting friendship.

In San Antonio, Rábago y Terán found new support from the San Fernando villagers for the proposed Apache missions. Those who a short time before had protested the very idea now admitted freely that the Apaches had kept the peace for five years. They advocated missions among them as the means to lasting peace. Captain Urrutia lent his voice to this appraisal, estimating there were four thousand Apaches to be missionized.[2]

Rábago y Terán, in his report written after his return to San Xavier, supported the findings of Lieutenant Galván. He suggested a solid fort of stone and mortar be constructed, with four curtains, defended by two guns each, adding that the commander should be a man of experience and proven integrity. He likely envisioned himself as that man, for Dunn suggests his report was not altogether objective. "Wishing to retain his command," Dunn says, "Pedro de Rábago probably saw in the Apache mission project a chance to prevent his company [at San Xavier] from being mustered out."[3] And clearly, time was running short for the ill-fated San Xavier project.

But still another expedition was to be made into Apachería. Both Galván and Rábago, on returning from their excursions to the San Sabá River, mentioned the indications of rich mineral deposits. Perhaps these reports were written in all honesty. Yet they might have been made with the hope of inducing settlement of the wild country of the Apache. Whatever lay behind the reports, no sooner had they been submitted than several of the more adventurous settlers of San Antonio set out in search of these silver deposits.

Governor Barrios, the doubting Thomas in matters of missions among the Apaches, seems to have thought the reports worth investigating. He sent Bernardo de Miranda, the lieutenant governor, to explore the Llano River region for mineral deposits. Miranda, with twelve soldiers, an Indian interpreter, and five citizens, left San Antonio February 17, 1756.

Near Honey Creek in Llano County he found Cerro del Almagre—a hill of red hematite or red ocher—where his men, spurred

[2] *Ibid.*, pp. 369–376.
[3] W. E. Dunn, "The Apache Mission," *SWHQ*, Vol. 17, p. 384.

by dreams of easy wealth, quickly dug a shallow shaft or found a cave from which they gathered samples of ore. While the men took the ore samples, Miranda explored Honey Creek down to the Llano, which he followed to its juncture with the Colorado River. The party started back to San Antonio March 4. On the Guadalupe, Miranda met a group of Apaches, and the chief told him of rich silver deposits to be found six days' journey above the Llano, in Comanche country, describing it as a mountain of pure silver.

This seems like a rather obvious attempt by the Apaches to play the Spaniards off against their enemies, the Comanches, and doubtless the story of the mountain of silver had no other basis. It appears to parallel the stories of the cities of gold told to the gullible Coronado in an effort to lure his troops onto the Great Plains, where the Indians believed they would perish.

In his report to Governor Barrios, Miranda declared the Cerro del Almagre mines were so numerous that he could guarantee a claim to each inhabitant of the entire province of Texas. The report and the ore samples were sent to the Viceroy. An assay was made, but the three-pound sample was much too small for the test to be conclusive.

Miranda and the citizens who had made mining claims then were asked to send at their own expense thirty mule loads of ore to Mazapíl, a Mexican mining town seven hundred miles from the purported mine. Miranda agreed to pay the cost himself, on condition that he be placed in command of a presidio at Los Almagres. The Viceroy agreed to this on November 23, 1757, more than twenty months after Miranda had made his find. Presidio de San Luis de las Amarillas and Mission Santa Cruz de San Sabá already had been established on the San Sabá River near Menard. Miranda, having been sent on an expedition to the missions in East Texas, never returned to extract his thirty *cargas* of ore from the rich mine he claimed to have discovered.

The reasons for Miranda's failure to open the mine and establish the presidio are not clear. But his report and his failure to pursue his advantage—if indeed he had an advantage to pursue—had an effect on the San Sabá establishment. Before the stockade of Presidio de San Luis was completed, its commander was asking permission to move his garrison to the Llano River region to work the Almagres Mine.[4]

[4] Castañeda, *Our Catholic Heritage*, III, 379–382.

Winds of Change

Miranda's report may have had an important effect also on the later settlement of the entire region, for it gave rise to some of the most phenomenal, though outlandish, legends Texas has ever known. Men who looked for the mines in later years fought the Indians, the wilderness, and each other. But after a German prince heard the rumors three quarters of a century later, his people came to settle the country.

Galván had first brought the omen of change to the San Sabá River country in 1753. A year later the winds of change wafted elsewhere. The curtain opened on the final act of the drama which determined the future course of North America. While officials in Mexico City were making plans for Don Pedro de Rábago y Terán to visit the San Sabá, the opening gun sounded in the French and Indian War. The French and the English were prepared to fight to a decision. Whichever side won, it meant trouble for Spain.

A Common Tie

It is remarkable how often throughout the history of Texas missions fear of French intrusion prompted the Spaniards to establish mission settlements. In 1722, for example, Presidio de La Bahía and Mission Nuestra Señora del Espíritu Santo de Zúñiga were founded at the site of old Fort Saint Louis. Twice moved, they finally were based on the San Antonio River near present Goliad in 1749.

This was just a year after the first of three missions was founded on the San Xavier River (now San Gabriel), near present Rockdale in Milam County. Here, too, the French influence was felt.

A common thread often links two missions, or a whole group of missions, and it frequently is difficult to dissect one mission from the group. In this case the thread runs from the San Xavier missions and presidio to those founded nine years later on the San Sabá River, and thence to the missions of El Cañon on the Nueces. It is necessary, therefore, to treat the San Xavier venture as a forerunner of the San Sabá Mission and Presidio.

The garrison of Presidio de San Xavier, after a temporary move to the San Marcos River, finally made up a part of the San Sabá garrison. The physical properties of the San Xavier missions were moved to the San Sabá Mission. The names of many of the priests and soldiers which appear in the San Xavier story appear also in the San Sabá adventure. But the relationship goes much farther.

The Indians gathered in the San Xavier missions had to be won

A Common Tie

away from the French, who had established trade relations with them. And, being enemies of the Apaches, they had to be protected from them. To accomplish these tasks the Spaniards necessarily employed a large guard of soldiers.

Years later, after the Mission San Sabá had been founded for the Apaches, members of the tribes dealt with at San Xavier, resentful of this alliance, came to the new mission on the San Sabá River. They assumed a guise of friendship, and the soldiers who had associated with them on an amicable basis at San Xavier were ready to believe them peaceful. Thus the savages, whose purposes were destruction and murder, gained admittance to the stockade.

The same man who directed Presidio de San Xavier de Gigedo also was to have command of Presidio de San Luis de las Amarillas. He was Captain Felipe de Rábago y Terán, who was intimately involved in the life—and the death—of both establishments. His violent misdeeds at San Xavier led to his removal as leader of that presidio, though eight years later his name was cleared. He was reinstated as commander of his garrison, which by then was part of the garrison of the presidio on the San Sabá. Castañeda says:

> Were one inclined to reflect on the consequences of a man's misconduct, Captain Felipe Rábago y Terán might be held responsible for a series of misfortunes that brought down upon the Spaniards the relentless enmity of the northern tribes, which resulted in the destruction of the Mission of San Sabá.... The failure of the San Xavier missions, as a consequence of his ill-advised conduct, caused the officials in Mexico to accede eventually to the removal of the original presidio to the San Saba River [to protect the Apache mission there]. To befriend [the Apaches] proved a serious error, which resulted almost in the loss of Spanish power in Texas.[1]

The string of far-flung outposts on the frontier of New Spain constituted a heavy drain on the Spanish treasury; the cost of colonization in Texas now was exceeding what it yielded in immediate returns. With these outposts strung across Texas from San Juan Bautista to Los Adaes—not to mention the extensive colonization effort elsewhere—the resources of the government of New Spain were spread thin. Regardless of how worthy a

[1] C. E. Castañeda, *Our Catholic Heritage*, IV, 99.

proposed new venture might appear, government officials were forced to take a sharp look before granting approval.

The reports of Juan Galván and Don Pedro de Rábago y Terán had upheld the feasibility of establishing a mission among the Apaches on the San Sabá. But it still remained for the officials to find a place from which they might recruit the large garrison deemed necessary to man the new presidio. This ultimately meant awaiting dissolution of the San Xavier missions and presidio.

For eight years the sons of Saint Francis labored to bring their religion to Indians, mostly of the Tonkawa family, gathered on the San Xavier River from a region which extended down the Trinity to the coast. For a time the little valley blossomed with activity. More than one thousand Indians received instruction from the padres. But then, plagued by a combination of tragic circumstances, this missionary effort languished and died. The mission buildings crumbled away, and the fields were reclaimed by the wilderness.

In the short life of the San Xavier missions is found a moving story of heroic devotion to duty, and of missionary zeal and fervor seldom surpassed. But curiously mixed into the story are dark human passions: lust and greed, hatred and cruelty.

Like the San Sabá project, the San Xavier mission proposal was discussed, investigated, and argued before finally being authorized. Approval for the establishment of three missions was granted in 1747, Fathers Santa Ana and Dolores having been the prime movers. Mission San Francisco Xavier de Horcasitas was established temporarily in 1746 and given permanent status in February, 1748. The missions of San Ildefonso and Nuestra Señora de la Candelaria followed.[2]

The missions met trouble from the start. Raiding Apaches drove away the mission Indians. Disputes arose between the missionaries and the antagonistic governor, Pedro del Barrio y Espriella. Before a permanent presidio was authorized, thirty soldiers with Lieutenant Juan Galván in charge were assigned to protect the missions. The soldiers only complicated the work of the priests, maltreating the neophytes, causing them to run away, or encouraging them to insubordination. Galván, who had won a reputation for being antagonistic toward the missionaries, failed

[2] H. E. Bolton, "The Founding of the Missions on the San Gabriel River, 1745–1749," *SWHQ*, Vol. 17, pp. 323–379.

A Common Tie

to discipline his men and sided with Governor Barrio in thwarting the mission effort. An epidemic of smallpox raged among the mission Indians in May, 1750, claiming forty lives.

Finally authorization for Presidio de San Xavier de Gigedo came through in 1751, and Captain Felipe de Rábago y Terán, later to head the presidio on the San Sabá, was named commander. No sooner had the Captain arrived than he began to berate the mission project, proposing to move it to the San Marcos River, reopening a controversy that had thrived for six years previously. But that was not the worst of Rábago y Terán.

While in San Antonio recruiting soldiers and settlers for San Xavier, he had had intimacies with the wife of Juan José Ceballos, a San Antonio citizen who had enlisted in his company. En route to San Xavier, Ceballos learned of the adulterous affair and protested to the Captain. Rábago, charging the man with threatening a superior officer, placed him in chains.

The situation festered. Father Miguel Pinilla of Mission Candelaria, who was serving as chaplain for the garrison, sought to end the affair but succeeded only in bringing Rábago's wrath down on Ceballos. The cuckolded husband eventually managed to escape and took refuge at Mission Candelaria. Rábago vindictively attempted to get Father Pinilla removed as chaplain.

The padres cringed at the effect of the scandal on the work of the missions. They tried in vain to make peace with Rábago, then wrote to the College of Querétaro, petitioning to be recalled. Father Dolores himself, who had been the moving spirit in the founding of the missions and the presidio, now asked the Viceroy to have the San Xavier Presidio removed, preferring to risk the depredations of hostile Indians rather than the excesses of the licentious Captain. If his request could not be granted, he implored, then the missionaries should be relieved of their work at San Xavier, for their usefulness had ceased.

Relations between the priests and Captain Rábago worsened steadily, as the Captain encouraged lasciviousness among his men by rewarding them for procuring his women. The neophytes found themselves deprived of their wives and daughters, who were made to serve the Captain in his lust. It was beyond the abilities of the padres to correct these abuses, and their work among the Indians was rendered impossible.

The trouble came to a head after the wife of a soldier named

Arucha told in her confessional of intimacies with Corporal Nicolás Carbajal, and shortly afterward the scandal became public. Carbajal accused Father Pinilla of violating the seal of the confessional and of defamation of character. Rábago issued an order prohibiting Father Pinilla from ministering as chaplain to the garrison and banishing him from the presidio.

Father Pinilla struck back with a decree of excommunication, which was delivered to the garrison by Father Juan José de Ganzábal. Most of the soldiers soon were penitent, however, and within a short time, all were granted absolution. But there was to be no lasting peace at the missions.

Abused by the soldiers and hard-pressed to understand the strained relations between the soldiers and the missionaries, the Coco Indians fled from Mission Candelaria May 1, 1752. Rábago saw in their flight the opportunity to perpetrate a heinous crime that could be imputed to them.

Ten days later Father Pinilla and Father Ganzábal were taking their evening meal with Juan José Ceballos. A shot rang out, and Ceballos fell from his chair. Father Ganzábal ran to the door, and, as he peered into the darkness, an arrow struck him in the heart.

A few days later, in San Antonio, an Indian named Andrés of the Sayopín nation, who had been living at San Xavier, admitted shooting the fatal arrow for the reward of a horse. He implicated four soldiers from the presidio. But Andrés soon retracted his confession, and the murders were blamed on the Cocos.[3]

Even so, Rábago faced a prolonged investigation. He was relieved of command, imprisoned in México for a time, and tried before various courts. Eight years passed before final disposition of his case. In the meantime he was assigned to take charge of the garrison of Presidio del Sacramento, in Coahuila.

The death knell had sounded for the ill-fated mission on the San Xavier. As if the hand of God had marked the spot in retribution of the sins committed there, the river ceased to flow, standing in stagnant pools. Most of the Indians had fled, and pestilence decimated the ranks of those who remained. Among the fatalities was Captain Miguel de la Garza Falcón, who had succeeded Felipe de Rábago y Terán as commander of the Presidio.

It took three years for the sufferers of San Xavier to get relief, and help came then only because Don Pedro de Rábago y Terán,

[3] Castañeda, *Our Catholic Heritage*, III, 241–338.

appointed to succeed Garza Falcón as captain of this presidio, was willing to risk official disapproval to alleviate the suffering. In order to keep the remaining Indians under the influence of the missions and to save the lives of the soldiers and missionaries, the uncle of Felipe de Rábago acted without orders in August, 1755, transferring the missions and the presidio to the San Marcos River, near the present town of San Marcos.

No sooner had the people settled in the new location than the friars—José López, Sebastián Flores, and Francisco Aparicio—petitioned Don Pedro to have the missions moved to the San Sabá. More than one thousand Apaches had come immediately to join the missions at San Marcos, and this large number could not be supported on this site, where irrigation was impractical and good agricultural lands were scarce.

The padres expressed willingness to go at once to the San Sabá, with or without a military guard, to establish a mission for the Apaches. Permission was denied, however, and the missions and the presidio remained at the San Marcos site more than a year, until November, 1756. The Apaches, whose mission desires were always just strong enough to keep the padres off balance, had left the missions long before that time.

By then the plan for a mission and presidio on the San Sabá already had been approved by officials in Mexico City. The San Xavier Presidio garrison was needed for this new venture, but the missions on the San Marcos could not be left unprotected. Moving them to San Antonio was contemplated. At this point, however, Father Mariano de los Dolores saw his long-awaited opportunity to get a mission established on the Guadalupe.

Father Dolores got the Mission San Francisco Xavier de Horcasitas re-established on the Guadalupe River some thirty miles from San Antonio, where it was deemed a presidio would not be necessary. The mission remained in operation at this site, near present New Braunfels, until March, 1758, with Father Miguel de Aranda and Father Francisco Aparicio instructing the Indian neophytes. Developments on the San Sabá River caused its abandonment.

A Plan Evolved

Spanish arms against the hostile Comanches, and therein lay the danger.[1]

Barrios, however, had already established his reputation as a dissenter by consistently opposing the project. His view got no consideration.

Dunn makes a significant footnote to the effect that in 1753 the French commandant at Natchitoches wrote to Barrios protesting plans of the Spaniards for establishing a presidio in Apache country. Barrios took occasion to put the French official in his place, though he himself was opposed to the project. He replied that since the Apaches were in the center of the province of Texas, and far removed from French jurisdiction, the matter could not possibly concern the French.[2]

The French had used such tactics before. In 1735 they had moved their settlement of Natchitoches from an island in the middle of the Red River to the river's west bank. The Spaniards raised a protest but failed to resist the move by force of arms. The French settlement remained on the west bank, in territory which the Spaniards considered to be theirs.

The Viceroy, in accordance with the recommendation of the *auditor*, referred the San Sabá project to the Junta, to meet February 27, 1756. In the meantime the Marqués de las Amarillas, for whom the new presidio was to be named, replaced Conde de Revilla Gigedo as viceroy, but the new viceroy did not interfere with the previously laid plans.

The council called for increasing the San Xavier garrison to one hundred men, twenty to be taken from San Antonio and the rest to be provided at the discretion of Viceroy Marqués de las Amarillas. The enlarged garrison was to be established on the San Sabá River. All property of the missions of San Xavier was to be transferred to the new site.

The new viceroy, on May 18, 1756, finally issued the decree putting into effect most of the recommendations of the council. Colonel Diego Ortiz Parrilla had been ordered the day before to succeed Don Pedro de Rábago y Terán as commander of the San Xavier Presidio. Don Pedro, who had become ill during the epidemic on the San Xavier River, had died several months previously.

[1] C. E. Castañeda, *Our Catholic Heritage*, III, 386–389.
[2] W. E. Dunn, "The Apache Mission," *SWHQ*, Vol. 17, p. 386.

A Plan Evolved

In the autumn of 1755, some thirty years after the aged Friar Francisco Hidalgo had offered to risk his life to go alone into Apache country to seek conversion of that tribe, action was taken in Mexico City toward establishing an Apache mission in Texas. On October 1 the *fiscal* reported favorably on the San Sabá project, which had been supported first by Juan Galván and then by Pedro de Rábago y Terán. The Viceroy, Conde de Revilla Gigedo, then referred the matter to the *auditor*, who raised some questions about how the proposed garrison of one hundred men was to be provided for San Sabá and suggested the plan be taken up by the Junta de Guerra y Hacienda.

At this point Texas Governor Jacinto de Barrios y Jáuregui uttered his final protest. He did not believe the Apaches when they promised to come and live in the proposed new mission, and he was supported in this disbelief by the Apaches' bloody history. The Governor was not opposed to converting the Indians, but he insisted that the practicality of such a project must be considered.

The most talked-of plan called for taking the San Xavier garrison and augmenting it with a sizeable number of soldiers from Presidio de Béjar to form the one-hundred-man garrison for San Sabá. But Barrios saw danger in reducing the San Antonio garrison. The accomplishments of the San Antonio missions might well be put to naught if the garrison were weakened. In the mind of the Governor, the Apaches merely wanted the protection of

Colonel Parrilla was ordered to remove the remaining neophytes of the San Xavier missions to San Antonio. He then was to leave immediately for the San Sabá, taking the San Xavier garrison of fifty men, plus twenty-two from San Antonio and twenty-seven recruits. He was to transfer all the property of the three missions of San Xavier to the new site, where he was to build a presidio and to establish three missions. Parrilla also received instructions covering enlistment of recruits. These instructions paralleled those given Felipe de Rábago y Terán for recruiting "men of good moral character" for the Presidio of San Xavier.[3]

Since it was not known within which jurisdiction the new site on the San Sabá River lay, Parrilla was to be subject directly to the viceroy until the question was settled. It was left unsettled for many years. In November, 1756, Governor Barrios held an investigation at Los Adaes, still the capital of Texas, to obtain testimony proving Texas' claim. This claim was based on the proximity of San Sabá to San Antonio, previous campaigns to that region, and priority rights in discovery and exploration. In 1765 the question was finally decided in Texas' favor.[4]

Just what challenge Parrilla saw in his new assignment on the San Sabá is left to the imagination. He actively sought the job. He was clearly a man of action, as shown later by his campaign from San Sabá against the northern tribes—and an egotist, as shown by his boastfulness and his efforts to excuse himself for all his mistakes. If he saw in the new assignment an opportunity to win glory for the Spanish Crown and to engrave the name Parrilla on the pages of history as well, he must have been disappointed.

Parrilla had enlisted as a soldier in Spain in 1734 and had served in Spain until 1740, when he was sent to Cuba to fight in the Almanza regiment against the English. A few years later he had been transferred to the garrison of Vera Cruz with the rank of captain of dragoons. Then in 1749 he was sent to Puebla to quell a native revolt. Shortly afterward he was appointed governor of Sinaloa and Sonora and was captain of Presidio de San Miguel de Horcasitas.[5]

At the time of the Pima rebellion in Sonora in 1751–1752, he

[3] "Instrucción que deberá observar el Coronel Dn. Diego Ortiz Parrilla," September 1, 1756, A.G.M., Historia, Vol. 95, pp. 181–188.
[4] Dunn, "The Apache Mission," *SWHQ*, Vol. 17, p. 386.
[5] Castañeda, *Our Catholic Heritage*, III, 391.

A Plan Evolved

became involved in a violent row with the Jesuit priests, which he was to recall with bitterness when the tenacity of the Franciscans at San Sabá put him in an unfavorable light.[6] He was promoted to the rank of colonel in 1755, when he probably was not much past forty years of age.

On the basis of this record he was chosen to carry out one of the most delicate and important missions of his time. The failure of the Mission San Sabá can hardly be attributed to his leadership. Like many good men, he was defeated by circumstance, having come at the wrong time to the wrong place, through no fault of his own.

Parrilla was but one of two strong personalities to be associated with the San Sabá project. While he was to command the garrison of Presidio de San Luis de las Amarillas, the efforts to convert the Apaches at the Mission Santa Cruz de San Sabá were to be directed by Father Alonso Giraldo de Terreros, whose career as a missionary rivaled that of Colonel Parrilla as a soldier. As is frequently the case with strong personalities, these two were to clash. It is difficult to determine if the clash materially affected the fate of the San Sabá project. And it is equally difficult to say that it did not.

Alonso Giraldo de Terreros was born June 19, 1699, at Cortegana, Huelva, in Spain, a province which furnished many missionaries to the Indian mission movement in New Spain. He received the sacrament of baptism in the parish church when he was ten days old. While he was yet a small child his parents took him to México. He prepared himself for missionary work at the College of Querétaro and entered the priesthood July 14, 1721, when he was twenty-two years old.[7]

Father Terreros worked among the Indians of East Texas and served as guardian of the College of Querétaro. Later he was sent to San Juan Bautista to serve as president of the missions on the Río Grande. Throughout New Spain he was known for his living faith and missionary zeal, his concern for his fellowman, and his desire to spread the Christian Gospel among the savages.

---

[6] Paul D. Nathan (trans.) and Lesley Byrd Simpson (ed.), *San Saba Papers*, p. 135.

[7] Isabel Flores de Lemus, *Un Gloria de Cortegana: el mártir, Fray Alonso Giraldo de Terreros*. Pamphlet printed in Spain and provided by Doña María Jesús Catilla de Terreros, Cortegana, Huelva, Spain.

When tragic difficulties pursued the San Xavier missions, the guardian of Querétaro called upon him to restore peace, as he had done at the missions on the Río Grande, though circumstances prevented his carrying out this assignment. He founded the Mission San Lorenzo in Coahuila for Texas Apaches in 1754, and though this mission was short-lived it doubtless had a bearing on Father Terreros' readiness to undertake conversion of the Apaches at the San Sabá Mission.

Having gone to Querétaro shortly after the founding of San Lorenzo Mission, Father Terreros had begun work on a plan for expanding activity among the Apaches. On April 29, 1756, he was summoned for a personal conference with the Viceroy. He reached Mexico City May 9 and learned that his cousin, Don Pedro Romero de Terreros, was considering sponsorship of missions for the Apaches on condition Friar Alonso would be placed in charge of the new conversions. The padre readily agreed to accept the directorship.[8]

The zealous friar went from his conference with the Viceroy to talk with his cousin. Together they ironed out some of the details of the plan. The padre suggested to his cousin that the new missions be founded for the Apaches and for the other tribes located to the north of San Juan Bautista. He also proposed that Don Pedro give four thousand pesos during the first year to each mission founded, paying the cost of as many as twenty missionaries. The stipend for the second year, he said, should be two thousand pesos for each mission, with fifteen hundred for the third.

Don Pedro Romero de Terreros had attained a position of high wealth and prominence since coming to New Spain. The Viceroy had conferred with him on the proposed development of Los Almagres Mine of Bernardo de Miranda, and it seems that the Viceroy consulted him frequently on other matters as well. Born in Spain, Don Pedro had been educated at the University of Salamanca. When he was called to New Spain by the unexpected death of his brother he decided to remain, possibly to take over management of his brother's properties. The decision paid off, for he amassed a considerable fortune from the mines of Santa Brígida and La Viscaína in Pachuca.

Don Pedro was not a miser. He believed in using his wealth to

[8] Castañeda, *Our Catholic Heritage*, III, 391.

A Plan Evolved

help those less fortunate than himself. Many charitable institutions benefited from his liberal contributions, and he was founder of the National Pawn Shop in México. As some present-day philanthropists have built libraries and endowed universities, he chose to support missions for the Apaches.

By July, 1756, formal details of the plan were worked out, and Don Pedro, in his name and that of his wife, pledged himself and his heirs to bear all the expenses incurred in founding of missions for the Apaches in Texas during a three-year period. After that the government would be responsible for their maintenance. Father Terreros was to be placed in charge, and the missionaries were to be selected alternately from the Colegio de la Santa Cruz de Querétaro and the Colegio de San Fernando de Méjico.

The military expenses were to be borne by the royal treasury. The mission property of the suppressed San Xavier missions was to be turned over to Friar Alonso, and Don Pedro was to pay for it a just price to be determined by qualified appraisers.[9]

Some years later, on September 23, 1768, Don Pedro Romero de Terreros was granted the title of Conde de Santa María de Regla by King Charles III in recognition of his services to the Crown and his support of the Apache missions in Texas.

The Terreros plan was developed independently of the San Sabá plan, but when the Viceroy's advisers received the Terreros proposal they recommended that the two be combined. Formal approval of the agreement was given August 20, 1756, and the Viceroy issued new instructions, merging the two plans and placing Friar Alonso at the head of the new missionary undertaking.

One part of the agreement to which Don Pedro Romero de Terreros affixed his signature seems, in the light of later developments, to have been somewhat prophetic:

> If on account of death, resignation or any other legitimate reason, Fray Alonso Giraldo de Terreros should cease to be the director of the new conversions, I still pledge myself to support this spiritual conquest, provided the missionary or missionaries appointed to succeed him in office meet with my approval.[10]

[9] *Ibid.*, pp. 391–393.
[10] Juan Agustín Morfi, *History of Texas*, II, 355.

Pilgrims' Journey

A Spanish mission like those planned for the Apaches on the San Sabá River was more than just a church in the wilderness. It usually included a group of small houses arranged on a square, where the mission Indians lived; carpenter, blacksmith, and tailor shops; looms, granary, and kilns; houses for soldiers assigned to protect the mission; and cemetery, garden, and orchard. These buildings generally were enclosed by a stockade wall with fortified gates. Outside the village, or mission, were irrigated fields, cultivated by the Indians, and beyond these were pastures for the mission livestock.

The mission's main purpose was to Christianize the Indian. Another important purpose was to teach him civilized customs and habits, to transform him from a savage into a useful citizen who would help to populate and to defend the vast regions to which Spain laid claim in the New World. The mission was designed to supplement the military outpost, or presidio, in holding and extending the Spanish dominion.

The task of the priests was to teach the Indians various trades —how to till the soil, to work the looms, and to make baskets or pottery—as well as to give them religious instruction. They also endeavored to teach the Indians to manage their own affairs, to form their own organization for local government, and to administer their own justice.

The presidios established near each mission or group of missions were responsible for protecting the settlements from hostile Indians and for holding the frontier against foreign aggressors. They furnished the mission a small guard of soldiers to help the priests instruct and discipline the neophytes in the faith. These establishments housed, in addition to the soldiers assigned to the presidios, women and children, the families of the soldiers.[1]

[1] C. E. Castañeda, *Our Catholic Heritage*, III, 27–30.

Hence, it is understandable that the job which lay before Parrilla, who was to command the presidio on the San Sabá, and the priests who were to found the mission, was a large one.

On September 1, 1756, Colonel Parrilla received detailed instructions for transferring the San Xavier garrison to the San Sabá River, and for increasing the garrison from fifty to one hundred men. He was instructed to make a thorough exploration of the country on his arrival. If the site selected for the presidio and missions was not to his liking, he was to choose one that was more suitable. This point in his orders later caused much anxiety among the priests, who came to feel that he used it as an excuse for unnecessary delays.

The buildings were to be constructed of timber as economically as possible, with the plans to be submitted to the Viceroy for his approval. With the San Xavier fiasco fresh on the minds of the officials, Parrilla was advised to accord the missionaries the proper respect, to treat the Indians with kindness and generosity, and to encourage them to learn Spanish. Both Indians and soldiers were to work the fields in an effort to produce enough food to prevent failure of the venture because of starvation. Trade with other provinces was to be encouraged, and the entire region developed as far as possible.

Parrilla was given authority to recruit in México the twenty-seven men needed to complete his garrison, which he did on his way north. At San Juan Bautista, on the Río Grande, he met Father Terreros, who had brought nine families of Tlaxcalteca Indians from Saltillo to be used as instructors for the neophytes of the San Sabá missions. The head priest, together with the other padres assigned to work in the new missions, left San Juan Bautista a few days ahead of Parrilla. With Father Terreros were Fathers Joaquín de Baños and Diego Jiménez, from the College of Querétaro, and Fathers José de Santiesteban and Juan Andrés from the College of San Fernando de Méjico. They arrived in San Antonio December 14, 1756, to find Parrilla already there, getting ready to proceed to San Marcos.[2]

---

[2] *Ibid.*, pp. 394–395; Father Alonso Giraldo de Terreros to Don Pedro Romero de Terreros, February 26, 1757, A.M.S.F. A discrepancy of dates will be noted in succeeding chapters between this and other versions. I rely on dates given by Father Terreros and other principals in letters written from San Antonio and San Sabá, in A.M.S.F.

Father Francisco de la Santísima Trinidad, who had been procuring supplies for the mission, caught up with the group before it reached San Antonio. As he made purchases he sent orders for payment to Don Pedro Romero de Terreros. One of these, written at Saltillo October 29, was for payment of sixteen hundred thirty pesos to Don Blas María de la Garza Falcón, captain of Presidio de Santa Ana de Camargo on the Río Grande, for twenty-one mules with harness and a quantity of corn.[3]

Also arriving with the priests was Father Francisco de Lara, whose name appears frequently in the correspondence of the other priests and Parrilla, but who is never identified. It seems likely he was the chaplain or parish priest of the Presidio and its families until early in 1758, when he returned to México; a guard of soldiers was sent to escort his replacement to San Sabá.

On the San Marcos River, at the temporary establishment that had lasted more than one year, the destitute garrison of San Xavier still waited. The soldiers were in need of new guns and horses; their uniforms were in shreds. It is a virtual certainty they warmly welcomed their new commander, who was to take them away from the scene of their misery.

On December 22 Parrilla completed moving the garrison to San Antonio in preparation for the journey to San Sabá. He found that the Indian neophytes were already relocated in a temporary mission established on the Guadalupe River, near present New Braunfels.

Those destined for San Sabá were to spend the winter in San Antonio, and, at the request of Father Mariano de los Dolores, Colonel Parrilla inspected the temporary site of the Mission San Xavier on the Guadalupe and made a favorable report. Thus encouraged, Father Dolores asked Father Terreros to include the Guadalupe mission among those to be financed by the gift of Don Pedro Romero de Terreros. As trustee of the grant, Father Terreros was hardly in position to grant the request.

He explained to Father Dolores that the site on the Guadalupe was outside the prescribed area for the new missions. Father Dolores took offense at the refusal, and the result was a schism which was to set the San Sabá venture off on the wrong foot. The equipment from the suppressed San Xavier missions had been

[3] "Libranzas y cartas" of Fray Francisco de la Santísima Trinidad, October 29, 1756, A.M.S.F.

Pilgrims' Journey

turned over to Father Terreros under terms of Don Pedro's grant, and this act furthered the antagonism.

But Father Dolores' resentment had deeper roots. He had labored continuously for more than fifteen years to win establishment of missions among the Apaches. As a result of his efforts the San Sabá plan had materialized, independently of Father Terreros. Yet Father Terreros, seemingly because he had a rich relative, now was to be placed in charge of the missions to convert the Apaches. Disappointment grew into bitter opposition.

Father Dolores' bitterness was understandable, yet regrettable, for it caused a split in the group waiting at San Antonio to proceed to San Sabá in the spring. The group gathered around Father Dolores, unfortunately, included Colonel Parrilla. The opposing faction was headed by Father Terreros and Father Trinidad, and the two factions soon were embroiled in an open feud, portending no good for the forthcoming venture on the San Sabá River.

Petty bickering was not the only ominous sign that troubled those waiting to start the journey to San Sabá. Soon after Colonel Parrilla and Father Terreros arrived at San Antonio, messengers were sent to the Apaches inviting them to come to San Antonio and meet the founders of the new missions. A group of Lipans, led by two chiefs, came bearing apologies for the absence of the other Apache tribes: the Natages, Mescaleros, Pelones, Come Nopales, and Come Caballos. The Lipans gave assurance they were eager to be congregated in the new missions, but it struck Parrilla that they were even more eager for the gifts that were being distributed among them. In a private report to the Viceroy, Parrilla said it appeared to him the Apaches were as treacherous as ever. He was fearful, he added, of the outcome.[4]

Perhaps these forebodings caused Parrilla to delay the start of the journey longer than Father Terreros considered necessary. In any event, he undoubtedly understood at this point a great deal more about the coming venture than he had previously: that the San Sabá Presidio, protecting a mission for a tribe of Indians almost wholly disinterested in the first place, was to stand as a buffer against an unknown tribe of savages to the north, who

---

[4] Parrilla to the viceroy, Marqués de las Amarillas, February 18, 1757, A.G.M., Historia, Vol. 95, p. 191; Castañeda, *Our Catholic Heritage*, III, 395–396.

were enemies of the Apaches. He may have foreseen, too, that he was about to be drawn into another dispute with the missionaries, such as the one between himself and the Jesuits in Sonora some years earlier.

On February 18, the date of his secret report to the Viceroy on his opinion of the Apaches, he also penned a letter to Don Pedro Romero de Terreros, in which he stated his misgivings:

> The state in which we have found the Apaches is so different from what I expected that I assure you the method of their pacification is a major concern to me.... To establish the mission and maintain it would be considered improper under the laws which we are given to observe.[5]

Parrilla may have been referring to the paralleling authority given the military and the religious. Since the soldiers and the priests viewed life in a different light, they were bound to clash. In the whole mission effort each circumstance was judged by two sets of standards. Indecision and confusion flourished.

Blame for the lamentable quarreling that poisoned relations between the soldiers and the missionaries, says Simpson, must be laid to the mistaken policy of the Crown in setting up these two parallel and inevitably conflicting agencies. The missionary was trained to the belief that his life reached its fulfillment in "the crown of martyrdom," and he joyously sought out occasions for exposing himself to death for the glory of God. While the missionaries sought martyrdom, the soldiers' duty was to keep them from attaining it. The soldiers naturally resented the missionaries' contempt for danger, which exposed the whole community to extermination and made the soldiers' job of defending the frontier extremely difficult.[6]

Parrilla, being an egotist, probably felt that he should be placed in overall charge of the San Sabá project. While he pondered the coming venture and balked at moving out for the San Sabá River, Father Terreros became more impatient.

With reason to be edgy, considering the spiteful treatment he had received from Father Dolores, Father Terreros accused Parrilla of purposely delaying the departure in an effort to spoil the success of the enterprise. He, too, expressed his misgivings in

---

[5] Parrilla to Don Pedro Terreros, February 18, 1757, A.M.S.F.
[6] Lesley Byrd Simpson (ed.), *San Saba Papers*, p. 155 n.

Pilgrims' Journey 47

letters to Don Pedro. He first wrote his cousin on February 24, with some foreboding of his own: "I fear [this venture] may cost me my life, although after some years of working with those of this land. It already has me weary by its bad treatment. Today one adjusts to one task, with salary never seen, and tomorrow is met with other trials." [7]

The reason for his despondency, the padre wrote, was that he found himself without men for some types of specialized work to be done at the missions. He asked Don Pedro to send "one or two carpenters, one or two blacksmiths, some laborers, and field hands," together with a personal representative to handle correspondence and payroll.

At this point he apparently was still credulous of the Apaches, recounting that "they have visited us frequently in bands of 300, 200, and other lesser numbers. We have given them gifts of corn, tobacco, sugar loaves, etc., in order to harvest their souls."

He noted that the Indians had been eager to please in their dealings with the Spaniards and the Indians of the missions and had maintained the peace for eight years.

"Toward the beginning of March, we will leave to inspect the site [on the San Sabá] with the intention of remaining there and beginning the foundations."

Two days later he wrote again, still expecting to begin the inspection tour March 1 but now apparently realizing that Parrilla's delaying tactics would prevent actual start of the missions: "I am violent at the loss of the early planting time." [8]

Father Terreros told his cousin he had reminded Parrilla that 1,000 *fanegas* of corn delivered to San Sabá would cost 5,000 pesos, indicating his concern over the extra expenses that would result from not reaching San Sabá in time to put in a crop. Indeed fear of being held accountable for the huge costs of the project seems to have troubled each of those who now wrote to Don Pedro, and to have had a hand in the bitter feelings among the principals. But the costs seem to have troubled Don Pedro not at all.

Some five hundred Indians of both sexes had arrived at San Antonio in bitter cold, Father Terreros wrote, and they had been

[7] Father Terreros to Don Pedro Terreros, February 24, 1757, A.M.S.F.
[8] *Ibid.*, February 26, 1757, A.M.S.F.

given the usual gifts. He noted that Parrilla suffered much from the cold.

He wrote of a hate campaign being conducted against him, the basis of which apparently was his refusal to approve inclusion of the Guadalupe mission under Don Pedro's grant, enclosing a sheet of paper which he said was to be his answer should the Viceroy ask Don Pedro about the matter.

"For all I can ascertain, I am to leave the first of March to make the inspection of the San Sabá, Florido (Concho), and other rivers."

To the missionaries it now seemed that everything was in readiness, but Parrilla still dallied. Blaming lack of pasturage at San Antonio, he ordered a move to the San Marcos River to get the livestock in condition for the long drive. Soldiers, missionaries, supplies, and Tlaxcalteca Indians all moved to the San Marcos to be ready to start from there for San Sabá. Father Terreros saw the move as having no purpose but to squander Don Pedro's money.

Don Pedro, meanwhile, was getting letters from another source. The writer was Father Francisco de la Santísima Trinidad, apparently one of Father Terreros' few allies in the feud with Father Dolores and Parrilla, who later was to author a document called "Vindicta del Río de San Sabá." Dunn quotes extensively from this document, saying its purpose was to put on record "the truth" regarding opposition to the enterprise.[9]

In a letter dated March 7, Father Trinidad described the delaying tactics of Parrilla, quoting the military commander thus:

"We will go to San Sabá. I will examine with the fathers not only this river but others which are found in the vicinity and will survey all the lands. If San Sabá does not permit the planting of missions and presidio, to be maintained in this particular spot, according to orders, we will report to the superior governor so a convenient one may be determined."

Father Santísima Trinidad saw in Parrilla's statement the possibility of delay and an additional burden of feeding the Apaches merely to keep them peaceful without accomplishing their conversion. Of San Sabá he said: "If it happens that some cloud is formed there that interposes the end, you will know they [Par-

---

[9] W. E. Dunn, "The Apache Mission," *SWHQ*, Vol. 17, pp. 391–397.

Pilgrims' Journey

rilla and Father Dolores] have maneuvered it all. I cannot state it more clearly." [10]

Writing again on April 1, he sounded another prophetic note:

> The happy progress for which your good intention and zeal aspire cannot result, because the purse is being emptied more than is intended. Since the religious are peevish, the Spaniards disgusted and the Indians vagabonds and cowards, nothing can be accomplished but [for them] to abound in restlessness and lose their souls. . . . Each day creates major difficulties: indiscipline in the soldiers, grave suspicions in the Indians, and almost total dejection in the ministers.[11]

He went on to offer in detail a plan whereby the difficulty between Parrilla and the missionaries could be circumvented. It proposed that the Viceroy annually appoint the San Sabá Presidio commander, with Don Pedro given, in exchange for managerial services, the title of colonel and the authority to name the Presidio captains.

Though mines at San Sabá did not offer to yield much silver, the padre said, this arrangement would serve to "draw you out with luster, avoid discord and win the Indians and to avoid that which your credit suffers in opinions."

Nothing came of the proposal. Five days after this letter was written, on April 5, 1757, Parrilla ordered sixty-one soldiers, the missionaries, and the Tlaxcalteca Indians to return to San Antonio and to take up the march from there to San Sabá. Most of the supplies and the livestock were left in the temporary camp under guard of the remaining thirty-nine soldiers, to stay there until sent for.

Parrilla's strange movements, some historians have said, were a precaution against surprise attack, as he was still fearful of the Apaches and their treachery. His behavior was denounced by Father Trinidad, who seems to have been as adept as Father Dolores at suspecting someone's motives. He said the purpose was to cause greater expense to Don Pedro Romero de Terreros.

Parrilla's real intent, however, seems to have been to prevent establishment of the mission and the presidio on the San Sabá River. He planned, as Father Trinidad had stated, to make an inspection. He was confident that after the inspection was made he

---

[10] Father Trinidad to Don Pedro Terreros, March 7, 1757, A.M.S.F.
[11] *Ibid.*, April 1, 1757, A.M.S.F.

could persuade the government to cancel the entire project. But he reckoned without considering the missionary zeal of the Franciscan friars.

Although Parrilla may have been motivated in part by prejudices, he was an experienced military commander, and he viewed the task of conducting the caravan to the San Sabá in military perspective. He was aware of the dangers posed by the penetration of the raw, unsettled country, the land of a sanguinary tribe of Indians noted for their ferocity. He was aware of the logistical problems of founding a new settlement: He could easily calculate the supplies needed for the garrison, but the number of Indians that would join the missions and the amount of supplies needed for them were unknown factors. He attended to these problems as best he could. Before the march began, he had gathered fourteen hundred head of cattle and seven hundred sheep, as well as a quantity of other necessities.

From San Antonio the expedition followed the established trail to the Pedernales and Llano Rivers, marked by Juan Galván and Don Pedro de Rábago y Terán, and thence on to its destination. Camp was made near the present town of Menard on April 17.

PART II
Life of the Mission

A Mission Founded

The story of the Mission Santa Cruz de San Sabá is one of Apache perfidy, Spanish gullibility, and the disastrous consequences of both. Despite the persistent urging of the Lipans for missions, and their repeated promises to submit to them and become Christians, not one single Indian was to be seen on the San Sabá River when the missionaries arrived. As the Spanish caravan passed through the Puerto de Baluartes and descended into the valley, it was greeted only by echoes from the rockbound hills.

The six Franciscan friars, bringing the message of salvation to this wild land, accepted the absence of converts philosophically at first. The priests (some of whom had joined the group since it left México) were disappointed, but they hoped the Apaches would come in time. Causing grave concern, however, was Parrilla's insistence that this trip was only for making inspection, in consequence of which he had left the supplies on the San Marcos River. The padres suspected the Commander would attempt to use the absence of the Apaches as an excuse for calling off the project. In this assumption they were correct.

Parrilla and his men examined the site recommended by Lieutenant Juan Galván, now a member of Parrilla's own company, and by Don Pedro de Rábago y Terán. Then they spent five days exploring the San Sabá River to its source. After the exploration, during which not one Indian was seen, the Colonel and his aides met in council with the missionaries on April 23.

Parrilla was outspoken in favoring abandonment of the project. The suggestion was anathema to the padres, who informed

Parrilla they would return to México and report his behavior if a mission were not founded at once. The Colonel was forced to yield. At the insistence of Father Terreros, he sent on May 4 for the supplies and soldiers that remained on the San Marcos.

Rankled by conflict within the group of Spaniards, haunted by doubts as to the intentions of the Indians, the missionaries and the soldiers now found a healing solution in hard work. The padres were bent on building two missions, one for the Querétaran missionaries and one for those of the College of San Fernando. They set to work on the Querétaran mission site on the south bank of the San Sabá River, a short distance from Don Pedro de Rábago's Holy Cross Ford.

From timber available nearby they built quarters for the missionaries and a temporary church. A typical mission village took shape inside a strong stockade of logs. Along the river they cleared fields and planted crops and started an irrigation ditch.[1]

While the friars busied themselves with the Mission, Colonel Parrilla looked after construction of barracks for the soldiers and quarters for their families at the site of the new Presidio de San Luis de las Amarillas. "The Presidio," says Simpson, "was a rude and primitive affair: a log stockade with a couple of gun platforms, and a number of mud and straw huts for living quarters." [2] The stone structure was to come later.

At other Texas missions soldiers of the "protecting" presidio had harassed the Indian neophytes in the faith and had thwarted the priests in their effort to convert the savages. Hoping to avoid a similar experience, the missionaries placed the San Sabá Mission three miles downstream from the Presidio and on the opposite (south) bank of the river. While this placement reduced the likelihood of military meddling in mission affairs, it rendered impossible defense of the Mission in case of attack.

Early in May, Father Benito Varela, who knew the Apache language, went in search of the Indians, who still had not put in

---

[1] W. E. Dunn, "The Apache Mission," *Southwestern Historical Quarterly*, Vol. 17, pp. 396–397.

[2] Paul D. Nathan (trans.) and Lesley B. Simpson (ed.), Introduction, *San Saba Papers*, p. xvi. I have found no confirmation of the use of mud, or adobe, but it seems doubtful because of the nature of the soil at this location.

A Mission Founded

their appearance. Contacting the soldiers remaining on the San Marcos, he learned, according to an account of an Apache squaw, that a band of Tejas had attacked the Apaches on the Colorado River, and the Apaches had been forced to flee.

When El Chico, a Lipan chief, visited San Antonio about that time, Father Mariano de los Dolores rebuked him for not keeping his promises. The aggressive friar admonished him to go to San Sabá at once.[3]

Had the Apaches stayed away from the mission on the San Sabá River, the Spaniards probably would have abandoned the mission project after a time without having suffered from the wrath of the Comanches and allied northern tribes. The Apaches, however, behaved in such a way as to insure disaster for the new Spanish settlement.

In mid-June the Franciscans at San Sabá found a glimmer of hope as some three thousand Apaches of both sexes arrived from the south and camped near the Mission. Overjoyed, the padres went out to greet them and offered them presents, but the tribe was sullen. When the missionaries invited them to enter the Mission, the Indians said they had not come for that purpose. They were about to begin a buffalo hunt and were preparing for a campaign against their old enemies, the northern tribes.

Yet the Apaches managed to stir the hopes of the padres. El Chico, the chief who had been rebuked by Father Dolores, professed willingness to enter the Mission. But another chief, called Casablanca, was bent on making a campaign against the Comanches and the Tejas to avenge the attack on the Colorado, where his brother had been killed. His was the greater influence.[4]

Among the band of Indians were two or three that were ill, one of whom was the brother of a chief. The Indians gave their consent for the priests to attend to the sick and permitted them to baptize the chief's brother. They promised to return and enter the Mission after their hunt and after just one more blow at their enemies.[5] The Apaches' false promises met with the priests' gullibility, and in the combination were the makings of disaster.

With heavy hearts the padres watched the Apaches disappear over the hill on their way to hunt buffalo on the northern prairies.

[3] C. E. Castañeda, *Our Catholic Heritage*, III, 398.
[4] Dunn, "The Apache Mission," *SWHQ*, Vol. 17, p. 399.
[5] Jacinto Marfil to Don Pedro Terreros, October 6, 1757, A.M.S.F.

That some of the missionaries were losing heart was readily apparent to Father Terreros, who was doing considerable soul-searching himself. He may have been unduly headstrong in forcing Parrilla's hand and insisting on the mission founding. Now his feelings appear to have been a mixture of his own wish to retire and of his determination to see the project through to the finish.

On June 29, with rheumatic pains shooting through his arm and crumpling his fingers, he took up his quill to write to his cousin, Don Pedro, using the trunk of a tree for a table.

> From San Antonio I have given account of my arrival, suffering and such things; now from this encampment of La Santa Cruz de San Sabá and the bank of this river. We arrived happily after spending twelve days en route from the San Marcos River, which we left on April 5, with no more purpose than that of inspecting the land. We have found it with all those desirable conveniences, and I am determined to fulfill my obligations.[6]

He told of the exploration of the area, saying Parrilla had chosen the ones who were already decided against the site to make the inspection. Those who were opposed to remaining, he added, were suggesting that the missionaries should be left there alone. "Having arrived at the site, we found it not inhabited by the Indians, whom we have been courting in San Antonio. I was determined to send for the train, part of which was on the San Marcos River, and the rest in San Antonio. It has not arrived."[7]

He then wrote circumlocutiously of the sinister relations, expressing the fear that "the brothers" would continue to lose spirit and suggesting his own distress—"All the hell that is conjured for me!"[8]

Before he had finished writing, the supply train from the San Marcos was arriving. Then the Mission president closed his letter: "This writing is upon the trunk of an oak tree, surrounded by others. I remain with a pain in the shoulder which catches my whole arm and has put my fingers to sleep. I believe it is rheumatism of some severity."[9]

---

[6] Father Terreros to Don Pedro Terreros, June 29, 1757, A.M.S.F.
[7] *Ibid.*
[8] *Ibid.*
[9] *Ibid.*

A Mission Founded

This letter apparently was written after the three thousand Apaches appeared the first time, but Father Terreros, probably because of the keen disappointment that they had not remained, made no mention of them until later.

The Indians had gone on north. Just what the Apaches did on this expedition of hunting and warfare is not definitely known, of course, but Bancroft offers a suggestion. He says the Apaches boasted of their alliance with the Spaniards, causing the northern tribes to form a league for the destruction of their new foe.[10] It seems likely also that in raiding the camps of their enemies they left behind some of the items they had received as gifts from the Spaniards at San Sabá, indicating that the Spaniards were responsible for the attacks. If this is the case, then the beginning of the end for San Sabá—and the forward movement toward the Great Plains by the Spaniards—may be traced to this one Apache expedition.

Before many days had passed, the Apaches returned to San Sabá with much buffalo meat from their successful hunt, and the missionaries dared to let themselves hope again. Though the Apaches stayed near the Mission for a few days, they refused to tarry longer. During their stay they appeared uneasy, casting furtive glances about them as if guarding against the approach of an enemy. After their brief sojourn the Indians hurried on southward, leaving the padres more destitute in spirit than before.

On July 4 the Mission president wrote again to his cousin, Don Pedro:

> It is my understanding the Indians are yet more of a mind to go, because of the partiality only to the Ipandes [Lipan]. More than three thousand souls have presented themselves to us on this river, although we do not hope soon to reduce the remaining factions. These comprise, according to reliable information, great numbers, not to be compared with those referred to.[11]

Father Terreros wrote also on that date to the Viceroy and to the guardian of the College of Querétaro, informing them of the seemingly hopeless situation but expressing his willingness to stay at his post if they deemed it advisable.

Father Trinidad also wrote to Don Pedro regarding the Apaches' visit, saying that only part of the group were Lipans.

[10] H. H. Bancroft, *The Works of Bancroft*, XV, 645.
[11] Father Terreros to Don Pedro Terreros, July 4, 1757, A.M.S.F.

There are many others more numerous that are called Natajes, although they communicate less with the Spaniards, but the Ypandes say they also will come. It is doubtful that they will place themselves in the mission, because they hunt for meat, and they had here many prayers and corn to eat and did not want them. One of the chiefs that govern the mob had the audacity to say that they never would come to the mission, having many times given us their word in Mission San Antonio. The other chief said [they would come] on returning from the hunt. [The Mission president] told them that he did not want to let them go, that they should leave their women and children, that we might keep them and help them. They doubted their settlement and considered themselves well off with a free and vagabond life.

This is in substance the state of these miserable ones, which we look upon with great pain. God in His infinite mercy give them light, to come out of their great deceit.[12]

Both Father Terreros and Father Trinidad, in their July 4 letters, manifested a change in attitude toward the Presidio commander. Wrote the Father President: "All my fellow religious and I are very much obliged to Colonel Don Diego Ortiz Parrilla." [13]

Noting Parrilla's "zeal for both majesties," Father Terreros suggested that it might be to the advantage of Don Pedro and the entire project if he could put in a good word for the Colonel with the Junta de Guerra y Hacienda.

Father Trinidad wrote that after leaving San Antonio the Commander appeared to be reformed, and he attributed the change to Parrilla's escape from the influence of those at San Antonio whom he considered to have been wronged—undoubtedly meaning Father Dolores.

"The dispatches that the Reverend Father President sent you seem to give credit to the different appearance of the gentlemen, together with what he has given me to understand on various occasions.... I must suspend my judgment." [14]

But there was to be no permanence in Father Trinidad's suspension of judgment.

The same courier who carried the letters of Father Terreros and Father Trinidad also carried one from Parrilla to the Viceroy. On June 30 Parrilla wrote the Marqués de las Amarillas, vowing

[12] Father Trinidad to Don Pedro Terreros, July 4, 1757, A.M.S.F.
[13] Father Terreros to Don Pedro Terreros, July 4, 1757, A.M.S.F.
[14] Father Trinidad to Don Pedro Terreros, July 4, 1757, A.M.S.F.

A Mission Founded

there was no hope for success of the Missions. He suggested it would be better to give up the project and remove his garrison to the Río de las Chanas (Llano), where Bernardo de Miranda had discovered Los Almagres Mine, to which he had never returned. He wrote:

> Of the minerals of this part of the north [the vicinity of San Sabá], it is not possible to make formal judgment until other inspections are made, and with better understanding than has been practical. For that reason I do not give news of them.[15]

The Viceroy, in his answer written September 30, tartly reminded Parrilla that it was his duty to direct all his energies toward success of the San Sabá project, which had been placed in his trust.

Three missions had been planned for San Sabá at the beginning. When the missionaries arrived to find no Indians, they had lowered their sights, planning to build two. But now, with one mission built, and no Indians available to teach, they had no heart for building a second one. The Mission Santa Cruz de San Sabá was the only one to grace the site. It was the Querétaran mission. The mission for the College of San Fernando was never built.

Yet it was the Querétaran missionaries who asked permission to return to México, leaving two of those of San Fernando to look after the mission with Father Terreros. Thoroughly frustrated, the missionaries felt the uselessness of their presence here. The new mission afforded them no opportunity whatever to serve. Some of them felt it would be better to return to México immediately, rather than to continue the fruitless effort.[16]

Father Varela was the first to go, returning to Querétaro. Fathers Joaquín de Baños and Diego Jiménez wistfully watched his departure. On July 5, not yet three months from the time they had left the San Marcos, they too wrote to Querétaro asking permission to return. The courier who carried the letters of Father Terreros and Father Trinidad and Colonel Parrilla probably carried theirs as well.

Fathers Baños and Jiménez wrote that they saw no hope whatever that the Apaches would submit themselves to missions. They complained also that they had been deceived by Father Terreros,

---

[15] Parrilla to the viceroy, Marqués de las Amarillas, June 30, 1757, A.G.M., Historia, Vol. 95, p. 194.

[16] Castañeda, *Our Catholic Heritage*, III, 399–401.

who apparently had led them to believe one of them would be placed in charge of the Querétaran mission when it was founded.

Fathers Baños and Jiménez, in addition, foresaw the possibility that they would have to share the responsibility for squandering Don Pedro de Terreros' funds on missions that had no chance of success.

> Even if Don Pedro should supply everything for three years, who could answer for the consequences at the end of that time? . . . We find no reason why we should remain with this enterprise, which we consider ill-conceived and without foundation from the beginning.[17]

The schism formed during the previous winter in San Antonio still lingered with the missionaries on the banks of the San Sabá River.

The requests of Fathers Baños and Jiménez, like that of Father Varela, were granted after a time, and when they departed only Fathers Santiesteban, Trinidad, and Terreros were left at the new mission.

Father Terreros was willing to let Don Pedro and the Viceroy decide whether the project should be continued. Although his early enthusiasm had been cooled by the Apaches' indifference, he was learning a lesson in patience.

On July 20 the Mission president, who had repeatedly written of the persecutions he suffered, wrote to Don Pedro to reassure the Mission sponsor that he would remain at his post.

> Like a soldier I strike, to serve a mission the time that God has given me to live, but not as president, more than faith dictates. I direct this business badly. . . . In successive service to God, the King, and the public, I commit myself to protect all, to gorge the ticks, and suffer rheumatism. For our Divine Majesty I wish to do it, for it coincides with the benefit of eternal life.[18]

---

[17] Dunn, "The Apache Mission," *SWHQ*, Vol. 17, p. 401. Fathers Baños and Jiménez apparently had a long wait for permission to leave. Father Jiménez endorsed one of Father Trinidad's payment orders with date of August 28 (A.M.S.F.).

[18] Father Terreros to Don Pedro Terreros, July 20, 1757, A.M.S.F.

Storm Clouds

Time required to send dispatches from San Sabá to Mexico City and to receive a reply seems to have been about four months. The spate of letters written from San Sabá early in July reached the capital in September. A lieutenant from the Presidio, probably Joseph Joachín de Eca y Músquiz, carried the dispatches and gave a personal summation to the viceroy, Marqués de las Amarillas.

The Viceroy, in receipt of letters from both Parrilla and Father Terreros, took up with his advisers, the *auditor* and the *fiscal*, the question of whether the project should be continued. Replies were written September 30, but it was at least mid-October before Lieutenant Eca y Músquiz left Mexico City to return with them to San Sabá. On October 6 the Viceroy's secretary, Jacinto Marfil, wrote to Don Pedro Romero de Terreros at Pachuca, asking him to send as soon as possible any letters he wished the Lieutenant to carry to San Sabá.

This slowness of communication, and the great deliberation which marked every action on the frontiers of New Spain, contributed greatly to the downfall of San Sabá, as well as to the failure of the Spanish effort on the entire northern frontier.

With news of the large number of Apaches that had camped near the San Sabá Mission, officials in the capital appraised the situation more optimistically than was warranted. This is revealed by Marfil's letter to Don Pedro. The Viceroy's secretary seems to have been of the opinion that many of the Indians still remained at the Mission. He wrote that one of the chiefs had stayed while the other departed to hunt buffalo and make war on their enemies.

To Captain Parrilla and the missionaries, this appeared as a renunciation ... a lack of faith and open denial. But they give one an idea of the character of these barbarians, and they say they are full of spirit, astute, and more civilized than others, that they go well-dressed, and finally that they have responded to efforts to settle and convert them.[1]

He then recounted how the Indians had given the missionaries leave to treat the two or three ill ones among them and to baptize the brother of a chief.

In view of these things, he said, the opinion of both the *fiscal* and the *auditor* was that Parrilla, the priests, and the Presidio should be maintained at their present site and that they should continue the cultivation and settlement of the Apaches "because one cannot find a motive or cause that would influence its abandonment." [2]

The court, he said, had celebrated the news, adding that King Ferdinand VI had a tangible reward in store for Don Pedro for his part in the project. But Don Pedro was to have a long wait.

> Write to Father Terreros, giving him your pledge, as there is no undertaking so great as that work. ... Parrilla has enough luster and practice; Father Terreros above all has the virtue and efficacy and is well-conducted with spirit and apostolic zeal to proceed in the fruits of his labors and work.
>
> The Indians, says the lieutenant, respond a great deal to kindness, and this is a great opportunity to be able to save their souls.
>
> You should examine this news and shortly write to Father Terreros and send me as quickly as possible a letter to be given to the lieutenant. We only wait for your reply for him to leave.[3]

In response to this letter, Don Pedro replied that he was willing to keep his part of the bargain. The Viceroy then asked Father Terreros to stay and wait for the Apaches to come.

How different the situation appeared at a distance from the harsh reality at San Sabá! How easy it was to judge from afar. It might have seemed like a great opportunity in Mexico City, but on the faraway San Sabá River there was little cause for optimism.

---

[1] Jacinto Marfil to Don Pedro Terreros, October 6, 1757, A.M.S.F.
[2] *Ibid.*
[3] *Ibid.*

Storm Clouds

The priests and the officers of the Presidio occupied themselves with administrative details while they waited without hope for the Apaches. They felt great concern over the tremendous cost to Don Pedro de Terreros of maintaining the establishment for no apparent reason.

On November 1 Parrilla wrote to Don Pedro, saying the Mission president was "adjusting the expenses to need," urging Don Pedro to continue to write cheering letters to his cousin. "I could not fail them [the missionaries] or fail in my understanding with the motives and reasons that I have tried to apply in all that has occurred."[4]

The state of the heathen Apaches, he said, was no different.

His own situation corresponded to that of Don Pedro, suggested Parrilla, because he had obtained a great herd of cattle for the missions, and much money would be lost in their care without hope of recompense.[5]

As the chilling winds of autumn whipped down off the Llano Estacado, small bands of Apaches began to appear at the Mission San Sabá. They were in a hurry to move on and would partake of the padres' hospitality but briefly, giving only empty promises that they would return.

As these little bands scudded southward like sparrows before a storm, a dark omen hung over the isolated mission. The Indians had a reason for their sudden migration, and the Franciscan priests were certain they were not simply headed for their wintering ground. Like animals fleeing a forest fire they came, glancing behind at the pursuing flames or sniffing the air for the acrid smell of smoke, ever hurrying on.

Then the friars and the commander of the Presidio began to receive reports that the northern tribes were gathering for an attack on the hated Apaches, hopeful of destroying them with one blow at the mission and presidio on the San Sabá River. The Spaniards of the new settlement may have been slightly incredulous at these reports, for the Apaches had never gathered there in any numbers.

Autumn dragged into winter, but the threatened attack did not

[4] Parrilla to Don Pedro Terreros, November 1, 1757, A.M.S.F.
[5] *Ibid.*

materialize. Both the soldiers and the padres ceased to be alarmed at the rumors, and began to prepare themselves for a severe winter.

Norther after norther blew down from the Plains, bringing snow, ice, and bitter cold.[6] The days dragged by at the Presidio de San Luis de las Amarillas. Between 300 and 400 persons, including 237 women and children, lived at the Presidio. Their lives were confined to a set routine within a limited area, like that on a ship at sea—the changing of the guard, herding the cattle and horses in the pastures, brief and cautious hunting trips to supply the larder with fresh game. But each day was always the same. The only real breach in the monotony was arrival of a supply train from San Antonio.

Father Terreros, meanwhile, moved unconsciously toward his destiny, which he welcomed and possibly even longed for. He began the new year on January 1, 1758, by writing his cousin Don Pedro for the first time in almost six months, acknowledging two letters that he had received, one of which apparently had chided the father for his persecution complex.

> I remain cognizant of the persecution [wrote the padre to Don Pedro] ... The causes of God our Lord and Father and the determination of the soul have not divided themselves from a design of the man of faith. This prepares the soul to suffer past and future persecutions, and all which the season will bring. This is the mode that we have found at San Sabá: Farther on there is a better life, and nothing is needed to show the road when it is guided.[7]

The Mission president wrote of a patent that had been given Father Mariano de los Dolores, naming him commissary and visitor, "not only of the old missions of my college but also of the ones which we will place henceforth," including the projected ones at San Sabá.

> I am considered abandoned and unfit for this particular. Therefore my cousin would not restrain me from retirement and abandonment of

---

[6] Parrilla makes repeated reference to severity of weather (Paul D. Nathan [trans.] and Lesley Byrd Simpson [ed.], *San Saba Papers*, pp. 93, 132, and 137), as does Father Terreros in his letter to Don Pedro Terreros on February 12, 1758 (A.M.S.F.). Also see Father Molina's statement, *San Saba Papers*, p. 91.

[7] Father Terreros to Don Pedro Terreros, January 1, 1758, A.M.S.F.

Storm Clouds

the canonical charge and that of yourself. But I will not retire, for quitting is not easy, until so much is evident to me of the patent, by effect of which Trinidad is ordered to the Mission of San Antonio.[8]

Father Terreros revealed that he had arranged for returning to Father Dolores, the ornaments, bells, and "all the items for celebrating the Holy Sacrifice," from the San Xavier missions for use in the mission on the Guadalupe River. Lieutenant Juan Galván, who conducted supply trains from San Antonio, was to deliver them. Father Dolores had written both to him and to Parrilla, conferring on the best method of congregating the Apaches, and Father Terreros was grateful.[9]

On February 1 Father Miguel de Molina arrived at the Mission Santa Cruz de San Sabá from the College of San Fernando. Father Francisco de la Santísima Trinidad already had departed, apparently for San Antonio, still leaving the Mission with only three missionaries: Father Molina, Father Santiesteban, and Father Terreros.

Father Molina wrote on February 11 to inform Don Pedro of his arrival at San Sabá:

I found your cousin the Reverend Father Friar Alonso, accompanied by Friar Joseph Santiesteban, who received me with full heart of charity, and I rejoice. . . .

Each day offers them new embarrassments and difficulties in this new conquest, by the hardness of the Indians who do not give themselves to be convinced by the good treatment and gentle procedure that has been practiced with them.[10]

Lieutenant Eca y Músquiz and three soldiers were getting ready to depart for México to escort the new parish priest back to the Presidio. They would take the letters now being written. Father Francisco de Lara, if the supposition is correct that he was the first parish priest, already had departed.

Father Terreros and Colonel Parrilla, having been in council, had decided on a different future course for the mission project, for as yet its purpose had not been realized. They hoped to obtain official approval of the Viceroy for the two of them to journey to Mexico City to explain their plan. But their letters regarding the

[8] *Ibid.*
[9] *Ibid.*
[10] Father Molina to Don Pedro Terreros, February 11, 1758, A.M.S.F.

plan were couched in such vague terms that the plan itself can only be guessed at.

Father Terreros wrote on February 12 to his cousin Don Pedro: "We do not find ourselves sufficient for the attainment of the benefits to which we aspire." [11]

He hinted that, should he accompany Parrilla to México, he would not return, though he would be sorry to abandon the project. But he continued to feel himself persecuted, and it seemed to be "the desire" that he abandon. Just whose desire he did not specify. The persecution had reached its peak, he said, with the patent conferred on Father Dolores as commissary and visitor of the missions.

> They deny me the families of the missions of San Antonio, alleging that the Great Father cannot have power to continue with the Indians who come. This I write you that you may know, that the Indians do not have more will than their teachers. In addition to what Lara has exposed on this subject, I say that although the Indians come, existing in these parts, one cannot but hope for success and good in the disposition.[12]

Father Terreros wrote of the severely cold weather, of illness, and of the death of some of the livestock:

> I write this as they are dragging from the corral the horses which died last night. . . . It is not known at the presidio how many have fallen in the horse pasture. . . . The steward just arrived from the care of the sheep, six hundred head, which were well except that twenty-seven of them died last night, twelve cows and the oxen, apart from the cattle that were sent to Parrilla with fifteen head of oxen and the cows which were maintained three days in the corral with the grass from which the huts are made.[13]

The Mission president seemed obsessed with the idea of his own death, as he had been from the start of the project. There is an air of mystery about the entire letter. He mentions sending his signature in blank "in order not to grieve Lara," asking Don Pedro to "tell Lara by mouth that which cannot be confided to the pen."

[11] Father Terreros to Don Pedro Terreros, February 12, 1758, A.M.S.F.
[12] *Ibid.*
[13] *Ibid.*

Storm Clouds 67

The next day Father Terreros wrote to the commissary general and to the Viceroy. He assured the former:

All Hell is joined to impede this enterprise, but I hope in God that it will be attained by means of that which Colonel Don Diego de Ortiz Parrilla asks of His Excellency, associated with the uselessness of Father Giraldo, for whose matters, if His Excellency concedes the exposition of them, I ask Your Most Reverence your leave, license, and permission to pass to that court.[14]

To the Viceroy he wrote that because of experience with the Indians the means most conducive to their hoped-for subjugation had become apparent. Only by coming to México in person, he said, could the proper explanation of such an arduous enterprise be communicated, or its importance duly emphasized.

On this premise, Most Excellent Sir, I, on my own account, and in the name of all our religious, appeal to the benignity of Your Excellency for approval, and to your well-known diligence in the service of both Majesties, praying for your approbation and consent, so that Colonel Don Diego Ortiz Parrilla and one of ourselves may proceed to your court with all the speed the situation requires.[15]

Of the Apaches he wrote:

They continue their good cooperation, but their promises of submission are sometimes pretexts of delay, some alleging illnesses and disagreements among them, while others in their perplexity make frivolous proposals and lack the unity to settle in the towns. But it is true that some evidences of particular friendliness continue to indicate favorable response to our efforts.[16]

Parrilla also was busy writing letters to be taken by Lieutenant Eca y Músquiz, to both Don Pedro and the Viceroy. To the latter he wrote:

Bearing in mind the nature of the locality and the condition of the heathen Indians to be reduced here, we felt that new authorization and

[14] Father Terreros to the commissary general, February 13, 1758, A.M.S.F.
[15] Father Terreros to the viceroy, Marqués de las Amarillas, February 13, 1758, A.M.S.F. Translated by Nathan as Doc. 1 in *San Saba Papers*, pp. 1–4.
[16] *Ibid.*

sanction of Your Excellency are needed, which would speedily be strengthened by face-to-face instructions from Your Excellency.[17]

Before the letters reached México, disaster struck at San Sabá. The question of whether Parrilla and one of the missionaries should come to México to discuss their plan, whatever it was, was muted.

After Father Molina's arrival and the departure of Lieutenant Eca y Músquiz with the dispatches, the Mission settled back into its old routine. But as winter waned rumors of a planned attack by the northern tribes began to fall on the Spanish settlement like the thump of war drums.

Then, on the night of February 25, a band of Indians swooped down on the pasture where the livestock was grazing and stampeded the horses. Joseph Antonio Flores, sergeant of the guard at the pasture, said the attack occurred about midnight. The animals scattered in all directions. Sergeant Flores and his men set out immediately to round them up. At daylight they picked up the trail, which told them the fifty-nine missing horses were being driven by Indians both on foot and on horseback.

Colonel Parrilla ordered Sergeant Francisco Yruegas, with fourteen soldiers, to pursue the Indians and recover the horses. The patrol returned after twelve days, weary from hard riding over rugged country. The soldiers had found eight dead horses left along the trail by the Indians but recovered only one live animal.

The country was crawling with Indians, armed and ready for battle, the sergeant's men explained. This report spread like a prairie fire through the garrison, striking fear into the already fearful women and children, as well as the soldiers.[18]

The cordon was tightening, the northern tribes gathering in a common cause. Colonel Parrilla was impressed by the story of Sergeant Yruegas and his men. Having sent a detail to escort a supply train en route from San Antonio, he now dispatched four soldiers and two servants to warn the escort.

The six men, led by Corporal Carlos de Uraga, camped for the night on the Pedernales River. At dawn the next day they were attacked by twenty-six Indians. Four of the group were wounded,

---

[17] Nathan-Simpson, *San Saba Papers*, p. 7.
[18] Deposition of Joseph Antonio Flores, in *ibid.*, p. 58.

Storm Clouds

but all succeeded in joining the supply convoy. The two most seriously wounded proceeded to Presidio de San Antonio de Béjar for treatment.[19]

A messenger from Lieutenant Juan Galván, in charge of the supply-train escort, brought word of the attack on the Pedernales to Parrilla, who included this information in a warning to Father Terreros at Mission Santa Cruz de San Sabá. Corporal de Uraga, he was informed, had noted that the Indians which attacked the small group consisted of Tancagues (Tonkawas), Bidais, and Yojuanes. Of this the Corporal was certain, for he had been associated with these tribes at Presidio de San Xavier.

Colonel Parrilla immediately ordered Sergeant Tomás de Ogeda to make a reconnaissance of the road between the Presidio and the supply train. Then he and his men were to reinforce Lieutenant Galván's escort, boosting its strength to twenty-two men. The supply train consisted of two strings of fifty pack animals each, with three muleteers to accompany each string.

From the hills to the north and the east, smoke signals rose, spiraling toward the sky in an ominous cloud. Parrilla repeatedly urged the padres to forsake their mission and seek protection in the Presidio. When they spurned his plea, he urged them at least to move closer to the Presidio, but again they refused. On March 15 Colonel Parrilla sent a soldier, Luis Padilla, to the mission three miles down the river with a message for Father Terreros, requesting the priests to come to the Presidio and advising them that Parrilla himself would come to the Mission that afternoon to escort them.

The messenger was rebuffed. If Padilla had no news besides the theft of the horses and the attack on the six soldiers on the Pedernales, said Father Terreros, then he saw no necessity to abandon the Mission and give up the care of his people and property. The Mission president maintained that his establishment was well-protected by its stockade. The Mission buildings, he noted, were safer than those of the Presidio, because they were

---

[19] *Ibid.*, pp. 58–59. W. E. Dunn ("The Apache Mission," *SWHQ*, Vol. 17, p. 404) and Castañeda (*Our Catholic Heritage*, III, 401) recount that four prospectors on the Pedernales River were attacked by Indians on March 9 and fled to San Sabá for protection. This appears to be a garbled version of the same incident, traceable to a letter written by Father Mariano de los Dolores.

covered with tile to resist fire. The Presidio buildings had roofs of reeds or straw; the fort's stockade was long, necessitating a large number of men to defend it. The message, said Father Terreros, was superfluous and the suggestion unnecessary, although he appreciated them.[20]

Despite this reaction Colonel Parrilla still went to the Mission that afternoon and had a long talk with the priests. With the refusal of the padres to move nearer the Presidio, he urged them to give up working in the fields until the threat had passed [21] and suggested other measures for the increased security of the Mission. Father Molina recalled later that these were to have been put into effect the very next day.

Parrilla had provided the Mission with a guard of eight soldiers—all he felt he could spare from his garrison in view of other demands on his troops—and with two light cannon, ammunition, powder, and muskets. The total number of persons there appears to have been thirty-five. This number included the three priests and the eight soldiers. The soldiers were Corporal Ascensio Cadena, Andrés de Villareal, José de los Santos, Vicente Gutiérrez, Juan Leal, Enrique Gutiérrez, Lázaro de Ayala, and José García. There were four San Antonio Mission Indians and their wives, two Apache Indians, the steward, Juan Antonio Gutiérrez, and his wife, Corporal Cadena's wife, and about ten servants, including a number of young boys who were sons of soldiers.[22]

Parrilla, with the practiced eye of a military leader, saw that the thirty-five persons could not hold out long against a sustained attack. But he had problems of his own at the Presidio. Besides the twenty-two men assigned to escort the supply train, four had been sent to the Presidio de Santa Rosa to meet the new parish priest who was coming to the San Sabá Presidio, three to the mission on the Guadalupe River, and eleven to guard the livestock

---

[20] Deposition of Luis Padilla, Nathan-Simpson, *San Saba Papers*, pp. 95–97.

[21] *Ibid.*

[22] Compiled from various depositions, Nathan-Simpson, *San Saba Papers*. Castañeda and Dunn both say that the Mission guard consisted of five soldiers instead of eight, and that the total number of persons at the Mission was seventeen. Nathan and Simpson clearly show these figures to be in error. What became of the nine Tlaxcalteca Indian families which Father Terreros brought never has been explained.

Storm Clouds

in the pasture some twelve miles west of Presidio de San Luis. Ensign Diego Ramón was in prison in Mexico City by order of the Viceroy.

Parrilla's problem was complicated by the women and children at the fort. The refusal of the missionaries to come into the Presidio and their insistence on maintaining their establishment apart from it created further complications. With lookouts keeping constant vigil, he alerted the garrison to the danger and took what measures he could to make certain the Indians did not catch the Presidio by surprise. Beyond that there was little he could do.

Parrilla, in this time of crisis, put his trust in armed might. The missionaries put their trust in God.

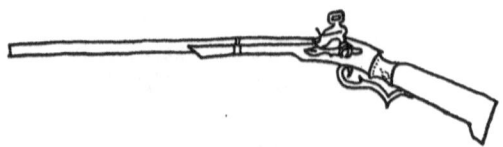

Crown of Martyrdom

As the mantle of night closed over the San Sabá Valley, an aura of peace seemed to envelop the little log mission on the south bank of the river. The padres said evening prayers and retired to their cells for quiet meditation. While the servants finished the day's chores, the eight soldiers from the Presidio set the guard for the night.

Out among the shadows a more sinister movement was taking place. From all directions, from many tribes, the shadowy figures came, advancing stealthily under the cover of night toward the point of rendezvous. While the little mission slept, they held their council of war.

The night passed, and the Franciscan padres arose to begin their daily routines. Father Terreros finished saying mass, and Father Santiesteban started the second service. Then, with the first rays of the sun peeking into the valley, the morning stillness was shattered by a burst of savage yells in the direction of the river. Someone inside the stockade, or just outside it, saw the mass movement and shrieked the alarm: "Indians!"

Before sunrise a member of the Mission guard, Juan Leal, age fifty years, had gone to the riverbank near the Mission to cut some stakes for an enclosure Father Terreros wished to build. Leal looked up from his work a short time later to see the hundreds of Indians, covering the country as far as he could see. They were swarming across the ford a short distance upstream, where the river makes a bend and flows north. As the Indians' war cry split the air, Leal ducked among the willows at the river's edge, but he was too late. Two Indians rushed at him with their lances, though a third came to his defense, arguing with the first two in the Tejas language. Leal's protector, apparently intent on keeping the advantage of surprise, took him by the hand and led him toward the Mission.

On the way they came upon the wife of the chief steward, Juan

Crown of Martyrdom

Antonio Gutiérrez, whom the Indians had stripped of her clothing. Leal removed his coat and put it around her. When they reached the Mission, they found the courtyard filled with savages, the stockade surrounded, and the road to the Presidio cut off.[1]

At the first alarm the Mission guard had hurriedly closed the gate. The soldiers inside the stockade took their positions in readiness for attack, as hordes of savages on horseback swarmed around the Mission, firing their guns as they came. As the gate closed, the Indians halted at the stockade wall. Assuming a conciliatory attitude, they spoke to the guards in broken Spanish and gave assurance of their friendly intentions. They did not want to fight the Spaniards, they said; they sought only their enemies, the Apaches.

Despite the repeated warnings of impending attack, apparently neither the padres nor the Mission guard had made a plan for dealing with it when it came. If there was a plan, it now was forgotten in the confusion. Although the chiefs of the savage horde declared their friendly intentions, their faces were smeared with black and red war paint, their bodies clad in war costumes made of animal skins, their headdresses adorned with tails and feathers. They were armed with guns, sabres, and lances. The largest number of the Indians were Comanches, but the group included also Tejas, Bidais, Tonkawas, and others.

While the Indians conversed with the guard, Father Miguel de Molina ran to the chapel to tell Father Santiesteban to suspend the service and prepare for attack. Father Santiesteban dismissed the mass but remained before the altar. He placed himself in the hands of God as he knelt to pray.

Father Molina hurried on to the room of Father Terreros, where several of the women and the servants already had taken refuge, to discuss the situation with the Mission president.

Ascensio Cadena, corporal of the guard, meanwhile, had observed the Tejas, Bidais, and Tonkawas among the horde of

[1] Deposition of Juan Leal, Paul D. Nathan (trans.) and Lesley Byrd Simpson (ed.), *San Saba Papers*, pp. 73–77. The description of the ford where the Indians crossed is Father Molina's (*ibid.*, p. 84). The author has determined this site to be at the mouth of Miller Draw, the only place where the River flows north and where a strategic approach could have been made.

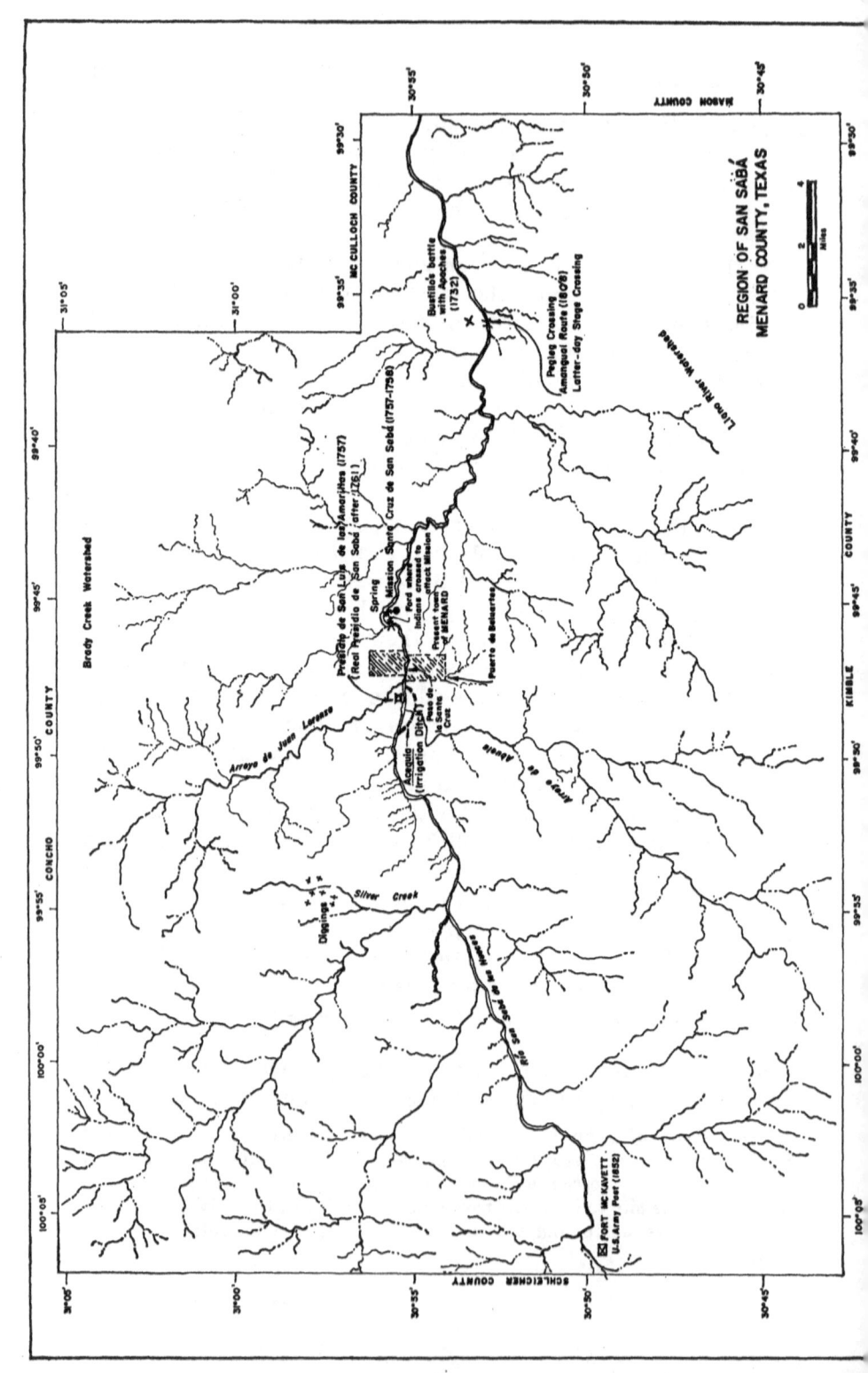

Indians. Since he had dealt with these tribes peaceably at San Xavier, their declaration of peace now seemed logical to him. Forgotten, or unknown to him, was the fact that these same tribes were the ones who had attacked the six soldiers on the Pedernales River just a few days before. Cadena went to Father Terreros and assured him that the Indians had come in peace—an error which made the savages' job easier and which hastened the fate of their victims.

After talking with Corporal Cadena, Father Terreros and Father Molina went into the patio. Father Molina gives a description of the sight that confronted them:

> [I was] filled with amazement and fear when I saw nothing but Indians on every hand, armed with guns and arrayed in the most horrible attire. Besides the paint on their faces, red and black, they were adorned with the pelts and tails of wild beasts, wrapped around them or hanging down from their heads, as well as deer horns. Some were disguised as various kinds of animals, and some wore feather headdresses. All were armed with muskets, swords and lances, and I noticed also that they had brought with them some youths armed with bows and arrows, doubtless to train and encourage them in their cruel and bloody way of life.[2]

There were, perhaps, a few seconds during which the padres had a choice of action; but in the confusion, intensified by the conflict between Corporal Cadena's appraisal and what they saw with their own eyes, they did not act. The savages soon eliminated the possibility of choice. Observing the indecision and the apparent fear of violence written on their faces, the Indians began to dismount from their horses and swarmed around the gate. They removed the bars and poured inside, filling the stockade with some three hundred of their number.

At Father Molina's suggestion, gifts of tobacco and trinkets were distributed to the chiefs in the stockade. He himself handed four bundles of tobacco to the principal chief, a fierce-looking Comanche, whose war dress and red jacket, the priest noted, were decorated after the manner of French uniforms. He was fully armed. The chief, who had remained on his horse, took the tobacco with a scornful laugh which struck Father Molina as a knife in the heart.

[2] "Informe de Fray Miguel de Molina," March 22, 1758, A.M.S.F.; translated by Nathan, *San Saba Papers*, pp. 84–92.

In his own mind Father Molina knew the Indians' visit would end in tragedy. He did not have long to wait for proof. The Indians scattered throughout the Mission, stealing food and utensils from the kitchen, taking the clothes of the soldiers from their quarters and the horses from the corral. When all the horses were gone, the Indians asked Father Terreros for more. Hoping to get the savages outside the stockade, Father Terreros told them there were no more horses at the Mission, but there were many more at the Presidio. A Tejas chief asked the Mission president to give him a note to Colonel Parrilla. Father Terreros went to his room to write the note.

Andrés de Villareal, who had charge of the Mission cannon, had been at his post when the Indians first swarmed around the Mission. As the Indians came, firing their guns, a musketball struck him under the shoulder. While Corporal Cadena went to Father Terreros to convince him that the Indians were peaceful, Villareal spoke with Chief Steward Gutiérrez and several others, who already had decided the Indians were bent on mischief.

While Father Terreros was writing the note to the Presidio commander, Villareal came into his room to advise him against sending the message. Villareal himself was wounded, he told the priest. The Indians were stealing everything they could lay hands on, and he was convinced they had not come in peace. But the padre continued to write, saying there was no choice.

On finishing the note, he told the soldier to find a comfortable place to take shelter, since he was wounded, and to conceal himself as best he could. Then Father Terreros went out and handed the note to the Tejas chief, assuring him that with the message he would be welcomed at the Presidio.

The chief then led Father Terreros' own horse from the corral. When the friar objected, the chief placed the muzzle of his gun on the horse's head. Father Terreros, frightened by the gesture, waved him on, and the chief, followed by a number of warriors, rode off for the Presidio.[3]

It now was too late for anything but appeasement. Hoping to avert bloodshed, the padres pretended not to notice the shameless abuses of the Indians as they sacked the Mission. They talked

---

[3] Deposition of Andrés de Villareal, Nathan-Simpson, *San Saba Papers*, pp. 68–72.

amicably with some of the Tejas Indians, who assured the fathers that they meant no harm to the Spaniards; they were looking for the Apaches, who had killed some of their people in a battle on the Río Florido (Concho). The two Apaches in the Mission had been concealed in the Father President's room, which was protected by a guard of soldiers.

In a few minutes the Tejas chief who had set out for the Presidio returned, his face aglow with anger. He said he had been received by a volley of shots and that three of his warriors had been killed and another wounded. Father Terreros suspected the chief was lying, because he had not had time to reach the Presidio,[4] but he offered to return with him to the fort.

The last horse was brought from the corral, and Father Terreros, accompanied by a soldier, José García, started for the gate. But the Tejas chief, meanwhile, had disappeared into the crowd. The priest and the soldier rode toward the entrance, hoping to find the chief outside the stockade. As they were about to ride through the gate, a shot rang out, and Father Terreros, who had refused to forsake his Mission in the face of adversity and danger, fell from his horse, mortally wounded. The shot was followed by a volley, and the soldier García fell lifeless from his horse.

The other Spaniards in the stockade fought their way through the savages to reach a haven in the buildings. Lázaro de Ayala and Enrique Gutiérrez, a son of the chief steward, did not make it. They were shot and cut to pieces in the patio.

Father Molina and eight others, most of them wounded, gained the President's room and barricaded themselves in, preparing to sell their lives dearly. Father Santiesteban had remained at prayer, and as the Indians moved to sack the chapel they came upon him still at the altar. They showed him no mercy.

From the buildings where the Spaniards had sought refuge, they saw the Indians set fire to the stockade, against which they had piled wood and tinder. It now was apparent that while the Indian chiefs had talked of friendship their comrades had been

---

[4] There seems to be a possibility that the chief was telling the truth. Though the chronology does not jibe and the Indians, by all accounts, fired the first shot, a group of soldiers coming from the Presidio did fire on a band of Indians. Note the account of the relief patrol in the next chapter, which raises the possibility that the soldiers fired on the Indians before the attack on the Mission actually had begun.

making ready for the fire. The massacre started as soon as the wood was ready and the roads covered.

Confident that the fire would destroy the Spaniards who had sought refuge in the buildings, the Indians continued their pillage of the warehouse, where all the supplies for the three projected missions were stored. The images of the saints in the chapel were cut to pieces, the cattle in the corral were killed, and everything that could not be carried away was wantonly destroyed.

From the rooms where the Spaniards took refuge, they fired at the Indians through the loopholes, with some effect. This defensive action led to the injury of Father Molina, for an Indian returned the fire through a small window in the President's room. The bullet struck the priest in the right side of the chest, after grazing the window shutter and piercing his arm with flying splinters.

The group remained in Father Terreros' room until midday, the Indians paying them little heed. As the savages busied themselves with their plunder, the Spaniards escaped from the burning building into a house next to the church. The enemy discovered the move, however, and kindled the fire and shot their guns into the building. The group then fled on into the church itself.

Those who had gathered in other buildings apparently had similar experiences, for in the afternoon they too came to the church, where the survivors were united into one group. Juan Leal brought in the cannon and mounted it on some chests facing the entrance. With the cannon and muskets the Spaniards continued to fire at the Indians in the stockade.

The survivors, all gathered in the church, were alerted sometime after dark by the barking dogs and the shouts of the Indian sentries. Prayers crossed the lips of the besieged, for they knew the hopelessness of a counterattack from the Presidio.

Escape

After talking with the wounded soldier Villareal, soon after the Indians had come, the Mission's chief steward, Juan Antonio Gutiérrez, turned to a shepherd named José Gutiérrez. José, twenty-two years of age, may have been a son of the Steward, who apparently had several. Steward Gutiérrez felt he could depend on the young shepherd to carry a message that he now knew to be vitally important. He told him to go to the Presidio and tell Colonel Parrilla what was going on at the Mission.

The Indians were watching to see that no one left the Mission. Armed with a musket, young Gutiérrez scaled the wall of the stockade next to the river and darted for the cover of the timber that grew along the riverbank. An Indian sentry saw him and leveled his musket. The bullet struck the barrel of José's rifle, tearing away a piece of the muzzle.

At the Presidio the messenger breathlessly told how the Indians had swarmed over the Mission after gaining entry by professing friendship. Their warlike intentions were evident, he declared, for most of the savages carried French firearms, bullet pouches, and large powder horns, while others had lances and bows and arrows. Their costumes, he noted, were those of war.[1]

Colonel Parrilla, who already had issued orders to two different

[1] Paul D. Nathan (trans.) and Lesley Byrd Simpson (ed.), *San Saba Papers*, pp. 43–45.

scouting parties, gave a command, and a messenger hurried to overtake one of the parties still near the fort. The party, led by Sergeant Joseph Antonio Flores was ordered to make an inspection of the Mission area. Flores was to determine the intentions of the Indians, and if necessary to reinforce the Mission guard with the eight men under his command.

Sergeant Flores and his men already had crossed the River at the ford nearest the Presidio when Parrilla's messenger overtook them. They then ascended a hill south of the river to get a view of the road to the Mission. The road, for almost two miles, was crowded with hostile Indians. The Mission stockade was completely surrounded by savages firing their muskets, and more were coming to join them.

A band of Indians in column formation was marching toward the Presidio, and Sergeant Flores and his men advanced to confront them and learn their purpose. When the Indians got within musket range, they fired a volley at the soldiers. Three men—Joaquín García, Luis Chirinos, and Joseph Vásquez—fell. The other six men made a defensive withdrawal, under continuous fire until they reached the nearest ford and recrossed the San Sabá River. One of the six, wounded, was cut off from the crossing and had to leave his weapons and his horse to swim the River and reach the Presidio.[2]

As Sergeant Flores returned to the Presidio he saw three Mission Indians running toward him. The Indians told him they had been able to escape from the Mission because they were outside the stockade cutting wood when the hostile savages came. They had taken cover and watched the murderous onslaught of the northern tribes. The Comanches and their allies, they said, had set fire to the Mission stockade and houses, killing everyone in them.

Parrilla formed a picture in his mind. Sergeant Flores had estimated that the Indians numbered about fifteen hundred (later raised to two thousand), with others still coming, apparently bent on attacking the Presidio. The Colonel called a hurried council of his officers and other soldiers of long experience in Indian warfare.

[2] Sergeant Flores says in his deposition (*ibid.*, pp. 46–52) that Vásquez fell when the Indians fired. Vásquez himself (*ibid.*, p. 81) is quoted as saying that he was struck down by a lance.

Escape

The Presidio garrison was reduced to less than one-third of its complement of one hundred, with the detail of twenty-two men escorting the supply train and twenty-seven assigned to guard the horses and cattle in the pastures. When the first messenger had come from the Mission, Parrilla had sent three men to gather in the soldiers, servants, women, and children encamped in the pastures a dozen miles away.

Considering these things, the council decided against dispersing the Presidio forces further; the Mission, it appeared, already had been destroyed, its occupants murdered. The Presidio lay exposed to similar attack. The Indians' number was so great that any detachment sent out from the Presidio could easily be overwhelmed.

Parrilla gathered the 237 women and children into one building. The horses were herded into the stockade to prevent the Indians from driving them off. As the horses were being brought in, several Indians were seen in the treetops and on the high bluffs south of the San Sabá River, watching movement to and from the Presidio.

In an effort to draw the garrison out into the open, the Indians set fire to the grass around the fort. But the soldiers remained inside the stockade until sunset.

As the sun sank behind the hills, the plaintive sound of the Indians' victory chant rose from the burning Mission. Sergeant Flores, with fourteen soldiers and three Indians, set out from the Presidio, taking a circuitous route to reach the Mission after dark. Flores sent the three Mission Indians ahead to scout, and they returned with the news that sentries guarded the main body of Indians. The savages were celebrating their victory with songs and dancing.

The sergeant and his men moved closer, but they found the sentries alert. As the Mission dogs began to bark, the Indian guards called to each other in warning. Flores noted the dwellings and other Mission buildings were still in flames, giving off an intense light that was to the soldiers' disadvantage.

On orders issued previously by Parrilla, two soldiers separated from the Flores party and started for the supply train as the rest made their way back to the Presidio. These two men were to inform Lieutenant Galván of the attack and to tell him to conceal the supply train off the road. He then was to make his way with the other soldiers and the muleteers to the Presidio by the safest route. The two messengers, Joseph Trujillo and Pedro de Rivera, then were to go on to San Antonio to carry news of the massacre.

It was an uneasy night at Presidio de San Luis de las Amarillas. The garrison remained on continuous alert, in anticipation of an attack on the Presidio at daybreak.

As Sergeant Flores and his men approached the Mission, causing the dogs to bark and the Indian sentries to shout to each other, those imprisoned inside the Mission's burning church were alerted to their opportunity to escape. With the attention of the savages diverted, they found an unguarded exit. Stealing out a few at a time they made their escape along a path to the east. Among the fugitives from the inferno were Father Molina, Corporal Cadena, Andrés de Villareal, José de los Santos, Vicente Gutiérrez, and Joseph Vásquez, one of the soldiers from the Presidio who had sought to reinforce the Mission that morning.

Also escaping were Juan Leal; Joaquín Valdés; Nicolás de los Reyes, a muledriver; the Indian Ignacio, an interpreter of the Apache language, and his wife; the wives of Corporal Cadena and Steward Gutiérrez; and those of the three Mission Indians who had fled to the Presidio. A young son of the Steward, two Apache Indians, and seven other young servants, the sons of soldiers, also escaped.[3]

The nighttime expedition of Sergeant Flores, though it was unable to attack, had provided an opportunity for the besieged to escape undetected. But there was one who still lived who could not escape. The steward, Juan Antonio Gutiérrez, whose rifle had taken its toll of the hostile Indians, lay unable to move because of a severe wound in the thigh.

One soldier, not identified by name, made his way directly to San Antonio, where he was the first to reveal the Mission massacre. He told of carrying Father Molina from the burning church on his back. They were detected and fired upon, he related, and the soldier fell to the ground unconscious. When he regained his senses, the priest was not to be seen. The soldier was wounded in the shoulder, and from the position of the wound he concluded

[3] Compiled from the various accounts, *ibid.*

Escape

that the bullet had passed through the body of the priest. The soldier did not rest until he had reached San Antonio.[4]

But Father Molina was not dead. In his deposition he said nothing of the incident recounted by the soldier. Perhaps the man, fearing he would be punished as a deserter, was seeking to make himself out a hero first. He also told another falsehood at San Antonio, relating to Captain Urrutia that he had tried to reach the San Sabá Presidio after his escape and had found it under attack.

Father Molina had set out alone from the ravaged Mission, making a wide sweep to the south, staying with hidden paths. Two days after the attack, March 18, he reached the Presidio, feverish from his wound and weak from hunger.

Perhaps the most unusual experience of the massacre was that of Joseph Vásquez, one of Sergeant Flores' relief detail. When on the morning of March 16 Sergeant Flores and eight men had set out to give relief to the besieged Mission, the squad became disorganized under the fire of the large band of Indians it encountered. Only Vásquez was able to slip through the barbarians to the shelter of the woods along the riverbank.

There was a canyon between the hillsides and the river, and the small band of Spaniards was caught in it when the Indians opened fire.[5] Flores saw three of his men fall—Joaquín García, Luis Chirinos, and Vásquez. He presumed all of them to be dead.

Vásquez was struck down by a lance thrust. The Indians stripped him of his clothing and left him for dead. But Vásquez regained consciousness sometime later, with a throbbing pain in his chest, where the lance had struck him, and without clothes. The enemy was all about.

Vásquez was about halfway between the Presidio and the Mission. The San Sabá River lay between him and the Presidio. The Mission, he could see, was in flames, and the enemy surrounded it. Whichever way he went, his chances were slim. Despairing of hope for his life, Vásquez, who was twenty-six years old, decided

[4] Nathan-Simpson, *San Saba Papers*, Doc. 7, p. 12; W. E. Dunn, "The Apache Mission," *SWHQ*, Vol. 17, p. 410.

[5] Accounts of Flores and Vásquez, Nathan-Simpson, *San Saba Papers*, pp. 52, 81. Flores' party must have been in the vicinity of present downtown Menard. No canyon, or ravine, now is in evidence. The group was probably caught between the bluffs and the River.

to try to reach the Mission to get a priest to hear his dying confession.

He dragged himself through the brush toward the burning Mission, and for a time he thought he would make it. Then two Indians standing watch by the flaming stockade seized him and threw him into the flames. But Vásquez rolled clear of the fire. There was a burn on his hand, but the pain in his chest was so severe he hardly noticed the sting of the burn. He lay still on the ground where he had fallen, and the Indians left him there. From a half-open eye he could see that someone was shooting at the Indians from the Father President's room. He saw one Indian fall dead, and others were being carried away as though dead or badly wounded.

Watching his chance, Vásquez picked himself up and ran, with what seemed like his last ounce of strength, to the Father President's room. He knocked on the door and called feebly for a priest to hear his confession. Naked, burned, and bleeding, he was admitted.

Some have written that Vásquez, on reaching the Mission, "confessed before dying." But he did not die that day. He lived to give Colonel Parrilla a complete account of what had happened to him, and around him. It was he who, despite his wounds and fatigue, took note that seventeen Indians were killed by the Spaniards. Three were killed on the road to the Presidio by himself and his companions; José de los Santos, firing through loopholes, killed five, the servant Nicolás de los Reyes, six. The chief steward, Gutiérrez, killed three.

That night, when the survivors of the Mission massacre stole through the darkness to make their escape, Joseph Vásquez was among them.[6]

---

[6] Deposition of Joseph Vásquez, Nathan-Simpson, *San Saba Papers*, pp. 80–83. The deposition of Father Molina is translated (*ibid.*, p. 89) as follows: "After we had spent the night in the room where we first took shelter, about eight o'clock the following morning, the soldier Joseph Vásquez came to the outer door, seeking confessions." This translation appears to be an error, for Father Molina says nothing to indicate that the Spaniards passed a night at the Mission during the attack, and all other accounts contradict this rendition. Observe that the number of Indians—three—which Vásquez says were killed on the road from the Presidio corresponds with the number which the chief cited as he explained to Father Terreros his men's attempt to approach the Presidio.

Scene of Death

As the sky paled on the crisp morning of March 17, those within Presidio de San Luis de las Amarillas were taut with expectancy. Dawn was the customary time for the Indians to attack, and the Presidio garrison would not be caught off guard. But the attack did not come.

It was evident that the Indians who had destroyed the Mission Santa Cruz de San Sabá and murdered its defenders remained among the trees along the river and behind the rocks on the hill. From time to time they appeared in small numbers, attempting to lure the soldiers out into the open.

The futility of making sorties from the Presidio had been thoroughly demonstrated the day before. Parrilla ordered a roll call of troops and found that he had a force of fifty-nine soldiers and three armed servants. Some of that number, he noted, were ill, but they were ready for duty. The attack, which had not come at dawn as expected, could come at any time.

The day was spent in an attempt to strengthen the Presidio's defenses. "Now," said Parrilla later, "our principal objective was to protect what we still had."[1]

Guards were organized and trenches dug to give protection to the garrison and the large number of persons, who, making their homes outside the stockade, had come inside the fort on learning of the attack on the Mission.

[1] Paul D. Nathan (trans.) and Lesley Byrd Simpson (ed.), *San Saba Papers*, pp. 49–50.

Without moving outside the stockade, the garrison remained alert throughout the day. From time to time, when the Indians moved too close to the fort, the soldiers fired on them. Though the Indians employed every trick to provoke the garrison to come out and attack, they themselves would not attack. The soldiers refused to fall into the baited trap.

At dusk Lieutenant Juan Galván, the twenty-two soldiers of his supply-train escort, and the six muleteers approached the Presidio cautiously. They scouted the approaches after dark and found that the fort was surrounded by hostile Indians on three sides. The approach from the east had been left open. By this route the detail reached the Presidio.

As Galván's men came into the fort, the drums and the bugle were sounded and one of the cannon was fired. The gates opened and closed. The Indians, too late, learned that the garrison had been reinforced. Taking the drum and bugle calls and the cannon shot as a demonstration of the Spaniards' confidence, they began their withdrawal.

When dawn broke the following day, March 18, there was no attack. Early that morning Sergeant Francisco Yruegas, with twelve soldiers and four scouts, set out on foot to ascertain the movements of the enemy. The party returned about noon with the report that the Indians were marching away to the north, leaving lookouts behind them.

That morning, as the scouting party left the Presidio, the horses had been taken out to pasture. Kept inside the stockade for two days, the animals had been fed only the straw used in thatching the roofs of the buildings. Now, with the report that the enemy was still near, though retreating, the horses were brought back inside the stockade.

During the morning Father Miguel de Molina reached the Presidio. Having made his escape from the Mission by taking hidden paths to the south of the San Sabá River, he had spent two nights in the open, without food or shelter. His wound, just above the right nipple, was badly in need of attention. As he was in no condition to give a log of the Mission massacre, Parrilla did not ask him for his account until four days later.

Most of the survivors apparently had reached the Presidio ahead of the priest, but none of them knew the fate of Father Santiesteban. The fugitives reported that they had not seen him killed, but that they had known nothing of his whereabouts after the savages began the attack.[2]

On receiving the report that the Indians were withdrawing, though still near, Colonel Parrilla took precautions for the safety of the fort. Then with Lieutenant Galván, Sergeant Flores, Sergeant Yruegas, and twenty-five soldiers, he set out to view the scene of death and destruction at Mission Santa Cruz de San Sabá.

Charred remains and ashes marked the spot where Father Terreros and his companions had risked martyrdom rather than abandon the site of their labors for safety at the Presidio. Near the entrance to the stockade, Parrilla and his men found the body of the Mission president, with two bullet wounds and a lance thrust in his breast. The body of José García lay nearby.

Two more bodies were seen inside the gate, both badly burned and almost unidentifiable. Only a portion of the head of one was intact. It was recognized as the remains of Lázaro de Ayala. Flames had consumed all but one leg of the other, and this was identified as belonging to the Steward's son, Enrique Gutiérrez. The four were buried in the cemetery near the church, which now was nothing more than a smouldering ruin.

The other Mission buildings were devastated also, the embers still aglow. Bales of tobacco, boxes of chocolate and soap, barrels of flour lay about, broken and burning. The crates of church ornaments had been broken to pieces and burned. Sacred jewels and pictures were smashed into useless fragments. Parrilla noticed that the effigy of the Holy Saint Francis had been overturned and the head severed from the body. He picked up the figure and carried it with him.

Continuing their search, the soldiers found near the ruins of the church the corpse of the steward, Juan Antonio Gutiérrez, who had been unable to travel when the other survivors had made their escape from the burning church. His eyes had been pried

---

[2] *Ibid.*, p. 65. C. E. Castañeda (*Our Catholic Heritage*, III, 404) says Father Molina and the others watched through the loopholes as the savages severed Father Santiesteban's head from the body and tossed it about like a ball. This apparently was not the case, for none of those from whom Parrilla took statements could tell him the fate of Father Santiesteban before his headless body was found.

from their sockets and his scalp taken. They prepared his grave and buried him near the others in the church cemetery.

What the Indians could not steal they had destroyed. Even the cats of the Mission had been slain. In the corral the soldiers found the bloated carcasses of the eighteen oxen, used by the padres to haul their building logs and to work their fields. Nothing was found alive but a few rams and ewes, which were taken later to the Presidio.

The group from the Presidio made a diligent search for Father Santiesteban but found only some charred fragments of a religious habit. Taking the effigy of Saint Francis, several iron griddles, copper vessels, and some iron bars, which they were able to salvage, the soldiers started back for the Presidio, reconnoitering the south bank of the river on the way. They found the bodies of Joaquín García and Luis Chirinos, the soldiers of the relief party who had been slain at the time Joseph Vásquez was wounded. The two soldiers were buried near where they were found.[3]

Father Santiesteban still was missing on March 24. Parrilla sent Sergeant Yruegas with sixteen men to search. At about five o'clock that afternoon the party returned. The priest's body had been found among the ashes of the Mission. The head, severed from the body, was found later, in the ruins of the clothing storehouse. Father Santiesteban, who was thirty-nine years old at the time of his death, was laid to rest in the church cemetery beside Father Terreros, who was fifty-eight.

Eight persons had been slain by the Comanches and their allies in the massacre at Mission Santa Cruz de San Sabá. As late as April 8, however, Parrilla wrote to Viceroy Marqués de las Amarillas, and to Don Pedro Romero de Terreros that five of his soldiers, badly wounded, still had little hope of survival. It was observed that all the victims were killed with bullets or lances, none by arrows.[4]

[3] Nathan-Simpson, *San Saba Papers*, pp. 55–56. Apparently more extensive salvage was done later, for a lengthy inventory of items retrieved from the burned Mission is found in A.M.S.F. It includes a large number of various kinds of livestock which apparently were on a pasture not found by the Indians.

[4] Both W. E. Dunn ("The Apache Mission," *SWHQ*, Vol. 17, p. 410) and C. E. Castañeda (*Our Catholic Heritage*, III, 407) say ten were killed, listing Ascensio Cadena and Andrés de Villareal among those whose bodies were found in the Mission stockade. Villareal, however, reached the Presidio and

Scene of Death

Somewhere along the south bank of the San Sabá River the bones of the two martyred priests and the soldiers who died in defense of the Mission still lie in their secret graves. The Mission cemetery has never been found. Any markers erected by Parrilla's men have long since disappeared, covered by silt or swept away by the river's floods.

A state historical marker near where the Mission was located pays tribute to the two priests and the sacrifice they made in attempting to advance Christianity and the frontier of New Spain.

---

made a deposition to Parrilla. His account (Doc. 26, Nathan-Simpson, *San Saba Papers*, pp. 68–72) and those of other survivors say Cadena was with the group that escaped from the Mission. Alessio Robles (*Coahuila y Texas*, p. 521) and Bonilla ("A brief compendium," p. 53), on the other hand, say two priests and three soldiers were killed.

Frontier Terror

Anxiously, Colonel Parrilla awaited reinforcements from San Antonio, not knowing when a new attack might come. It was apparent that two thousand hostile Indians, many of them bearing firearms, would have little difficulty in destroying the Presidio as they had the Mission.

The two soldiers, Joseph Trujillo and Pedro de Rivera, whom he had sent out the night of March 16 with instructions for the supply train, had been ordered to proceed to San Antonio with an appeal for help. On March 24 they still were unheard from. On that date Parrilla wrote, "Considerable anxiety is felt here at the lack of word from the two soldiers."[1]

For fear that they had been unable to reach San Antonio, he dispatched two of the Mission Indians with letters to Toribio de Urrutia, the commandant of Presidio de San Antonio de Béjar, and to Father Dolores, the president of the San Antonio missions. Three days later the Indians, frightened by signs of the hostile tribes, returned to the Presidio, their messages undelivered.

The apprehension now had spread throughout the Presidio. Speculation as to the fate of Trujillo and Rivera was rife, and such speculation had the two soldiers meeting a most horrible end. The anxiety increased daily.

Parrilla also noted on March 24 that the supplies which had been hidden along the road the night following the attack, in order that the escort might hasten to reinforce the garrison, now had been brought to the Presidio. The horses had been sent to "a sheltered place, well provided with fodder, in order to strengthen

[1] Paul D. Nathan (trans.) and Lesley Byrd Simpson (ed.), *San Saba Papers*, p. 94.

Frontier Terror

them against the important tasks that may lie ahead." Severe winter weather persisted, with extreme cold and some snow, and the animals were in a weakened condition.[2]

On March 27, the same day the Indian messengers returned, nine Apache Indians arrived at the Presidio. They said Father Mariano de los Dolores had sent them from San Antonio with instructions to observe the state of affairs at the Presidio and the disposition of the enemy known to be present in the region. Parrilla regarded the Apaches with suspicion. For all he knew, no word of the attack had reached San Antonio. If these Indians were sincere, they could have obtained their information nowhere else.

The Presidio commander then ordered Lieutenant Galván to go to San Antonio to give a full report to Captain Urrutia and to Father Dolores.

The commander of Presidio de San Luis de las Amarillas had no way of knowing that word of the attack on the Mission had reached San Antonio March 19. It had been carried by the soldier who had fled after escaping from the burning Mission. This unidentified person confused the picture for Urrutia and others by saying he had tried to make his way to the Presidio and had found it under attack.

Nor did Parrilla know that the two soldiers, Trujillo and Rivera, had arrived the following day, bearing Parrilla's letter to Captain Urrutia. News of the massacre had passed like a shock wave through the settlement of San Antonio. Father Dolores ordered the Spanish settlers, missionaries, and soldiers on the Guadalupe River to come at once to San Antonio for safety, lest those at that mission also be slaughtered by the Norteños.

Governor Jacinto de Barrios y Jáuregui, who had foretold the fate of the San Sabá Mission in opposing its establishment, had similar fears. He first learned of the massacre April 3, while at Nacogdoches, and immediately set out for San Antonio to prepare the defense for the settlement. But the East Texas rivers and creeks were swollen by spring rains, and the Governor was forced to turn back.

Captain Urrutia, however, was unable to send help to San Sabá, since all but five of his men were on guard duty at the San Antonio missions. Father Dolores deemed it inadvisable to heed

[2] *Ibid.*, p. 93.

Parrilla's request for a force of mission Indians, for he feared they were not to be trusted away from the missions. But what seems to have most concerned the Captain and Father Dolores was the fear that Presidio de San Luis de las Amarillas no longer stood as a buffer between San Antonio and the northern Indians, and an attack on that settlement could be expected at any hour.[3]

Parrilla had stated in his letter brought by the two soldiers that he would keep Urrutia informed if he was alive and able to do so. But since the San Antonio commandant had heard nothing further he therefore presumed that the presidio on the San Sabá, along with the mission there, had fallen. But for fear of being "held blameworthy at some future time," as he so candidly expressed it, he sent out an appeal to Los Adaes, La Bahía, San Juan Bautista, Santa Rosa, and Nuevo León, asking those presidios to send him what help they could for the relief of San Sabá—and San Antonio. If assistance was not offered, the entire province of Texas could be lost to the hostile tribes, he wrote, adding that in his own opinion the attacking Indians were "incited by foreign political agents."[4]

But, on learning of the savage attack of the Comanches and their allies at San Sabá, each of the presidios was paralyzed by panic. They felt that they themselves were in danger of surprise attack from the daring savages, goaded by their victory.

Angel de Martos y Navarrete, governor of Coahuila, transmitted Urrutia's appeal to the Viceroy on March 25, describing the situation at San Sabá as follows: "The post is so remote ... and so isolated that no matter what I might wish to undertake in this urgent necessity, it would be of no avail because of the great distance and the extreme aridity of the whole region."[5]

Martos feared the Apaches, who had moved south in large numbers, and he dared not deplete his garrison lest these Indians take advantage of the weakness and attack the settlements. "In view of all these things, I have concluded that I ought

[3] C. E. Castañeda (*Our Catholic Heritage*, III, 407–408) says a lieutenant and eighteen men were dispatched to San Sabá immediately after word of the attack was received in San Antonio. If such was the case, Parrilla, in all his letters and depositions, fails to make mention of it.

[4] Captain Urrutia to Don Angel de Martos y Navarrete, March 20, 1758, Nathan-Simpson, *San Saba Papers*, pp. 8–9.

[5] Angel de Martos y Navarrete to the viceroy, Marqués de las Amarillas, March 25, 1758, Nathan-Simpson, in *ibid.*, pp. 24–25.

Frontier Terror

to strengthen and supply the frontiers of my command against whatever may occur." [6]

Martos also informed the Viceroy that Joseph Joachín de Eca y Músquiz, lieutenant of Presidio de San Luis de las Amarillas, had passed Monclova and had learned of "the unhappy news." Eca was on his way to Santa Rosa to meet the new parish priest whom he was to escort back to San Sabá. Martos continued:

> I have written to the Minister of the Treasury, the Marqués de San Miguel de Aguayo, requesting that he send me twenty-five men, fully armed, equipped and supplied. With these and with Lieutenant Eca y Músquiz, and others from this Province . . . some assistance may be given to San Antonio de Béjar.[7]

The dispatches, bearing the news of the attack on Mission Santa Cruz de San Sabá, reached Mexico City April 6. The Viceroy's advisers pondered Urrutia's appeal for help, and the question of whether troops from Mexico City or the garrisons of "the more distant stations" should be sent to the rescue of the settlements in Texas. The *fiscal*, Marqués de Aranda, ruled that the commanders of the presidios of the neighboring provinces should render the necessary aid, "regardless of their misgivings." The *auditor*, Domingo Valcárcel, concurred.[8]

The viceregal advisers failed to recognize the importance of the remote frontier, or to sympathize with the plight of the soldiers charged with defending it.

The Viceroy issued orders to the governors of Coahuila, Nuevo León, and Texas to send what help they could to the beleaguered Presidio de San Luis de las Amarillas. There was no response. The outlying presidios, poorly manned and inadequately equipped, simply did not have the capacity to send aid. The daring of the Indians of the north was unparalleled in the annals of Spanish Texas, and every commander along the frontier feared that his post might be their next objective.

Supplies were running low at San Sabá, for all the two thousand head of livestock, abandoned in the pastures because of the attack, had been driven off or scattered by the Indians. Those living at the fort, seeing that no aid came, lived in constant fear

---
[6] *Ibid.*, p. 25.
[7] *Ibid.*, p. 29.
[8] Marqués de Aranda to the Viceroy, April 6, 1758, in *ibid.*, p. 30.

of a new attack, and some of the soldiers were deserting, leaving their families behind to face the ravages of the Indians.

Such was the situation April 2, when Father Francisco Aparicio arrived from San Antonio, with the soldiers Trujillo and Rivera and three soldiers from the now abandoned mission on the Guadalupe. Father Aparicio brought a reply from Father Dolores to the Parrilla letters, carried to San Antonio by Lieutenant Galván.

Aid had not been sent, Father Dolores wrote, because

> ... I considered it difficult to send out reinforcements in sufficient numbers to defend themselves, in view of the large force of the enemy reported in your letter.
>
> This decision was arrived at because of reports among the Indians that the enemy intended also to destroy Guadalupe and to invade these missions. Since the Apaches in the vicinity of Medina are very numerous, it is suspected that some secret ambush is being prepared, in which our troops, if known to be widely scattered, might all be slain.[9]

Further on in the letter he said:

> I pointed out to the Commandant [Urrutia] that with five of his men, ten from the Missions, and eight more who were at the Presidio, he would have at his command 73 men for the relief of your Presidio. But instead of dispatching them with all speed, he issued orders in writing to the soldiers, and verbally to the governors, that not one Father or Indian was to leave the Missions, and that any garrison soldier who did so would be subject to severe penalties.[10]

Just who was to blame for the lack of help is not clear. Father Dolores first seems to assume the blame himself, then to hand it to Urrutia. "Whatever else this discrepancy may mean," says Simpson, "it is another instance of the confusion arising from the overlapping authorities on the frontier." [11]

In his letter Father Dolores also informed Parrilla that he had not received the ornaments and other items from the suppressed San Xavier missions which Father Terreros finally had agreed that he should have. "I was expecting all these things by the pack train." [12]

[9] Father Dolores to Parrilla, March 30, 1758, in *ibid.*, p. 123.
[10] *Ibid.*, p. 125.
[11] Nathan-Simpson, *San Saba Papers*, p. 126 n.
[12] Father Dolores to Parrilla, March 30, 1758, in *ibid.*, pp. 124–125. For an inventory of the Mission equipment which caused this squabble, see A.M.S.F. The equipment was valued at 1,231 pesos.

He told Parrilla that all available supplies would be sent to him, guarded by an escort of Indians from the San Antonio missions, by the soldiers who would bring Father Molina back to San Antonio, and by three families from San Juan Capistrano.

With this news, and the stock of supplies dwindling to the danger point, Parrilla two days later sent Sergeant Francisco Yruegas, with a corporal and fifteen men, to San Antonio with the string of mules to be used in bringing the needed supplies. Father Molina, still suffering from the chest wound he had received in the attack, was sent with the soldiers to San Antonio for treatment.

Since the attack Parrilla had busied himself in compiling a record of events pertaining to it. He feared that he would be held responsible for the success of the northern tribes in destroying the Mission and murdering the priests and the soldiers. In order to absolve himself he took depositions from the most responsible survivors and from others who had special knowledge relating to events of March 16.

To these he added depositions from the two soldiers sent to San Antonio the night of March 16, several formal statements of his own, various letters, and other documents.[13]

Not only did these papers preserve a record of the occurrences on the day of the massacre, but they provided Parrilla with a basis for understanding the new forces on the frontier. The salient aspects of the change were the large number of warriors which the northern tribes were able to muster, their firearms, and their skill in using these new weapons. In such large numbers, and so well armed, the Indians had the capability of destroying his Presidio with ease. Parrilla was deeply concerned, but he was not the only one who was apprehensive.

On April 2 he was presented with a petition signed by the ensign of the Presidio, Juan Cortinas, by the noncommissioned officers, and by the soldiers. Only Lieutenant Galván, who like Cortinas was a veteran of many years' service on the Texas frontier, refused to sign the petition; expressing confidence that his commanding officer would be able to reach the right decision.

Voicing the fear that the Indians would double their number

---

[13] See Nathan-Simpson, *San Saba Papers*, pp. 41-151, for translations of these documents.

and return to wipe out the Presidio, the company pointed out that reinforcements had not been forthcoming, even after twelve days; that the Indians could easily steal the garrison's horses and cut off its supply lines, leaving the Presidio "in deadly peril." [14] They asked the Colonel to move the Presidio to a safer place.

Though the petition was properly worded, expressing both courtesy and respect, it hit Parrilla's vulnerable spot—his egotism. Considering the petition as an affront to his ability as a commander and a threat of mutiny, he proceeded to interrogate the ensign and the sergeants, taking written depositions from each.

> I recognize that their misgivings require consideration, in view of present conditions in this territory and the increasing number of women and children at this Presidio. The reasons for future actions and procedures that I may adopt must also be made clear, and I must therefore discover the motive for the soldiers' decision to make this most unusual remonstrance.... This is to be done in order to ascertain why they joined together in preparing it, and whether they were subjected to influence or persuasion, or to any incentive other than those they acknowledge and describe as honorable, and whether they were influenced or swayed by foreign sources.[15]

But the soldiers had no mutinous intent, nor were they influenced by "foreign sources." They were aware of the dangers and were unnerved by the continual outcries of the women and children. They knew the Apaches would never congregate in missions at this site, and they did not want to see their wives and children murdered.

The newly arrived priest, Father Aparicio, soon showed himself to be in sympathy with the soldiers' desire to move the Presidio, and mission effort, to a safer place. Father Aparicio is another link between the history of the missionary effort of the Franciscan friars on the San Gabriel (San Xavier) River and that on the San Sabá. At the San Xavier missions he had endured the ravages of Captain Felipe de Rábago y Terán until the murders of Father José de Ganzábal and the luckless soldier Ceballos. Then he, with two other priests, had fled the ill-fated missions. The three friars

---

[14] Petition presented to Parrilla by members of the garrison, April 2, 1758, in *ibid.*, p. 108.

[15] Statement of Parrilla, in *ibid.*, p. 110.

had returned after the panic subsided, only to suffer drouth, epidemic, and other hardships.

Father Aparicio had been among the petitioners desiring removal of the San Xavier missions to the San Marcos River. After this transfer was accomplished, and after a large band of Apaches appeared at the new site, he had joined with the other priests in urging a mission for these Indians in their own country, on the San Sabá River. Though the priests had offered to go into Apache country without a garrison of soldiers to protect them, their petition was denied. Father Aparicio then served at the mission on the Guadalupe, until it was abandoned because of the attack on San Sabá.

Now Father Dolores was sending Father Aparicio to San Sabá, apparently to determine whether there was any hope of bringing the Apaches into missions at this site. He was instructed to work with any Indians who might come until the fate of this missionary endeavor was decided.

Father Aparicio had no sooner arrived at San Sabá than he realized the futility of any such hope. On April 5, just three days after his arrival, he formally requested abandonment of the site, suggesting removal of the missionary effort to either the San Marcos or the Guadalupe. The Apaches, he said, would never congregate at San Sabá after the terrible massacre. The Indians who had worked with him at the San Xavier missions had expressed their hatred for the Apaches. On the San Marcos, members of tribes formerly friendly to the Spaniards had told him they were friends no longer because the Spaniards had allied themselves with the Apaches and had established an Apache mission.

Since the massacre the Apaches had forsaken the San Sabá region, fleeing southward. Father Aparicio doubted that any of them would ever return, but, if they should return, he doubted that they would ever agree to stay here. Their enemies had found the way to the mission area and very likely would come again. Now that converting the Apaches seemed to be an impossibility, to remain at San Sabá, he asserted, was useless.[16]

While Father Aparicio was seeking abandonment of the San Sabá project, the viceregal government in México was taking

---

[16] Father Aparicio to Parrilla, April 5, 1758, in *ibid.*, pp. 127–130; Castañeda, *Our Catholic Heritage*, IV, 100.

steps to replace the martyred missionaries and to carry on the effort for which Fathers Terreros and Santiesteban had died. On July 19 the Viceroy wrote succinctly to Don Pedro Romero de Terreros. Awkwardly offering his regrets, he reminded him of the obligation which he had assumed, to continue support of the Apache mission despite the tragic outcome.

In correspondence to the Viceroy and the guardian, Father Joseph García, Don Pedro readily agreed to defray the expense of sending the new missionaries to replace those slain by the Indians and to pay for replacing lost supplies and equipment. He urged that delays be avoided, so that the heathen Indians could be instructed in the holy faith.

On September 7 the Viceroy notified Don Pedro that the commissary general had appointed Father Aparicio, already at San Sabá, and Father Pedro de Parras, at Mission Concepción, from the College of Querétaro. From the College of San Fernando he had appointed Fathers Junipero Serra and Francisco Palou.[17] But Father Aparicio soon returned to Mission Concepción, and the other three priests never went to San Sabá. The only explanation is that given by Father Dolores in a letter to the guardian dated February 11, 1759: plans could not be made for re-establishing the mission on the San Sabá River, pending the outcome of Parrilla's campaign against the northern tribes, which was to begin soon. This punitive campaign, however, was to have a different outcome from the one anticipated, placing matters in an entirely new light. The missionary effort on the San Sabá River had ended.

Fathers Serra and Palou, though never to reach San Sabá, were destined to win distinction elsewhere. The first became the founder of the missions of California, the second their historian.[18]

[17] The viceroy, Marqués de las Amarillas, to Don Pedro Romero de Terreros, July 19 and September 1, 1758; rough drafts of letters from Don Pedro de Terreros to the Viceroy and Friar Joseph García, September, 1758; all in A.M.S.F.

[18] Castañeda, *Our Catholic Heritage*, III, 408–409.

PART III
The Changed Frontier

Banner Borne by Pride

The importance of the San Sabá massacre may be seen in several different lights. Aside from later developments, the most significant points were these:

First, it represented the initial contact of the Spaniards with large numbers of hostile Indians equipped with firearms and skilled in using them. Up to now the Spaniards had held the advantage in their warfare with the savages. They had been able to protect themselves against the Indians' arrows by means of their leather jerkins and shields, but these devices were ineffective against musket fire, which the natives now accurately employed.

While interrogating Sergeant Joseph Antonio Flores, Parrilla asked whether in his thirty years of serving the King, in the presidios and on the frontiers, Flores had ever before seen so many hostile Indians equipped with firearms and so skilled in handling them as those he encountered on his way to aid the Mission the day of the attack. Flores

... replied that he had never seen or heard of hostile Indians attacking our forces in such numbers and so fully armed. Formerly the barbarians had fought with arrows, pikes, hatchets and similar weapons, against which the officers and soldiers of the presidios had held the advantage and had won many victories.[1]

According to Simpson,

Sergeant Flores' testimony is conclusive proof of the real cause of the Spanish defeat on all frontiers, namely the adoption by the Indians of

[1] Statement of Sergeant Flores, Paul D. Nathan (trans.) and Lesley Byrd Simpson (ed.), *San Saba Papers*, p. 53.

European techniques of warfare: horses, armor and firearms, in the use of which they became expert. Nothing else explains the success of the Apache and Comanche federations, which obliged the Spaniards to abandon any notion of further expansion to the north, and indeed, put them permanently on the defensive.[2]

Testimony gathered by Parrilla revealed also that the attacking Indians included Comanches, Tejas, Tonkawas, Bidais, and others who had never made war on the Spaniards before. Hence the second point of importance is that, as a result of allying themselves with the Apaches, the Spaniards had made new enemies. These new enemies, regardless of other events linked with the San Sabá Mission episode, were certain to have an effect on future efforts to extend the Texas frontier of New Spain, for they controlled the area to the north.

Furthermore, these new enemies, incited by the alliance of the Apaches with the Spaniards, had formed a strong alliance themselves. With their superior numbers and firearms they aroused apprehension among the Spaniards. They also dissuaded the Apaches permanently from congregating in missions on the San Sabá River. Therefore, the San Sabá massacre resulted in ending the missionary endeavor at this particular location.

A third significant point is that the San Sabá massacre marked the beginning of Comanche warfare with the white settlers in Texas. Sergeant Flores, the thirty-year frontier veteran, said he had not heard of hostility by the Comanches "in this part of the north, but he did know that the Comanches in New Mexico had done as much damage as they could." He mentioned that the Comanches had captured several persons and were still holding them as prisoners in New Mexico.[3]

Newcomb notes that the Comanches had stolen horses in New Mexico as early as 1705, "thus marking the arrival of the greatest horse thieves of them all." They would stand as a barrier to settlement of the Plains, not only by the Spaniards, but by the Texans and the Americans as well. Until 1875 they were the principal and most stubborn adversaries the Texans had.[4]

Until the last years of their independence they raided through much of the state, to say nothing of Mexico, and killed or captured men.

[2] *Ibid.*, p. 53 n.
[3] Statement of Sergeant Flores, in *ibid.*, p. 55.
[4] W. W. Newcomb, Jr., *The Indians of Texas*, pp. 88, 155.

Banner Borne by Pride

women, and children, carried off what loot they could, and burned the rest. Not only did the Comanches valiantly battle the Spaniards, Mexicans, Texans, and Americans but they conquered the original Indian residents of the southern plains—the eastern Apaches, Tonkawas, and others.[5]

The Spaniards had planned the Mission and Presidio of San Sabá as a base from which to penetrate the Great Plains. They had visualized, first, the development of a flourishing town, then of the entire region, and, second, the establishment of trade routes across the Plains country to New Mexico after the country to the north and the west had been explored. But the nature of the Indians who inhabited that region called for a change of plans.

"The first Plains Indian tribe to discomfit the Spaniard in his northern advance [says Webb] was the Apache; the second was the Comanche."[6]

In seeking to subdue the Apache with missions on the San Sabá River, the Spaniards had incurred the wrath of the Comanche, exchanging an old enemy for a new one. "... when they traded an Apache for a Comanche, they found themselves in possession of a tiger in place of a wildcat."[7]

With destruction of the San Sabá Mission, the Comanches served notice to the Spaniards that they militantly opposed any further advance toward the Plains and demonstrated that they had the force to prevent it.

Parrilla was not ready to admit that the Comanche barrier was insurmountable; yet he knew that he would need help from the other presidios in order to overcome it. With these thoughts in mind he took measures which would lead to the next major episode in the San Sabá story, and which, coupled with the Mission massacre, would shape still further the pattern of history.

The Presidio commander bundled up the depositions he had taken regarding the massacre and sent them to Viceroy Amarillas. Then on April 8 he spent all day, and probably part of the night, writing his own letters and reports. He wrote to Don Pedro Romero de Terreros, enclosing a copy of Father Molina's testimony regarding the attack on the Mission.

As Parrilla interpreted the events of the past month, the north-

[5] *Ibid.*, pp. 155–156.
[6] W. P. Webb, *The Great Plains*, p. 116.
[7] *Ibid.*, p. 118.

ern tribes did not look on the attack as a success in itself, but rather as a step toward total destruction of the enterprise. What had happened would count but little, as would be seen in counting the toll of future depredations, Parrilla predicted. The Apaches, he noted, continued to promise to join missions, "though never doing so on this river because of their terror of their enemies." [8] Molina expressed similar views in the document which Parrilla sent to Don Pedro.

> The number and resourcefulness of these enemies of religion, divine and human, is very great, and the inhabitants of this region cannot be converted, even by the strongest efforts and the best planning, unless the territory between this river and our own settlements is occupied by our troops. For it is likely, if in this case the attackers numbered about two thousand, equipped with at least one thousand firearms, that in another attack their numbers will be still greater because of the many nations now involved in the war. Intent as they are on robbery and plunder, they will not desist from such activities, nor cease to carry out their diabolic schemes. Therefore I consider it impossible to reduce and settle these Apache Indians along the San Sabá, or for many leagues round-about, even with the aid of the King's forces; nor will they be pacified by the utmost favor and aid. For having become aware, as they have done, of the evident threat and danger from their enemies, they are certain to try to escape from them, as they are now doing.[9]

Parrilla, in his report to the Viceroy, offered three proposals in such tedious wording that historians—and probably the Viceroy also—have had difficulty in determining just which course of action Parrilla himself favored.

What Parrilla wanted was, first, to remove any blemish, real or imagined, from his record. In the first of his three proposals, he explained in great length that he could in no way be held accountable for neglect in the massacre and destruction of the Mission. His innate egotism shone through in such statements as, "I have remained silent about the special and conspicuous merit I have earned by my unselfishness, diligence, and disregard for my own life and personal comfort." [10]

---

[8] Parrilla to Don Pedro de Terreros, April 8, 1758, A.M.S.F.

[9] "Informe de Fray Miguel de Molina," March 22, 1758, A.M.S.F.; translated by Nathan in *San Saba Papers*, pp. 84–92.

[10] Parrilla to the viceroy, Marqués de las Amarillas, April 8, 1758, Nathan-Simpson, *San Saba Papers*, p. 133.

He said implicitly that the stubbornness of the missionaries themselves had brought the downfall of the Mission, recounting how he had repeatedly urged them to move to the Presidio; "Only by resorting to force, your Excellency, could I have succeeded in removing the religious, as I had attempted many times to do." [11]

Here he recalled with bitterness his row with the Jesuit priests during the Pima rebellion in Sonora (1751–1752), and how their esteem for him had turned to vituperation when he had to assume the duties of magistrate. The mistakes for which he had been criticized, Parrilla wrote, did not exist. "All my actions and procedures have been adopted only after careful thought and attention, which always guide me in the discharge of my duties, so that I shall never neglect to apply the proper measures when they are called for." [12]

Since the massacre, the Commander continued, the soldiers and their families—numbering almost four hundred persons—were anxious to abandon the Presidio. "I have reason to believe that one by one they will desert if they become discouraged, even if they have to leave their families behind, as some have already done." [13] But, as for himself, Parrilla would remain at the post alone rather than abandon it without permission.

His position was made somewhat untenable, he pointed out, by the way the Indian tribes here differed from the ones dealt with elsewhere. The northern tribes, he explained, were more numerous than those of the south, and traveled in larger bands. They had obtained firearms and a supply of ammunition by trading with the French, were mounted on good horses, and had learned modern methods of warfare from the Europeans. Thus they were a more formidable enemy than any tribe encountered previously, and the present site was too much exposed to their attacks. The Apaches, having been afforded little protection by the Spaniards, were not likely to congregate at San Sabá. They had fled southward and taken up their abode on the San Marcos and Guadalupe Rivers.

Then came the first of the three proposals: The northern Indians should be punished for the outrages they had committed at the Mission. Whether the Presidio was moved, Parrilla said, a

[11] *Ibid.*, p. 134.
[12] *Ibid.*, p. 135.
[13] *Ibid.*, p. 136.

campaign should be made into the country of the Norteños. If something was not done to give them a taste of Spanish might, he opined, they would lose all respect for the Spaniards and would be encouraged to attack other outposts. Recalling his successes in fighting the Indians in Sonora, he offered to lead such a campaign himself if the Viceroy deemed it advisable. And this assignment, it seems, is what Parrilla really wanted. For next to being an egotist he was a man of action.

Then came an alternate proposal. During his year on the San Sabá River, he related, he had sent out exploring parties to determine if there were mineral deposits in the region. His men had visited Los Almagres on the Llano River and had obtained some samples of ore, a quantity of which was smelted at Presidio de San Luis de las Amarillas and found to contain silver. It appeared, said the Colonel, that twenty-five pounds of ore would yield an ounce and a half of silver.[14]

Other samples of ore had been carried by Lieutenant Eca y Músquiz on his most recent trip to Santa Rosa, in Coahuila, for more accurate assay. There three times as much ore was needed to produce the quantity of metal Parrilla expected to get from twenty-five pounds.

Parrilla sent José de Guzmán to Mexico City with his personal report on the possibilities of the Almagres mine and of another deposit which he said had been found near the headwaters of the Llano. Guzmán, a veteran miner and frontiersman, had explored both sites. The Commander's message suggested that the Presidio de San Luis de las Amarillas could be moved to either of the two sites, or to some point halfway between, from which protection could be afforded to settlers at both. As in the case of the proposed campaign against the Indians, Parrilla suggested that the matter should be carefully studied by the council in San Antonio.

Parrilla's plethora of ideas gets a little confusing at this point. He made a third proposal which called for moving the Presidio

[14] Remains of this smelter later gave rise to the Bowie or Lost San Saba Mine legend, treated in Chapter 22. A nugget picked up there in 1962 was analyzed for the author by the Department of Mining and Metallurgy, Texas Western College. It was found to have this composition: iron, 4.5 per cent; lime, 18.43 per cent; alumina, 6.32 per cent; and silica, 29.84 per cent. A fire analysis on the sample for gold and silver found no gold but showed 0.45 ounce of silver per ton of ore. For Parrilla's proposals regarding the mine and other possibilities see Nathan-Simpson, *San Saba Papers*, pp. 131–151.

temporarily either to the San Marcos River or to the Guadalupe, to await final disposition by the Viceroy. In something of a paradox, he said that the Apaches were more amenable now to being congregated into missions than ever before, and that several missions could be founded, on either of the two streams, for the Apaches and for the former neophytes of the San Xavier missions.

Viceroy Marqués de las Amarillas passed the various proposals of the Commander to his advisers, who, in short, attempted to rule out a campaign against the Indians and the quest of silver and to concentrate on Parrilla's suggestion to move the Presidio to a safer, and not quite so remote, location. A special council was called to take up the matter. For once the council did not see eye to eye with the viceregal counselors, but they finally came to an agreement.

To abandon the presidio on the San Sabá River would be an admission of fear. Spanish honor demanded its maintenance at all costs. This was essential, not only to vindicate Spanish prestige, but to insure the peace and safety of Coahuila and Nuevo Santander. To avoid recurrence of the Mission massacre, the missionaries should be ordered to live in the Presidio. But Parrilla should be instructed to hold his post, come what may.

The council voted unanimously in favor of authorizing a campaign to punish the northern tribes for the sacrilegious murders of San Sabá. The Viceroy approved the council's recommendations June 27, 1758. In line with the recommendations Parrilla was to lead the expedition, and he was instructed to call a special council in San Antonio to be attended by the governors of Coahuila and Texas, by Parrilla, and by other frontier officers, to plan the campaign. The various officials summoned were to be warned that failure to attend would be sufficient cause for suspension from office.[15]

While Parrilla waited at San Sabá for official reaction to his proposals, the tension increased among his garrison. Since destruction of the Mission in March no Indians had been living at the Presidio. The Comanches apparently were taking care to prevent the Apaches from gathering there, and their harassment succeeded also in keeping the soldiers on edge.

Small bands of Apaches came from time to time to the Presidio,

[15] C. E. Castañeda, *Our Catholic Heritage*, IV, 104–110.

while on their way to or from buffalo hunts and raiding expeditions. They never dared linger long, for fear the Comanches would surprise them there. These fears were not groundless.

During the summer a large force of northern Indians, probably Tonkawas, ambushed a band of Apaches a short distance from the Presidio. According to Parrilla's account, more than fifty of the Apaches were killed, with only a few managing to escape their death-dealing foes. Since this success—accomplished without interference from the Presidio—the northern Indians had become bolder. They now were seen frequently, prowling in the vicinity of the Spanish stronghold. They often came within sight of the Presidio to taunt the discouraged soldiers. Parrilla was fearful he might not be able to hold his post without additional men. He informed the Viceroy of these events and of his fears soon after he received instructions for planning the campaign against the Indians who had destroyed the Mission Santa Cruz de San Sabá.

Parrilla wrote on July 4 to Don Pedro de Terreros, sending papers which he said would certify that the deceased fathers of the Mission were satisfied with the captain's recent conduct.[16]

As always, Parrilla was eager to maintain his good name and to persuade others to esteem him as he esteemed himself.

The instructions for which Parrilla waited arrived early in August, when his garrison was taut with apprehension over the next move of the Comanches and their allies. He lost no time in taking the action set forth in the Viceroy's letter. In his reply to the Viceroy, under date of August 11, he announced he had already requested the governors of Texas and of Coahuila and the commanders of the other presidios to meet with him in San Antonio October 4.

The Viceroy had asked him to determine the attitude of the Apaches with regard to establishment of missions for them in the San Sabá region. Not until he and Lieutenant Eca y Músquiz went to San Antonio for the council session did Parrilla make contact with an Apache chief who could give him the information he sought. The chief told him that the Apaches were about to undertake a campaign against their enemies, that they had chosen to have no fixed habitat in order to avoid surprise attack, and that

[16] Parrilla to Don Pedro Terreros, July 4, 1758, A.M.S.F.

they would be ready to congregate at missions as soon as the campaign was over.

But the Apaches had dallied too long. Father Mariano de los Dolores, once the champion of missions for this wily tribe, now declared that the Apaches constituted the most serious menace to Spanish interests in Texas. There should be no temporizing, he said. At the end of the campaign the Apaches should be made to fulfill their promises; if they refused to do so within a reasonable length of time they should be considered enemies of the Spaniards and treated as such.

Although Parrilla had called the meeting in San Antonio for October 4, heavy rains and impassable roads prevented many of the officers from arriving until the end of the year. The council finally met on January 3, 1759.

During the Colonel's absence from San Sabá, a force of northern Indians, principally Comanches, surprised, in mid-December, a party of thirty-four Apaches near the Presidio, killing all but thirteen. The Apache survivors said their attackers included members of eleven nations, all armed with muskets. For several days the Presidio remained in a state of fear. On the night of December 22 the raiders hovered around the Presidio but departed without making an attack.[17]

The council in San Antonio agreed that at least five hundred men were needed for the campaign against the northern tribes, including presidial soldiers, volunteer militiamen, Tlaxcalteca Indians, and other mission Indians. The offensive should be directed against the Tehuacanas, Tonkawas, and Wichitas, including the Taovayas and Iscanis, all of which had taken part in destruction of the Mission San Sabá. Because the Comanche country was too far distant and unfamiliar, the Spaniards decided not to include these Indians in the campaign. It was deemed more prudent to hand them an object lesson by dealing severely with their allies who could be more easily reached. But ruling out the Comanches was not to be done so easily.

June was the time chosen to begin the punitive expedition, since grass would be plentiful and since carrying feed for the horses would not be necessary. Yet it was to be August before the

[17] Henry Easton Allen, "The Parrilla Expedition to the Red River in 1759," *Southwestern Historical Quarterly*, Vol. 43, pp. 57–58.

start was made. A four-month expedition was planned, at an expected cost of 59,000 pesos.

Father Dolores reported on the council by letter to Father Joseph García, the guardian of Querétaro, on February 11. Concern of the religious in the proposed campaign seems to have stemmed from two sources: They feared that absence of large numbers of soldiers would leave the settlements and missions open for attack; also, they realized, as pointed out by Father Dolores in his letter, that re-establishment of the San Sabá Mission and continued efforts to gather the Apaches hinged on the campaign's outcome. Father Dolores apparently feared for the safety of the settlements, and possibly for the outcome of the campaign, because of word received from Father Joseph de Calahorra in East Texas, and from the French commander of the fort of Reathitos. They warned that eleven Indian nations were gathering in preparation for an attack on San Sabá and San Antonio.[18]

When the Viceroy received the plans made by the council, he wavered, hesitant to authorize such an expensive undertaking. But his advisers, who at first had discouraged the campaign, now insisted on its necessity. On March 30 the Viceroy granted his approval. His misgivings were allayed shortly, for King Ferdinand VI, having been apprised of the recommendations of the Junta de Guerra y Hacienda made the previous June, recommended that the plan be carried out.

Undoubtedly the Viceroy's resolve would have been stronger had he known that, on the very day he issued his approval, the same daring tribes of the north had committed new depredations at the Spanish presidio on the faraway San Sabá River.[19]

[18] Dolores to García, February 11, 1759, A.M.S.F.
[19] Castañeda, *Our Catholic Heritage*, IV, 114–118.

The Great Mistrust

The council in San Antonio was held against a backdrop of growing tension between the Spaniards and the French in Texas. Since the discovery of Fort Saint Louis the Spaniards' fear of French encroachment had been an important motivation of the mission movement. Many times had this fear impelled officials of New Spain to accede to petitions of the missionaries for occupation of the remote areas of Texas. The Mission San Sabá was a case in point.

The history of the province was dotted with incidents manifesting the irritation of the colonial arms of the two European powers, which in their separate ways were attempting to woo the Indians of the region into their respective camps.

During his time as governor of Texas, 1750–1760, Jacinto de Barrios y Jáuregui had established an illicit trade with the French at Natchitoches. But in 1754 he learned that four Frenchmen, together with two Spaniards, had settled in Texas, near the mouth of the Trinity River, and were selling guns and ammunition to the Indians. An expedition led by Lieutenant Marcos Ruiz located the settlement some two leagues from the mouth of the Trinity and arrested Joseph Blancpain, two associates, and two Negro slaves. Blancpain revealed that he had expected fifty families to come from New Orleans to found a permanent settlement, with a chaplain who was to found a mission among the Indians.

In 1755 Barrios ordered Domingo del Río to visit the site on the Trinity again. From this visit it was learned that soon after Blancpain's arrest a boat had sailed into the mouth of the Trinity. When those on the boat were informed of the fate of the French traders, they sailed down the coast to the Brazos, then turned back toward New Orleans. Later four Frenchmen on horseback had come, and they too departed on learning the fate of the vanguard of the proposed settlement.

These events were considered in the light of the French penetration to Santa Fé, which had begun with the Mallet brothers in 1739, and in light of the treaty made between French traders and the Comanches and Jumanos eight or nine years later. The French appeared to be spreading around the Spanish frontier on the north and threatening, with their alliance with the Comanches and the Jumanos (probably Wichitas, in this case), to move down the Pecos River on the west. The Spaniards could not risk a French settlement on the coast. They countered by establishing Presidio de San Agustín de Ahumada and Mission Nuestra Señora de la Luz del Orcoquisac near the mouth of the Trinity in 1756.

Blancpain had died in prison in México, meanwhile, and his cohorts were sent to Spain for trial and life imprisonment. The whole affair naturally aroused the resentment of the French. Barrios, attempting to purchase supplies used by the Indians, found the French at Natchitoches sullen. The French explained that the high prices charged were due to the war with the English but Barrios suspected it was to make the Spaniards' trade with the Indians unprofitable. The French also placed an embargo on corn, which they previously had sold to the Spaniards.[1]

But now the Spaniards had a new complaint against the French. They suspected them of having had a hand in the San Sabá massacre. If Frenchmen had not actually participated, the Spaniards believed, they had provoked the Indians of the northern tribes to make the attack. Beyond a doubt the firearms which the Indians used were of French manufacture, though it seems the Spaniards had little room for complaint on this score; for the Spaniards had allowed the Indians to acquire horses.

France, in her attempt to colonize in the New World, was caught in the middle: The English pressed upon the French holdings from the east, while the Spaniards held her in check on the south and west. With the tide of the French and Indian War going against France, her dominions on the Atlantic and the Great Lakes were falling apart. These losses may have had a bearing on the behavior of the French in the Southwest.

[1] C. E. Castañeda, *Our Catholic Heritage*, IV, 53–73.

The Great Mistrust

They had watched the Spaniards' advance in Texas, and wondered how far they would push. The French were traders, primarily, and it was not difficult to foresee the day when the Spaniards would intrude upon their trading ground.

The feeling of mistrust between the colonial arms of France and Spain had played a major role in the establishment of Presidio de San Luis de las Amarillas and Mission Santa Cruz de San Sabá by the Spaniards over the protests of the French. The Spaniards had been motivated in part by a desire to Christianize the Apaches. But they were driven also by a fear that their failure to act would allow the French to form an alliance with this tribe, as they had with the Comanches.

Following the San Sabá massacre, the commander of the French outpost at Natchitoches, in Louisiana, wrote on August 19, 1758, to the Spanish governor of Texas, Jacinto de Barrios y Jáuregui. The French commander, Cesar Le Blanc, voluntarily informed Barrios of how two French traders had obtained from a Tehuacana village on the Red River a number of articles from the Mission San Sabá.

One of the traders, named Saint Quentin, had told of visiting the Indian village to find the savages celebrating a victory in a wild orgy of dancing. The Indians seized his goods and gave him in return some soiled pieces of silk, some gold and silver braid, a chalice, two silver cases containing stocks of sacred oils, two patens, and three metal plates. The Tehuacanas told him the Taovayas, who had accompanied them on their recent raid, had many articles of solid silver in their village a short distance up the river.

Saint Quentin said his first knowledge of the raid on the Mission San Sabá came from the Indians. He had seen in the village a number of scalps around which the savages were dancing, and had noticed one Indian wearing a part of the habit of one of the slain missionaries.

The Tehuacanas, Saint Quentin reported, already had wind of a proposed campaign against the northern tribes, and had sent scouts to keep them posted on the movements of the Spaniards. The Indians told the French trader also that they were expecting a band of Taovayas and Nasonis to join them in August (1758) to make a new raid on the Spaniards in the fall.

If the French had been responsible for the raid on the Mission

San Sabá, it seems strange that Le Blanc would admit to having in his possession some of the goods taken from there. The Frenchman may have written with a clear conscience, but the Spanish governor replied with an accusation that the French had incited the northern tribes to harass the Spanish outposts.

Le Blanc emphatically denied this charge, pointing out that he had returned the articles obtained by Saint Quentin at the risk of his life, yet the Spaniards had refused to make any recompense to the Frenchman for the goods he had lost in obtaining the sacred objects. Citing the Blancpain affair, he asserted that it was the Spaniards who were manifesting an uncooperative attitude.

Then Le Blanc made what might have been one last effort to save the Spaniards from their own foolishness. He warned them that the Wichitas (Iscanis and Taovayas), Tonkawas, and Comanches were negotiating a treaty and making arrangements to attack the Spaniards, who were greatly outnumbered by these Indians.

Governor Barrios transmitted this information to Colonel Parrilla at San Antonio just before the council convened to plan the campaign against the northern tribes. The Spaniards who gathered there were convinced thereby that the French were an accomplice in the hostility of the northern tribes. Before the end of the campaign they now were planning they were to be still more certain of it.[2]

The northern tribes, meanwhile, waged a war of nerves, to keep their enemies, the Spaniards, off balance from fear. In January, 1759, as the council was planning the campaign to avenge the San Sabá massacre, rumored plans of a new attack by the northern Indians on San Sabá Presidio and San Antonio reached it from sources other than the French. Father Joseph de Calahorra y Sáenz, in East Texas, sent a messenger to the Spanish governor to inform him of disquieting rumors he had heard while visiting among the Indians in the vicinity of Los Adaes and Nacogdoches. Called to minister to the Indians during an epidemic of measles and smallpox, he had learned the northern tribes were planning to make a determined effort to destroy the presidio on the San Sabá River and the San Antonio settlement "early in the spring."

[2] *Ibid.*, pp. 110–114.

The Great Mistrust

According to these rumors, the attack was being planned by the Tehuacanas, Tonkawas, Wichitas, Tejas, and numerous other tribes, who hoped to drive the Spaniards out of Texas.[3]

Then came a message for Parrilla from Ensign Juan Cortinas, who had been left in command of Presidio de San Luis de las Amarillas during Parrilla's absence. Friendly Indians who had visited the Presidio had warned Cortinas that the northern tribes soon would return to destroy the fort. Marauding bands had been seen in the area, he said, adding a plea for reinforcement of the garrison.

Governor Barrios, who was presiding over the council, appealed to the governor of Nuevo León to send one hundred men, which he felt were indispensable if destruction of San Antonio and San Sabá was to be prevented. But there were problems in Nuevo León, also, and the force so urgently requested could not be raised.

Parrilla hurried back to San Sabá to prepare for the impending attack. As the soldiers of the garrison worked to improve the defenses of the Presidio, however, they witnessed no signs to indicate that their efforts were necessary. From time to time a wandering band of Indians would stop to trade for a few days, but they had only excuses to offer when invited to stay and enter mission life. Their trading done, the peripatetic natives moved on. No Indians of the hostile tribes showed themselves.

It was a bleak winter, and the lack of forage caused the Commander to send the livestock to range some distance down the river, with a detail of soldiers to guard it. The livestock remained away from the fort during February and March. The soldiers had been cautioned to be on the alert for a surprise attack, but on the morning of March 30 the Indians had them surrounded before they were aware of their presence.

Shortly after sunrise one of the soldiers reached the Presidio to pant out the story of the surprise attack by a large horde of savages, all carrying firearms and well mounted. The Presidio commander hastily mounted a detail to go to the aid of the besieged soldiers. When the men reached the scene of the attack, they found scattered over the ground the naked bodies of their comrades, cut to pieces by the savages. Against the hills that rose

[3] *Ibid.*, p. 118.

from the San Sabá River, the soldiers could see the rear guard of the enemy, driving before them the seven hundred horses, mules, and cattle of the Presidio.

The soldiers watched helplessly as the Indians disappeared among the hills with the livestock. The small group briefly considered pursuing the enemy to recover the livestock and to avenge their slain comrades, but the Indians far outnumbered them. Pursuit likely would lead only to still greater loss for the Presidio de San Luis de las Amarillas.

Grimly, Parrilla appraised the status of his command. The stolen cattle represented the bulk of the food supply, and the garrison had only twenty-seven horses left. Now the soldiers would have to confine their activities to the Presidio walls. Scout reports told him that the Indians, made up of the same tribes that had destroyed the Mission a year earlier, had traveled only about twelve miles before halting to honor their slain warriors with a funeral chant. But to attack these Indians, with so few horses, would be foolhardy, for their numbers were many, and they were well armed.

Complicating the situation was the fact that a supply train had left San Antonio for San Sabá six days before and now should be nearing its destination. Destruction of the supply train would be tantamount to destruction of the Presidio.

Parrilla still was expecting the reinforcements that had been requested from Governor Angel de Martos y Navarrete of Nuevo León. He sent word to San Antonio that the additional force must be speeded on its way if massacre and capture of the supply train were to be prevented. While Martos y Navarrete had been unable to raise the force himself, he pleaded with the missionaries at San Antonio to send two soldiers and four Indians from each of the five missions to Parrilla's aid. But the missionaries were fearful that the Indians who had attacked San Sabá might attack San Antonio also. No aid was sent.[4]

Again the period of crisis passed, and Parrilla, on May 11, 1759, finally received orders from the Viceroy to proceed with the campaign against the hostile Indians of the north. When Parrilla reached San Antonio early in June, he found that none of his force for the campaign had arrived. Toward the end of July he was still waiting on some contingents.

[4] *Ibid.*, pp. 118–122.

The repeated delays were to jeopardize the expedition's success. For while he waited, Parrilla learned that the friendly Indians who had come to the presidio on the San Sabá River and to San Antonio had informed the northern tribes of the plans. The northern tribes had retreated to their own country to make preparations to resist the attack.

Mission of Vengeance

Parrilla's force came from the provinces of northern México and all the presidios in Texas. Each of the missions at San Antonio and those in Coahuila furnished Indian auxiliaries, and 134 Apaches joined the expedition as scouts and guides. When Parrilla reviewed his troops in San Antonio before starting for San Sabá, he had 360 presidial soldiers and volunteers, 176 Indian allies, more than 1,500 horses, several hundred mules, and a supply of dry beef, flour, corn, and beans.

The force bore little resemblance to the modern-day conception of a military expedition. Even the presidials were more *vaqueros* than soldiers. The militia was a motley crew of untrained men, and Parrilla later was to rue that fact. As the force was beginning to gather, he wrote the Viceroy of the "quality and conditions of the soldiers and people under arms of the presidios and frontiers." [1] Yet he failed to make allowances for their shortcomings when he went into combat.

Leaving San Antonio the middle of August, the force went first to the Presidio de San Luis de las Amarillas on the San Sabá River, which furnished five officers and forty-five men for the campaign. From San Sabá, Parrilla traveled north. Crossing the Concho River near the Painted Rocks (present town of Paint Rock), the expedition continued in the same direction and crossed the Colorado just below the present town of Ballinger, then angled off to the northeast.

Not all of Parrilla's force shared his enthusiasm for seeking out the enemy Indians and engaging them in battle. Many seemed

[1] "Consulta del Coronel Diego Ortiz Parrilla," November 18, 1759, A.G.I., p. 233.

Mission of Vengeance

to relish the fact that the Indians had been forewarned and had fled before the advancing troop, and they hoped to turn this into an excuse for turning back. Although the expedition advanced cautiously, only tracks of fleeing Indians and abandoned villages were found.

It would have been easy, Parrilla recalled later, to have returned without gain, and some of his officers pressed for such a course. But Parrilla, bent on avenging destruction of the San Sabá Mission,

> maintained appropriate firmness and applied all myself to the encounter with the enemy, ignoring suggestions to the contrary . . . until a *ranchería* of barbarians was overtaken.
>
> They thought themselves hidden from my vigilance and careful attention. Surprised by sagacious means, they had but the short time of one hour to ready the defenses of their habitation.[2]

The *ranchería* to which Parrilla referred was a Tonkawa camp, encountered after crossing the Clear Fork of the Brazos River near present Fort Griffin, in Shackelford County.

> At this time fifty-five were killed, one hundred forty-nine taken prisoners. . . . All those taken in this place were accomplices in the treacherous murders and thefts on the San Sabá River. They showed fragments of those ruins, and they were found with some horses and mules of my property and of the individuals of the Presidio of San Sabá, and one piece of the sacred habit worn by one of the reverend father missionaries shot by the cruelty of these gentiles.[3]

Parrilla's critics have berated him for not being satisfied with this initial conquest and for not turning back. But he had tasted victory, and his thirst for vengeance against the marauding savages was only partially slaked. In spite of Parrilla's shortcomings, he never tried to dodge responsibility for the decision to continue:

> The immediate return to our country could have resulted from a triumph so special, for not much had been hoped for; but I aspired to others. In compliance with the special orders of Your Excellency [the viceroy, the Marqués de las Amarillas] and of the tirelessness of my spirit, we continued in quest of those other delinquents, to reach the river which they inhabited.[4]

[2] *Ibid.*, p. 231.
[3] *Ibid.*, p. 231.
[4] *Ibid.*, p. 232.

The Tonkawa prisoners knew the location of the village of the Wichitas (Taovayas), and freely volunteered the information. Parrilla later recalled this willingness to inform with bitterness, for it was partly responsible for leading him on. The vanguard took one of the prisoners as a guide, placing him in irons to prevent his escape.

On what Parrilla referred to as "Day Seven," "when the prisoner guide had not yet shown the vicinity of the enemy, our vanguard was seen to leave in a gesture of attack." The force, which had covered six leagues, now was in the vicinity of present Spanish Fort, on the banks of the Red River seventeen miles north of Nocona, where the Taovayas village was found. As the vanguard of the Spanish force advanced to a thicket near the village, some sixty or seventy warriors broke out of the brush and charged.[5]

The Spaniards formed a front line to meet the attack. The Indians left three of their number dead and took flight by a wooded road, as the Spaniards pursued within musket range. The road came to an end in a sandbank along the river. Parrilla wrote later:

We pursued the fleeing enemy until our troop arrived at the front of the village of the Taovayas. Their reception, waiting at this advantageous place, made mockery of our diligence.

Finding hindrance to gaining the village, and being at the hands of the enemy, which had provoked us to come this far, we retreated a short distance to form a line and to consider the situation and place where they were found. Clearly seen within easy gunshot range was a village formed of large huts of oval shape, enclosed by a stockade and a moat. The winding entrance road was enclosed in the same way, with the gate toward the river, in which water runs more than a vara and a half deep. The entire stockade at the front was covered with Indians, armed and firing muskets. The attack was withheld until some forethought intervened.

But the enemy considered themselves secure in their fort. Those outside, with the help of those within, began to fire, attempting to cut off the wooded road in order to leave our troop in the sand, among four fires. First one then the other flank gave way. People on foot and on

[5] Parrilla, "Testimonio de Parrilla," October 7–November 18, 1759, A.G.I., p. 208. Details of the battle and the subsequent events chronicled in this chapter are based on the writer's own translation of this document except where noted.

Mission of Vengeance

horseback were taking a toll, and continued to fire in concert with those in the stockade.[6]

When the mounted Indians fired, the ones on foot handed them other loaded guns. The Spaniards made thrust after thrust at the fort, but the enemy force refused to yield. As night approached, after four hours of battle, two cannon were brought into the field and were fired eleven times at the fort, but the Indians only mocked the effect.

There arose more people on the sand, and they attempted furiously to cut off the retreat, taking the entrance to the wood, and to this effect marched by the left flank with great intrepidity and savagery. In this maneuver they lost people but not valor. For us there remained nothing else but to seek withdrawal in good order to the open field, since fire from the wood was encountered.[7]

The cannon were left in the field. The Spaniards were rattled, and many had fled, along with some of the Apaches and the mission Indians who had protected the flanks. Parrilla sought to work his force into a position of attack on the Indians who pursued them by the road to the wood, hoping to turn the cover to the Spaniards' advantage. But many of his men had deserted to the camp. Nightfall ended the battle, a merciful blessing for the Spaniards.

On reaching the camp, Parrilla methodically began gathering the information that would help him to determine his future course. He gathered estimates of the number of Indians they had encountered, and these ranged from two thousand to six thousand. He himself said only that

... the enemy exceeds in number all the people of this expedition, and they have the advantage in arms and determination.

From the Indian prisoners and from many of the Apaches who had knowledge of the people of this country, it was surmised that the enemy camp of the Taovayas nation had Comanches, Yaceales, Tehuacanas and many other nations of the north, who by foresight were gathered at the Taovayas village as friends and companions in the attacks on the San Saba River.[8]

The other officers expressed the sentiment that camp should be broken that night and the march for San Sabá begun immedi-

[6] *Ibid.*, p. 210.
[7] *Ibid.*, p. 210.
[8] *Ibid.*, p. 214.

ately. In his report Parrilla set out thirteen reasons for this proposal. The troop was completely discouraged. Desertions already had taken place; some of the soldiers had feigned return to the horseherd to secure new mounts in order to leave the field of battle and flee to safety. The troop was reduced by the dead and the wounded. It was not deemed advisable to risk loss of the 149 Tonkawa prisoners, whose salvation could be attained by leading them to the Christian country.

Many horses had been lost in the battle, and cold weather had begun "with force that corresponds to that in the far north." [9] With seven days of October gone, it appeared likely that the cold would remain until April, and under such severe conditions the horses could not possibly make the march. A glorious military exploit already had been attained, wrote Parrilla, because the Spaniards had crossed unknown lands to put their front line against the heathen Comanches and Taovayas on the river of their villages, forcing them to unite at one place to meet the Spaniards.

The chief of greatest acclaim among the Indians had been slain, along with more than fifty others at the village, in addition to those killed by the cannon, and many were wounded. It seemed, said the Commander, that "No further gain can be hoped for in view of these circumstances, the enemy and the terrain." [10] It had been demonstrated to the Indians, he added, that the Spaniards were not asleep, or abandoned, and that they were willing to face up to their enemies in the open field.

> The major part of our people do not have the qualities needed for opposing the forces and conditions of such intrepidity and vigor of the immediate enemy, because to the disgrace of being undisciplined, they added personal defects and a complete ignorance of the use of arms.[11]

Some of them were of "very strange professions," said the military leader: shepherds, tailors, laborers, cigar-dealers, shoemakers, peons from the mines. They were wholly unqualified for military service. "It does not seem just to expose the lives of these happy ones and gain triumph in such a manner." [12]

[9] *Ibid.*, p. 217.
[10] *Ibid.*, pp. 218–219.
[11] *Ibid.*, p. 220.
[12] *Ibid.*, p. 220.

Mission of Vengeance

The proposal of the officers to begin the homeward march was seconded by Father Tomás Arcayos, who served the expedition as chaplain, and by Father Santiago Pelaes, who served it as surgeon. The surgeon noted the many wounded, some near death, and others with "confused souls."

Parrilla examined an Apache chief, who had been sent out to bring fugitives from the wood, and other Indian scouts, who told him that the enemy Indians had returned to the fort. From downriver growing numbers of new Indians were riding into the village to give it reinforcement. Two giant fires were lighted in the village, and by their light the scouts were able to see that the enemy still guarded the stockade, though there were shouting and dancing within.

Colonel Parrilla then asked the captains to report the numbers killed, wounded, and missing from their companies, and it was found that a total of nineteen were dead and fourteen wounded. Nineteen had fled or had not yet found their way to the camp. The missing did not include the Apaches, most of whom had scattered.

Dead, wounded, and missing totaled fifty-two, which has led some historians to write that the Spaniards lost fifty-two men.[13] The defeat, therefore, has been exaggerated, some calling it the worst rout suffered by the Spaniards since Cortés' landing. But the important feature is not the measurement of defeat the Spaniards suffered, but their failure to accomplish what they had set out to do, and the hidden meaning of this failure. Parrilla, who can be described objectively only as an able leader when compared to many of his contemporaries in New Spain, was to do considerable head-scratching in an effort to understand this hidden meaning.

Of the nineteen dead, sixteen were Spaniards and three were Indians, including one Apache. Thirteen Spaniards and one Apache were wounded. Thirteen Spaniards and six mission Indians had fled or were missing, in addition to the many Apaches

---

[13] C. E. Castañeda (*Our Catholic Heritage*, IV, 130) says the Spaniards lost 52 men. H. E. Bolton (*Texas in the Middle Eighteenth Century*, p. 90) and L. B. Simpson (*San Saba Papers*, p. 155) give the same figure. H. E. Allen ("The Parrilla Expedition," *SWHQ*, Vol. 43, pp. 69–70) says 14 killed, 15 wounded, and 13 desertions besides the Apaches. Other sources fail to give a casualty figure.

"who had undertaken their retreat when the great violence arrived, with their horses and those of some Spaniards." [14]

The enemy Indians themselves had suffered heavy losses in holding their village against the Spanish attack. Parrilla wrote that more than 100 had been killed, including the 55 slain at the Tonkawa camp on "Day Two." The 149 Tonkawa prisoners which the Spaniards had taken boosted the total loss of the savages to more than 250—"A matter of satisfaction with which the retreat is undertaken." [15]

In contrast to the militiamen and the friendly Indians who fled from duty, many of the officers and the soldiers performed outstanding deeds of valor. Parrilla, grazed by two bullets, his horse shot from under him, took the horse of a soldier and returned to battle. A bullet creased the cuirass of Captain Manuel Rodríguez of Presidio del Río Grande. Captain Elías de la Garza Falcón of Presidio del Reyno had his clothing and equipment struck countless times by musket balls but was not harmed.

Francisco Espinosa of Charcas, in charge of the cannon, received only an injured leg in an accident with the gun carriage, although many of the enemy concentrated their fire on him in an effort to silence the cannon. Captain Angel de Oyarzún of San Luis Potosí, shot from his horse in the middle of the sandbank, was rescued from a withering fire, unharmed. Lieutenant Ildefonso de la Garza of Presidio del Reyno had his clothing pierced by numerous bullets before his horse was killed, but he was not hurt.

Bullets struck the saddle, the shield, and the ramrod of the sublieutenant of San Sabá, Don Domingo Castelo, and grazed his cuirass, without harming him. Lieutenant Santiago Moneo of Presidio del Río Grande counted hits on the cuirass, the shield, the saddle, and through the hat, and came out unscathed. Small wonder that "A festive function was launched by the *jefe* to Nuestra Señora del Rosario in thanksgiving and memory of the happy progress which happened this day." [16]

Considering all the information he had gathered, Parrilla decided to move the camp that night in order to be near water and

---

[14] Parrilla, "Testimonio," October 7–November 18, 1759, A.G.I., p. 223.
[15] *Ibid.*, p. 224.
[16] *Ibid.*, p. 226.

Mission of Vengeance 125

pasture for the horses and mules. The troop was arranged for marching in extended fashion, along the road that led onto the plain, so that those still hiding in the wood might have an opportunity to rejoin the force.

Finding the water and the pasture, the Spanish force halted to wait one day near the enemy, to make a reconnaissance, and to attend the wounded. Parrilla wished also to give those cut off from the main force an opportunity to catch up. From this camp he wrote a letter to Father Mariano de los Dolores, which gave the first news of the battle to Spanish settlements. He dispatched this letter to San Antonio by two Indian runners.

The day before yesterday we arrived at the renowned village of the Iscanis, or Chaguesas, which form the head of the Chaguacanes,[17] on the large river that runs through the French country, having experienced in more than one hundred leagues, which we have marched, a happy summit and the benefit of having at hand one hundred fifty of the enemy who march as prisoners, though many are badly wounded.

They left fifty-five dead and many vestiges of the attack and theft from the Mission of San Sabá, and some horses of the Presidio, in our command.

The enemy which inhabits this river, gathered in the said village, with the aid of many Comanches, came to meet us in the encounter. After they retreated we unloaded the mules to arrange the camp and horseherd in corresponding position. They [the enemy Indians] were charged by most of the troops and the Apache Indians, and having killed some of the enemy we pursued them to the village, where were found fenced cultivated land and a stockade covered with people, shooting from within. Outside were some on horseback, with others in harmonious arrangement. The force was large, its military instruction even greater.

Our people were intimidated, some killed and wounded and many fugitives of combat, even of the main body of the troop, since many are missing who fled with the Apaches. They left me seven times among the barbarians but without more regrettable misfortune for me than that of seeing the troops of the King of Spain without courage in the face of the French, who were directing the enemy Indians.

They gravely wounded my horse, and I received contusions from two bullets which overtook me, on the side and the left arm. The enemy kept themselves inside the fort, and I made night in the immediate area. Yesterday I retired to improve our position as to water and pasture for

---

[17] Indians of the village were Taovayas, a Wichita subtribe.

the horses and will not return unless the barbarians charge upon us, for our people remain frightened.[18]

Father Dolores copied the letter in one which he wrote to Father Diego Jiménez under date of October 20, 1759, the month and year of the battle on the Red River. Oddly, the transcript of this letter has Parrilla dating his communication: "Bear Camp, 200 leagues north of San Antonio, October 3, 1753." [19]

Father Dolores, summarizing in his own words a postscript to Parrilla's letter, told how the Yojuane (Tonkawa) Indian captives had deceitfully led the Spaniards to the Wichita village, where a trap had been prepared. After meeting the enemy in a bloody battle, the Indians turned as if to flee, leading the soldiers into the trap.

The Spanish force, he said, was caught in a dense wood, "filled with underbrush as with concealed enemies." Continuing the struggle on the plain of entry, they found this so sandy that the horses sank in the loose sand to their knees.

"The enemy charged the cannon," Father Dolores related, "and the colonel, with few people remaining, was able to retire to the camp, having remained in continuous movement, without eating or drinking water, from the break of day until sunset."

It was impossible to know how many had died, he said, because so many had fled. "This was to be expected of the cigar-dealers, tailors, shepherds and rabble who came to insult the Spanish Crown."

Father Dolores wrote that the two Indians who brought him Parrilla's letter

affirm only that they saw five of ours dead in the canyons: one Indian of La Concepción, another of San Joseph, three of San Juan Bautista, including one of Peyotes. One Spaniard named Joseph Hinojoso and the captain of San Luis, Don Juan Angel de Ortuza [sic], and some others are wounded, not dangerously, as are Francisco el Sordo and Xavier Pérez.

[18] Dolores to Jiménez, October 20, 1759, A.M.S.F.

[19] *Ibid.* The date of October 3 would indicate the battle was fought October 1. In his "Testimonio" Parrilla refers to the day of the attack on the Tonkawas as "Day Two," and that of the assault on the Taovayas village as "Day Seven," indicating dates of October 2 and 7. His letter probably was written October 9, not October 3, and of course the year was 1759, not 1753.

Mission of Vengeance

Of the deserters, up to six are found prisoners at San Sabá, and among them, one water tender named Gallardo, and twenty enemy Indians.

Of the Lipan Apaches, they were an important number of the campaign, behaving themselves very well with the Spaniards excepting in the greatest danger, as when their horses were killed, and in all proceeding regularly.

He closed the letter to Father Jiménez by asking him to send the letter on to the father guardian and reminding him to ask God's help for Colonel Parrilla, who was doing so much to repress the barbarity, which was aided by the French.

"The evident danger which is found consists of losing this province," he concluded.

As Parrilla's troop took up the march for San Sabá, says Bonilla, "The enemy pressed the rear guard closely as far as San Sabás but without further damage." Bolton adds in reference to the retreat that it became a rout. Simpson says the force, chased all the way to San Sabá, was saved from annihilation only by the Apaches, who fought a rear-guard action.[20]

But Parrilla's account gives no indication of a pursuit, and his normal procedure seems to have been to report everything in detail. He claimed: "We maintained ourselves three days in the camp, waiting for those that were protected by the fortified village."[21]

The retreat apparently was orderly, and the force reached San Sabá by a more direct route about October 25. Soon after arrival at San Sabá, Parrilla called the officers into council, asking them to determine if a new campaign should be undertaken against the Tonkawas (Mayeyes and Yojuanes) and Hierbipiames, also known to be enemies of the Spaniards.

The other officers of the campaign, however, had not been as impressed as was Parrilla by the ravages on the most advanced outpost of the Texas frontier. They were tired from the long trek to the Red River, their horses worn out. They held out against such a campaign, suggesting that the men rest at San Sabá until the first of December, when the troops gathered for the campaign

---

[20] Antonio Bonilla, "A brief compendium," p. 41; Bolton, *Texas in the Middle Eighteenth Century*, p. 90; Nathan-Simpson, *San Saba Papers*, p. 155.

[21] "Consulta de Parrilla," November 18, 1759, A.G.I., p. 239.

should be taken to San Antonio, with the surplus supplies, and then allowed to return to their homes or stations.

Parrilla had asked the council of officers also to determine by what extent his garrison should be increased in order to afford sufficient protection from the hostile Indians. They replied that the one hundred men regularly assigned to the Presidio were sufficient.[22]

That Parrilla was resentful and disappointed at the attitude of the council is shown by the fact that he did not allow the rest at San Sabá until December as suggested. Early in November, he left Captain Manuel Rodríguez of Presidio del Río Grande (San Juan Bautista) temporarily in charge of his garrison, since Lieutenant Joseph Joaquín de Eca y Músquiz was ill at the time. Parrilla and the campaign troop set out for San Antonio, where the force was to be disbanded.

On arrival at San Antonio, Parrilla finished compiling his own reports and those of the officers of the troop, which were forwarded to the Viceroy. By his calculation the force had traveled 220 leagues from San Antonio and 150 from San Sabá.[23] He wrote of the outcome of the campaign as though it were a great triumph, but in the back of his mind he was troubled. For he had observed firsthand the vast changes that had taken place on the northern frontier of New Spain, and that still further changes were in the offing.

The pivot was approaching.

[22] Castañeda, *Our Catholic Heritage*, IV, 132–133.
[23] "Consulta de Parrilla," November 18, 1759, A.G.I., p. 230.

Aftermath of Failure

Of Parrilla's campaign to the Red River, Dunn says:
"... The Spaniards were so badly defeated that it was declared that never had such a disgraceful rout been experienced since the landing of Cortés in New Spain."[1]

This is obvious exaggeration, for Dunn himself tells elsewhere of a campaign made in 1743 against the Apaches: "They had a force of two hundred men and were commanded by the governor of Coahuila, who fell into an ambush, was dangerously wounded and lost more than half of his men and almost all of his horses and equipment."[2]

Although the battle on the Red River has often been written of as a disgraceful defeat for the Spaniards, it was more in the nature of a standoff. Yet, while the carnage wrought by the Indians in repelling the Spaniards has been exaggerated, the significance of it cannot be. Parrilla's impotence against the northern tribes confirmed the conclusions drawn from the San Sabá massacre. The battle bore out all the more lucidly that the Spaniards, in their northern advance, faced a new type of enemy with overwhelming capabilities. The Spaniards' inability to deal with this new and more powerful force was demonstrated further.

The failure should have proved to the officials of New Spain the need for a different type of military system on the frontier. For while the militiamen—civilians pressed into service without benefit of training, whenever the need arose—may have been adequate when they held the advantage of firearms over bows and arrows,

[1] W. E. Dunn, "The Apache Mission," *SWHQ*, Vol. 17, p. 414.
[2] Dunn, "Apache Relations in Texas," *SWHQ*, Vol. 14, pp. 251–252.

they were adequate no longer. The enemy now was better armed, and more skilled in the use of arms, than were the Spaniards.

It should have proved also that presidios with small garrisons no longer were adequate tools on the frontier. The largest of the presidios was San Sabá, and it had one hundred men. Even the officers who took part in the campaign had ruled that this number was sufficient. The Spaniards consistently refused to profit by experience. Instead of acting, they reacted, repeatedly handing their enemies the advantage of determining their actions for them. By continuing on this course, the Spaniards were defeating themselves.

From the discovery of La Salle's Fort Saint Louis, the Spaniards had visualized a Frenchman behind every bush. Many times their fears were justified, for the French and Spaniards were face to face in the colonial struggle. While the Spaniards and the French were in the midst of this struggle, a third power was moving in to claim the spoils. This encroachment had never been more apparent than it was in the year 1759. On September 13— while Parrilla's motley crew trudged over the rolling hills of central Texas, meandering toward the Tonkawa camp on the Clear Fork—the Battle of the Plains of Abraham erupted. When the battle was over, the generals of both French and English armies lay dead. Quebec was in British hands.

In the remoteness of Texas, however, it was difficult to view the complete picture. Parrilla continued to see a Frenchman behind every bush.

To what extent the French actually figured in the battle on the Red River probably will never be known. Whether, as Parrilla stated, the French actually directed the attack of the Indians, or whether Parrilla merely was seeking to alibi his failure is one of history's secrets. But, whatever Parrilla's faults, he seems to have been conscientious, and he likely reported the battle as he saw it:

> They [the Indians] had made us understand clearly that they had many firearms, and a large provision of munitions, and that they were directed and guided by foreign instruction and a military doctrine very similar to that observed in our presidios of the frontiers of the Indies.
>
> All our people saw and distinguished clearly the French flag flying from the center of the stockade, and the military instruments of drum and fife. Even though these corresponded to those which the Indians

Aftermath of Failure

use, they were distinguished by their greater harmony and the manner in which they were used, in cadence, without interruption during the combat.

There were seen also many pieces of white clothing hanging upon the huts.[3]

The nature of the village itself, which was surrounded by a moat, caused Parrilla to suspect European influence on the Indians:

There were found some large fields planted in corn, and many other of beans, pumpkins and watermelons, all enclosed by a palisade....

It could be seen that one part of this village was fortified and the other was desolate, all the people having hastened to the fortified place.[4]

Beyond the corrals which held the enemy's horses the Comanche allies had set up camp, for their cone-shaped teepees were easily distinguished from the oval huts of the Taovayas.

Besides the French flag, the moat, and the general arrangement of the village, Parrilla reported also that the Indians had among them some "individuals who help them and govern them, because fourteen French were seen within the gentile village." [5]

Morfi, who could no more write objectively of Parrilla than of the Apaches, discounts the French signs. "The flag is of small consequence, it being an old custom in this country to present the natives with one whenever some agreement for trade was made with them." [6]

Nor do the stockade, ditch, and other defenses prove anything, he adds, because the natives had come to realize their value in the recent campaign against the Mission and the Presidio of San Sabá.[7] But Morfi overlooks the fact that there was no moat at San Sabá until after Parrilla's time.

"It must be admitted," says Newcomb, "that the Wichitas [Taovayas] had learned from the French something of defensive art, though just how much is difficult to ascertain.... Coronado

---

[3] Parrilla, "Testimonio de Parrilla," October 7–November 18, 1759, A.G.I., p. 212.

[4] *Ibid.*, p. 213.

[5] Parrilla, "Consulta del Coronel Diego Ortiz Parrilla," November 18, 1759, A.G.I., p. 238.

[6] Juan Agustín Morfi, *History of Texas*, II, 390.

[7] *Ibid.*, p. 391.

had found no stockaded villages in Kansas two centuries earlier."[8] But the real impediment to the Spanish advance at this point was the hostility of the Comanches, Wichitas, and their allies.

Webb comments,

> An examination of the records will show that it was the Apaches and Comanches, more often than the Frenchmen, the English, and the Russians, who caused the Spaniards to avoid the Great Plains. On no occasion did a European nation destroy a settlement on the northern Spanish frontier west of Louisiana.[9]

And yet the Spaniards always seemed to govern their actions by what the French did, or by what they feared they might do.

The failure at the Red River confirmed the conclusion that might have been drawn immediately following the San Sabá massacre: that the Comanches and the other tribes of the north had become an insurmountable obstacle to the northern advance.

It may seem in retrospect that Parrilla's campaign was hardly necessary to prove this conclusion, in view of the large number of Indians who attacked the San Sabá Mission. But one must remember that the human race has always been hesitant to accept new phenomena without first testing them thoroughly. If Parrilla had believed his own intelligence reports following destruction of the Mission—which stated that the attacking Indians numbered two thousand, half of them armed with muskets which they used skillfully—he might never have requested the campaign. Yet he could not believe that the savages were able to devise any military maneuver capable of defeating a large troop of Spanish soldiers and militiamen under his own competent leadership. The situation was too new for him to comprehend its import.

The Spaniards and the French shared the culpability for bringing the new set of circumstances into force. Each had provided the Indians with an important tool. The Spaniards had given them the horse, while the French had given them firearms. The firearm was the immediate instrument of warfare, but of the two the horse was more important in the long run.

The unfortunate campaign also provided a new tally for the Apaches' scorebook. Following the attack on the Mission by their hated enemies, the Apaches had been skittish. They observed that

[8] W. W. Newcomb, Jr., *The Indians of Texas*, pp. 254–255.
[9] W. P. Webb, *The Great Plains*, p. 116.

Aftermath of Failure

their new Spanish allies were not as valuable as they had hoped they would be. Had the Spaniards been victorious in the campaign, the Apaches might have reversed this decision. But here again, the standoff added the clincher. The Apaches now saw that the Spaniards lacked the capacity to protect them in missions. It remained for their crafty minds to contrive a plan whereby the Spaniards could still be of some use to them.

This is not to say that had Parrilla been victorious the Apaches would readily have congregated in missions. Nothing was farther from their minds. Yet if the Spaniards had carried sufficient force of their own to command the respect of the Apaches, and if they had been willing to face up to the Comanche barrier to the north, the Apaches could have been valuable allies in advancing the Spanish frontier toward the Plains. But instead the Apaches pegged the Spaniards as weaklings and determined to use them as pawns in continuing their longstanding war with the Comanches. The Apaches did not realize that their destiny was more closely linked with the Comanches than with the Spaniards.

When Parrilla reached San Antonio on November 18, 1759, he had much work to do. He completed his diary of the campaign and signed it in the presence of witnesses, one of whom was Bernardo de Miranda, discoverer of Los Almagres Mine. But he had more to report than the events of the campaign. There were conclusions to be drawn, and questions answered, some of which were to have a great bearing on the future of the Spanish settlement on the San Sabá River, as well as on the future of the northern Texas frontier.

Parrilla, despite what has been written by many chroniclers of his campaign, does not seem to have come limping home from the Red River like a whipped puppy. True he was eager to explain why he had been unable to take the fort at the Taovayas village, for he could see the implications it bore for the future of Spain's New World empire. But apparently he did not feel the need to apologize for his own efforts. In terms of military strategy he felt he had done well in the face of the many difficulties which confronted him, and had delivered to the Indians of the northern tribes far more than he had received in return.

As to my arrival all the inhabitants of the San Antonio River and the Reverend Father Missionaries of the five missions were already well-informed of the favorable effects of the expedition, and of the great number and condition of the enemy. Before the Indian auxiliaries and other soldiers had arrived, I was presented the two attached representations.[10]

These were requests from the council of the Villa de San Fernando and from the missionaries, asking him to assign forty additional soldiers to Presidio de San Antonio de Béjar. This fort now had only twenty-two men who would be unable to protect it if the northern tribes, aroused by the campaign, should descend to destroy the settlement. Parrilla took it upon himself to order forty soldiers to remain in San Antonio until the Viceroy could make known his superior wishes.

It would not be well, Parrilla wrote, "to reduce this land too quickly to the scantiness of people it had before."

He reported his action to the Viceroy, saying he himself would pay the soldiers for this added duty if he failed to prove that it was necessary—just as he himself had paid the soldiers he had placed at San Sabá to fill vacancies left by those killed as they guarded the horseherd the previous March, and by those who had deserted.

The remainder of the troop was disbanded, and Parrilla busied himself with writing his reports. The outcome of the campaign had been awaited before sending the missionaries appointed to re-establish the San Sabá Mission. Parrilla now was obliged to give an appraisal of the Apaches and the possibility of congregating them in Missions.

Reports of the conduct of the 134 Apaches who accompanied Parrilla's troop have been at variance, but the commander himself indicates they were valuable allies. True they were not trained soldiers, and he acknowledged his mistake in placing them on the flank as his force advanced on the Taovayas village. But by his account they merely scattered to fight as Indians rather than as soldiers: "The one hundred thirty-four were found constant in the critical moments and occasions which the campaign offered." [11]

He noted that the Apaches had to forage for their own food, and he found no reason to think ill of them. Nor could they be classified as deceitful in their promise to settle in missions. They

[10] Parrilla, "Carta Consultiva," November 18, 1759, A.G.I., pp. 184–185.
[11] Parrilla, "Consulta," November 18, 1759, A.G.I., p. 229.

Aftermath of Failure

had witnessed the Spaniards in an expedition against their enemies, but, in Parrilla's opinion, it was hardly enough to convince them that the Spaniards could protect them in missions.

Parrilla blames the Spaniards as much as the Apaches for the Indians' failure to congregate in missions. The Spaniards had failed to prove that they could live up to their part of the bargain; hence it was hardly reasonable to expect the Apaches to live up to theirs.

The Apaches, he continued, had withdrawn at the start of the campaign, feeling the need to stay far out of reach of their enemies with the 134 warriors away. As was their custom, they were occupied in dances and festivals in celebration of the triumph over their enemies. Therefore Parrilla could not obtain from them a statement of their intentions regarding missions; but he expressed the opinion that the Spaniards should continue to pursue an alliance with them. Information that these Indians were unreconcilable in their enmities was ill-founded, he said; the same Apaches and Ipandes (Lipans) that suffered the cruelties of these enemy tribes had amicable dealings and trade with them. It was noted that the Apaches had obtained 260 French muskets, powder, balls, and swords by trading with those who were supposed to be their enemies.

Here again Parrilla shows admirable perspicacity. He seems to understand the problem of the Apaches in defending their homeland against many aggressors, of which the Spaniards were one. If the alliance with the Spaniards failed to work for the Apaches, Parrilla seems to say, it was only natural that they form other alliances and begin treating the Spaniards like any other intruder.

Parrilla still had hopes that the Apaches would come to seek missions after their feasting. "They maintain that good relation that so many times has been communicated to your Excellency, and which they have just practiced in the campaign. . . . but not by this circumstance can we persuade them that they should come and form the villages."

While concerned with the mission effort, Parrilla saw somewhat greater significance in the new situation which manifested itself on the northern frontier. It was made up of three parts: first, the deplorable quality of the military forces, both presidial soldiers and militia, of New Spain; second, the foreign influence on the Indians of the north and the indications that other European nations, notably the French, were intruding upon Spanish territory; third, the new capabilities of the hostile Indians, who were amply equipped with firearms and munitions through trade with the French, and who possessed greater skill in using these arms than did the Spaniards themselves. These Indians, who had formed an intertribal alliance for the attack on the San Sabá Mission, still maintained the alliance, and, by means of it, they had strength greater than that of the Spaniards.

On the first point, Parrilla recalled that before the start of the campaign he had advised the Viceroy of his doubts in regard to the qualifications and character of the men being sent him to bear arms against the hostile Indians. The campaign had borne out his misgivings. The soldiers and militiamen had shown total disregard for his orders, and for the honor of Spain, refusing to apply themselves. Some were greedy, others ignorant, and still others "defectors in obedience." Such forces could not be expected to hold the frontier against such a capable enemy, he said.

"Our presidios, created for containing and converting the Indians, are considered sufficient when the force is unaware of the dexterity and great numbers of the gentiles and the instruction and assistance they receive from foreign sources."

The soldiers of San Sabá, said Parrilla, had been given instruction during the time they had been under his command, but they still did him no credit because of "the bad inclination of their nature and breeding."

Parrilla saw an ever-present danger that the French, allying themselves with hostile Indians, could drive the Spaniards from the frontier. He understood now that, in view of the great capabilities he had found among the enemy tribes, forestalling such a union would require concerted action to strengthen the frontier.

The presidio should be kept on the San Sabá River, he believed, though it should be reinforced by placing others near it. As he wrote to the Viceroy, he emphasized the importance of holding on to the gains that had been made. But Parrilla felt the inadequacy of trying to impart his knowledge of the problems on the northern frontier by letter. He included in his report to the Marqués de las Amarillas a request that he be allowed to come to Mexico City for a personal conference.

He may have had in mind exonerating himself for the failure

Aftermath of Failure

of the campaign, as some have suggested, but this motive is doubtful. It seems more likely that he felt he understood the situation on the frontier better than perhaps anyone else. He hoped to see this information converted into gain for his king, and this would be done only if he could convince the Viceroy that his appraisal was valid.

Because the Indians of the north always seemed to attack the settlement on the San Sabá River in March, he proposed to remain at his post until the time of greatest danger was passed, then proceed to México, with the Viceroy's permission. After completing his work in San Antonio, Parrilla returned to San Sabá to await the Viceroy's reply. It came the following April. He proceeded to the capital, arriving there about the first of August, 1760. On his arrival he found that an unanticipated cloud had gathered.

His campaign had been costly in many ways. It had cost the King's treasury almost sixty thousand pesos, in addition to the soldiers killed and the many horses and mules lost. Even the 149 captives from the Tonkawa camp proved to be worth little to the Spaniards. The Apaches had taken 97 of these, which they traded to the Spaniards for merchandise. Of the 52 held by the Spaniards, 25 died shortly after arriving in San Antonio in an epidemic of smallpox and dysentery. The survivors were sold into slavery, a practice strictly forbidden by law.[12]

The real benefit of the campaign might have been in the observations made by Parrilla, who most certainly was an astute observer. But the new viceroy, the Marqués de Cruillas, sent by a new king to replace the Marqués de las Amarillas, was to take precipitous action which would preclude even this benefit. In fact, his action was to nullify the gains that had been accomplished by means of the Spaniards' most northern advance on the Texas frontier.

When Parrilla reached México, he learned that Captain Felipe de Rábago y Terán had been absolved of charges made against him eight years earlier in connection with the murders at the San Xavier missions and had been ordered reinstated to his command. Since the San Xavier garrison comprised half the troops at Presidio de San Luis de las Amarillas, Rábago was to take command

---

[12] C. E. Castañeda, *Our Catholic Heritage*, IV, 132.

of that post. Parrilla protested this action but to no avail. The Viceroy appointed him governor of Coahuila instead.

Castañeda implies that the Viceroy relieved Parrilla of his command as a reprisal for the failure of his campaign against the northern Indians:

> He had been in charge of the largest and most important presidio in Texas, he had been entrusted to carry out the most important and pretentious expedition since the days of Marqués of Aguayo. But he had failed to reduce the Apaches and subdue or chastise the northern tribes.[13]

The Marqués de Cruillas, however, having just become viceroy, must have been under pressure to take action in Rábago's behalf. The source of the pressure is not known, but there appears to be no other logical explanation of why the new viceroy would precipitously replace a capable and conscientious commander with one of Rábago's caliber. Parrilla had the benefit of much valuable experience, which was being put to naught. He had established rapport, to a degree, with the Apaches, although he had not yet settled them in missions. He disdained his new appointment as governor of Coahuila, because he felt that he could serve God and King to better advantage on the northern frontier, where he had acquired experience and knowledge of that region unequaled by any man of his time.

The Marqués de Cruillas may have had one of the most difficult times to govern New Spain as viceroy. His regime began shortly after the San Sabá massacre and the ensuing punitive expedition against the northern tribes. It ended about the time the Marqués de Rubí, inspector general for King Charles III, of Spain, completed his inspection tour of the frontier outposts. But, if this was a difficult period during which to serve, Cruillas served with less distinction than the situation called for. When the times called for decisive action to hold what Spain had won by costly effort, he dallied. He let the presidios fall apart. While the frontier outposts as a whole suffered from the abuses of greedy and licentious commanders, he blindly replaced the competent commander of the most advanced outpost with a rogue.

Perhaps it is to the new viceroy's credit that he asked Parrilla to brief him on the situation on the northern frontier. Parrilla

[13] *Ibid.*, p. 139.

Aftermath of Failure

did so, apparently after winning a struggle with his own misgivings:

> On my arrival, I found myself surprised to be dispossessed of the command of that troop and of other commissions. I confessed to Your Excellency that I was confounded and embarrassed by that which does not employ the purpose of my coming. But now I realize I must obey blindly the superior precept of Your Excellency.[14]

The Viceroy asked to be informed on three points: the extent of the French influence among the enemy Indians, whether these Indians were receiving help also from the English, and finally "all that corresponds to the settlements on the San Sabá and San Antonio rivers" and the ravages of the enemy tribes against these outposts.

Parrilla answered these queries taking into consideration his observations during the campaign, his knowledge of the progress of the war between the English and the French, and the information obtained from many sources following the campaign, in his search for facts that would help him understand the new situation.

Dealing with the first point, he related that the prisoners captured during the campaign had told him the French lived among the northern tribes, instructing them in the use of firearms and other devices of war. To support this, he told of declarations taken in the presence of the governors of Texas and Coahuila from three Frenchmen, who had deserted the French fort at Natchitoches and sought asylum at Los Adaes.

These declared the style of their chiefs was to send Frenchmen in small squads of five or six men to live in the Indians' *rancherías*, to make trade and traffic with them in gunpowder, bullets, muskets, and other European arms. They declared to us also that they were among those of this destiny, sent by their superiors to the *rancherías* of the Indians who invaded the Presidio and Mission of San Sabá, at the time they went out with plans for a similar assault.[15]

He then recounted observations made during the attack on the Taovayas village on the Red River. All the Spanish officers had noticed the armament which consisted only of muskets and

---
[14] Parrilla to the viceroy, Marqués de Cruillas, November 8, 1760, A.G.M., Historia, Vol. 84, Part I, p. 108.
[15] *Ibid.*, p. 101.

lances; the ingenious arrangement for defense, with stockades and moats; the French flag; the well-ordered discipline.

Authentic testimony had been presented, he said, by Don Tomás Veléz Cachupín, governor of New Mexico, and by Don Jacinto de Barrios y Jáuregui, then governor of Texas. Barrios had noted that the French nationals who were apprehended had been provided with passports or licenses, and that they knew the language of the Indians in the provinces where they were found.

On the second point—whether the Indians were receiving help also from the English—Parrilla told the Viceroy that the English had made much progress and were intent on taking New Orleans. Two Apache Indians and a squaw, who had been prisoners of the Taovayas, had gained their freedom and fled to San Antonio. They reported having seen a number of white men who dressed in similar manner to the French but did not speak the language of the French, and who came from a different direction. These strange white men also gave the Indians firearms and demonstrated a strange weapon which fired a most destructive bomb. These white men, Parrilla said, undoubtedly were English. Obviously the English were intent on taking New Orleans and on moving into French, and possibly Spanish, territory.

He cited also a portion of a letter from Father Joseph de Calahorra, missionary minister of Nacogdoches: "The English hasten in their war with the French. It is said that they have taken Quebec, which is in Canada, and that five thousand English are marching to the Illinois. They occupy the lower part of this river." [16] From there they had but to descend the Mississippi to reach New Orleans. "This news seems to leave no doubt that the English also press their auxiliaries on the barbarian Indians, our enemies, and that in the present war with the French, they have made happy progress." [17]

The third point mentioned by the Viceroy left Parrilla plenty of latitude, which he used to full advantage. He was principally concerned with peace offers which now came from the Indians of the north, giving indication that they were not so happy, after all, with the outcome of Parrilla's campaign against them. Several tribes had made peace overtures through Father Calahorra at Nacogdoches, who had promised to relay the message to the Span-

[16] *Ibid.*, p. 104.
[17] *Ibid.*, pp. 104–105.

Aftermath of Failure

ish governor. The Indians received this promise with exultation, returning horses they had stolen from the missions, promising everlasting friendship, and saying they would even respect any Apaches who should congregate in missions. They promised also to return the cannons left by Parrilla at the Taovayas village.

Father Calahorra, reporting to the Governor, had urged that missions be established among the northern tribes. The policy toward these Indians should be changed, he said, and the Apaches should be abandoned, unless they agreed immediately to be reduced to mission life. Martos y Navarrete, the new governor of Texas, had turned to the Viceroy, and the Viceroy now turned to Parrilla.

Recalling how these Indians had gained admittance to the Mission Santa Cruz de San Sabá by pretending peace, Parrilla unhesitatingly branded them as treacherous, insisting that their promises of peace were not to be taken too seriously.

"To my meager understanding is known the false appearance of the babarians in their peace offers, it having been I who stood with the Catholic arms in their own land, it having been I who in reality put them to terror and fright." [18]

The actions of these Indians, he continued, manifest their peace offers clearly to be all fictions. It still remained advisable, he said, to seek the pacification of the Apaches, and their reduction to missions.

Castañeda says,

> The viceregal officials were once more puzzled. Could they now abandon the Apaches, assume a harsh policy toward them and adopt a policy of reconciliation and friendship towards the northern tribes? Pride and honor and the natural aversion of human nature to admit an error caused the opportunity to pass.[19]

It appears likely, however, that the Marqués de Cruillas was glad to use Parrilla's appraisal as an excuse for inaction. His administration seems to have been disinterested in launching new programs on the Texas frontier. It was hardly interested in maintaining the status quo.

Parrilla insisted that the Presidio de San Luis de las Amarillas should be maintained on the San Sabá River. It would be desirable

[18] *Ibid.*, p. 108.
[19] Castañeda, *Our Catholic Heritage*, IV, 146.

to augment the force of one hundred men stationed there by establishing another company of forty in the vicinity of Bernardo de Miranda's Almagres Mine on the Río de las Chanas (Llano River). This reinforcement would enable the Spaniards to offer greater protection to the Apaches, whose homeland was, in certain seasons, "a bloody theater of war." An additional garrison on the Llano would help also to free the Lipan Apaches from this constant danger of attack.

Many Spanish families already were going to the Almagres region to settle and work the mines. The encouragement of a new presidio would enable further settlement of the region. The Apaches would put aside the fear that had kept them from missions; foreign aggressors would be kept from the land; the treasury would be enhanced and the Catholic goals of conversion of the infidels attained, Parrilla believed. Regardless of whether this new company was established, he said:

> The Presidio de San Luis de las Amarillas should be maintained always on the San Sabá River. If, with the favorable effects of the campaign and the permanency of the presidio where it is, containment of the enemies is achieved, the Apaches will have more appreciation and esteem of our power. On the contrary, with abandonment and retreat of our people [from San Sabá], spirit would be given to the barbarous enemies to return to their hostilities.[20]

Simpson says a row between Parrilla and the mission colleges, apparently an outgrowth of the San Sabá massacre, grew very bitter and went on for years. Simpson cites Parrilla's difficulty with the missionaries at San Sabá as being typical of the feuding between religious and military which characterized the mission movement. He blames the "mistaken policy of the Crown in setting up these two parallel and inevitably conflicting agencies." [21]

Parrilla, however, showed himself well aware of this problem, for his final suggestion to the Marqués de Cruillas was for a *junta* of missionaries and presidial captains to iron out points of perennial controversy between them: the method in which the missionaries should ask for help, the number of soldiers needed by each mission and the duties they should have, the designation of lands for mission villages and presidios. The purpose would be to avoid

---
[20] Parrilla to the Viceroy, November 8, 1760, A.G.M., Historia, Vol. 84, Part I, p. 113.
[21] Nathan-Simpson, *San Saba Papers*, p. 155.

Aftermath of Failure

the "quarrels and disputes which each day offer themselves in the presidios of the Río Grande, San Antonio, La Bahía, and Espíritu Santo, to the end that all would observe their limits and that the planting and reduction of new settlements would not be upset by such disputes." [22]

This suggestion, like the others Parrilla made, apparently got no further. But had Cruillas taken advantage of Parrilla's perspicacity, the Spanish kingdom might have profited.

Parrilla, though he had his personal failings, had for the most part drawn the right conclusions. Though he may have tended to magnify the imminent threat of the French and the English and to underestimate the full potentialities of the Comanches and the other northern tribes by themselves, he recognized the new situation on the frontier for what it was. He recognized also the need for changes by New Spain in her manner of dealing with it.

Parrilla's thinking, however, was revolutionary, and it called for greater exertion on the part of the already over-taxed government of New Spain. It remained for the Marqués de Rubí, whose proposals differed from those of Parrilla, to instigate reforms on the frontier. Where Parrilla's plan was to strengthen the frontier in order to hold it against native and foreign aggressors, Rubí's was to withdraw and consolidate Spanish forces farther south.

Parrilla, for all his faults, saw things more clearly than his superiors at this point; but his vision bore no fruit. His discerning conclusions, based on his experience at the largest and most advanced outpost in Texas, were to come for naught, for his service there was being terminated. He was being replaced by one who lacked his insight, and who could acquire it only by walking many moons in the moccasins Parrilla was being forced to cast off.

During his "orientation period" Felipe de Rábago y Terán was to make many irrevocable miscues. They were errors which rendered the Spanish position at San Sabá still more untenable, pushing Spain toward the final pivot in its northern advance in Texas.

[22] Parrilla to the Viceroy, November 8, 1760, A.G.M., Historia, Vol. 84, Part I, p. 116.

PART IV
The Retreat

The New Commander

The tenure of Captain Felipe de Rábago y Terán as commander of the presidio on the San Sabá River is important because of its very ineffectiveness. Never able to adjust himself to the purposes of the government which he served, he persisted in setting his own course. He lacked Parrilla's character and judgment, as well as his respect for authority and obedience of it. Though he made some notable accomplishments of his own at San Sabá, these were nullified by his lack of judgment and by his refusal to pursue the goals set for him by the viceroy, the Marqués de Cruillas.

From the beginning the failure to place San Sabá under the jurisdiction of the governor of Texas, instead of making it directly responsible to the Viceroy, had created an unwieldy situation. The lack of liaison between the commander of San Sabá and the officials who governed the rest of the province made it almost impossible for them to pursue the same goals.

When the jurisdictional question finally was settled in Texas' favor in 1765, Rábago refused to recognize this decision, desiring to establish an independent jurisdiction of his own. This refusal was an insurmountable obstacle to cooperation between Rábago and the governor of Texas, Martos y Navarrete, and contributed to Rábago's ultimate failure, as well as to failure of missions for the Apaches.[1] On his return to Texas, Rábago played a definite role in hastening the time of the pivot.

That he could ever have been absolved of his previous conduct

[1] C. E. Castañeda, *Our Catholic Heritage*, IV, 187.

to be given another command post on the frontier is remarkable. When he was appointed commander of Presidio de San Xavier de Gigedo in 1751, he had just arrived in Mexico City from Spain with a royal patent from King Ferdinand VI. No sooner had he received notification of his appointment than he petitioned the Viceroy for one year's pay in advance for himself and the fifty men of his garrison, and an additional advance of six thousand pesos for the expense of constructing the new presidio. The presidio was never built. After Rábago was ousted as its commander a year and a half later, government officials had to ask him to return the six thousand pesos. It seems doubtful that he did.

Established as commander of the Presidio de San Xavier, he proceeded to ignore the instructions of the Viceroy for cooperating with the missionaries and treating the mission Indians with kindness. He baited the missionaries at every turn, harassed the mission Indians, and raped their women.

That he was behind the murders of Father José de Ganzábal and the soldier Ceballos, whose wife he had seduced, there is little doubt. But after an investigation that lasted eight years, during which Rábago had remained at Sacramento, Coahuila, he was exonerated.

Many protests arose at the news of his appointment to San Sabá. Colonel Parrilla, who was losing his command because of this maneuver, pointed out in his argument to the Viceroy that Rábago had never been commander of Presidio de San Luis de las Amarillas; the presidio he had commanded, San Xavier, had been abolished. Though the San Xavier garrison had been moved to the San Sabá River, it had been increased from fifty to one hundred men. Rábago could not be restored as commander of the garrison on the San Sabá, Parrilla contended, because it was a new post, and Parrilla himself was the only officer who had ever commanded it.

But the new viceroy, Marqués de Cruillas, had no intention of returning Parrilla to his command at San Sabá. Despite one of the most tarnished records in the history of New Spain, Rábago prepared to take possession of Presidio de San Luis de las Amarillas, the largest and most important presidio in the province. A tidal wave of apprehension swept Spanish Texas.

One of the strongest protests came from Father Mariano de los Dolores, who had been president of the missions of San Antonio

The New Commander

and San Xavier when Rábago's crimes were committed. The aged friar journeyed to México in a futile attempt to influence the Marqués de Cruillas.

Rábago's return to Texas, Father Dolores warned, could give rise to new disturbances, jeopardizing the peace of the entire province. The Apaches, he said, had become attached to Parrilla, who had founded the mission for them at San Sabá and had led the campaign against their enemies. To antagonize these Indians now by changing commanders, when the northern tribes were so resentful and when the French and English so active among them, was dangerous in the extreme.

In view of this argument, one of the Viceroy's advisers suggested that former Governor Barrios y Jáuregui be asked to make a report on points Father Dolores had raised. Barrios did not reply until after Rábago had taken possession of the presidio on the San Sabá River, but his response was a frank appraisal.

Barrios explained that Rábago, a young man with more money than judgment, had acquired wealth from the mines of Zacatecas before coming to Texas to take command at San Xavier. By Barrios' observations, he was domineering, overbearing, vain, jealous of command, and passionate. After the affair in Texas with the wife of Ceballos, he said, Rábago again had involved himself in an adulterous affair at Santa Rosa del Sacramento, in Coahuila. The woman in this case was the wife of an ignorant and unscrupulous soldier, Manuel Váldez, who had been consistently promoted and who now was second in command as Rábago's lieutenant at San Sabá, though he could not read or write.

And San Sabá, reminded Barrios, was the largest and most important presidio in Texas.

But no action was taken to remove the new commander of Presidio de San Luis de las Amarillas. Rábago's personal agent in México denied the charges and presented testimonials which apparently convinced the Viceroy.[2]

In fairness to Rábago, he may have made an earnest effort to reform after being ousted from his command at San Xavier. At least Father Diego Jiménez, one of the six missionaries originally sent to establish the Mission San Sabá, was able to see some good in him. When Rábago was given command of Presidio de San Luis de las Amarillas, Father Jiménez, who had remained at San

[2] *Ibid.*, pp. 148-150.

Sabá only a few months, was serving as president of the missions on the Río Grande, living at San Juan Bautista.

Father Jiménez and Rábago apparently had become close friends. When Rábago was assigned to his command at San Sabá, Father Jiménez was able to make certain suggestions to him regarding his conduct—and to have his suggestions accepted gracefully. Father Jiménez advised Rábago by letter to exercise discretion and to comport himself with circumspection in his new post. More pointedly, he advised him against bringing the Sayopín Indian Andrés to Texas.

Andrés, who had admitted killing Father Ganzábal at San Xavier, implicating Rábago and several of his men, had lived in Rábago's household since that time. After making his confession he had repudiated it, an act which made it possible for Rábago ultimately to be exonerated.

Rábago accepted the suggestion of Father Jiménez and left Andrés in Monclova, Coahuila. He thanked the padre for his friendly interest. Rábago, as witnessed by the testimony against him by Father Dolores, had alienated himself from the missionaries at San Antonio. The missions under control of Father Jiménez were the only ones which would furnish him supplies.

Rábago had made his way directly from San Fernando de Austria to San Sabá, opening a more direct trail, to miss San Antonio, because of the ill feeling against him there. He arrived September 30, 1760, and took possession of the post the following day from Captain Manuel Rodríguez, whom Colonel Parrilla had left in charge when he went to México.[3]

After inspecting the Presidio, Rábago reported on its condition to the new viceroy, explaining that the equipment was in poor shape, and that portions of the stockade had rotted away or were destroyed. There were, he said, six cannon with no artillerymen to operate them. While the garrison was at full strength in numbers, it contained a number of mere youngsters and some who were not soldiers at all.

For the poor condition of the Presidio, he excused Parrilla. The Comanches were said to be camped not more than thirty miles away, posing a constant threat. The necessity for posting a continuous watch hindered acquisition of supplies, as well as work to maintain the Presidio, he pointed out. The men must patrol the

[3] Rábago to the viceroy, Marqués de Cruillas, October 24, 1760, A.G.M., Historia, Vol. 94, Part I, pp. 4–5.

The New Commander

country to keep track of the movements of the Indians. They must watch closely over the horses and the cattle, escort supply trains, do guard duty at the Presidio, and accompany parties of friendly Apaches on their hunting trips to prevent their being attacked by the hostile northern tribes. And Rábago now was faced with the need of clearing timber around the Presidio, and of sending some men to northern México to obtain recruits and to purchase horses and cattle.

That Rábago was impressed with the importance of his new assignment is readily apparent. Echoing the position of his predecessor, Parrilla, he declared in his report to the Viceroy that Presidio de San Luis de las Amarillas was the bulwark of four provinces: Texas, New Mexico, Nueva Vizcaya (Chihuahua), and Coahuila. He said it should be maintained at all costs, for its abandonment would imperil the infant settlements in these provinces, and would put an end to any missionary effort among the Apaches. Abandonment also would embolden the northern tribes and cause the Apaches to feel they had been betrayed, he said; it would be an admission of failure.

In the hope of establishing a trail into New Mexico, Rábago sent out expeditions to explore the country to the west of present-day Menard. He claimed first to have explored the Concho River from its source to its juncture with the Colorado. Then, in the spring of 1761, he sent a party of forty men into an area now comprising Tom Green, Schleicher, Irion, Reagan, Upton, and Ward Counties. The patrol was gone twenty-four days, reaching all the way to the Pecos River. It apparently followed the stream from near the present town of McCamey to the present city of Pecos, Texas, where a large Indian village was found.

The circumstances which prompted this expedition are explained by Webb, who says that first the Apaches then the Comanches had thwarted the Spaniards in their northward advance.

> These were the two tribes that held, first and last, the southern end of the Great Plains region and that brought terror to all and ruin to most of the Spanish settlements whether presidio, pueblo, or mission, which lay around the borders of Apachería and Comanchería. The result was that as the Spanish line advanced northward it began to sag in the middle, folding itself round the Great Plains, not only leaving them unoccupied but practically unexplored.[4]

[4] W. P. Webb, *The Great Plains*, p. 116.

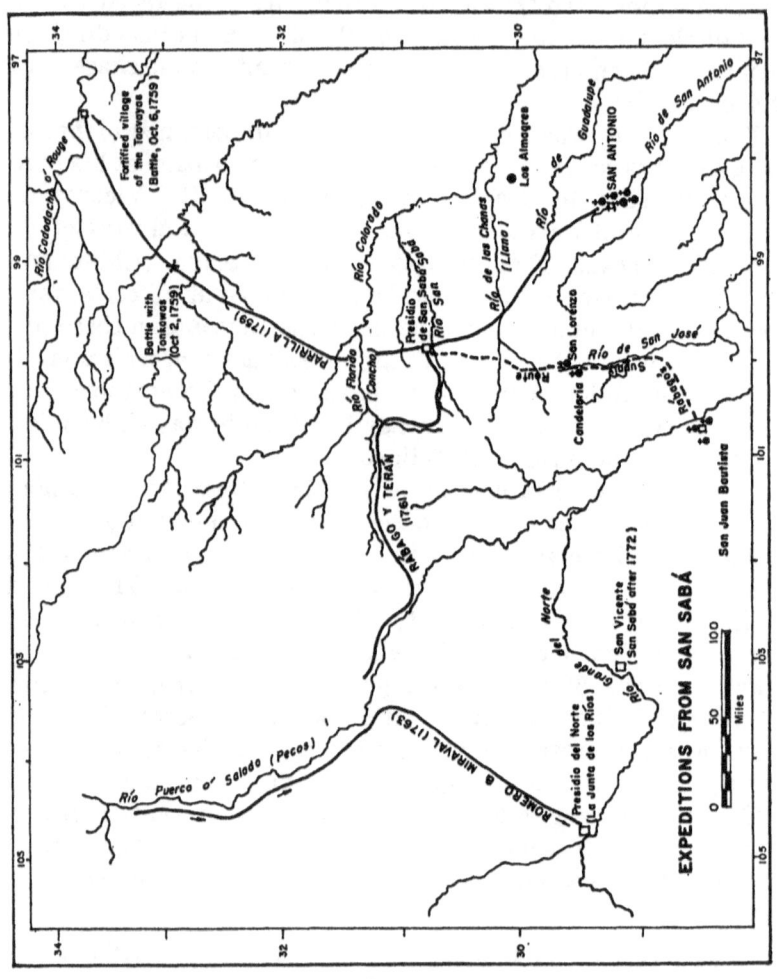

The New Commander

This "sag" had become evident long before 1761, with the line of Spanish outposts extending from San Juan Bautista northeastward to San Antonio and Los Adaes and skirting the Llano Estacado on the west by following the course of the Río Grande. San Sabá stood as a lone extension from the sagging line.

When the San Sabá project first was undertaken, the location was thought to be much closer to the settlements of New Mexico than it actually was. In fact, it was thought likely that the location was in New Mexico; hence the indecision about placing it under the jurisdiction of the governor of Texas. Plans had called for establishing trade routes between San Sabá and the New Mexico settlements.

Rábago's jab into the country to the west was an effort in this direction, but it accomplished little because of his failure to pursue the exploration further. From this expedition came a description of the country, including the location of springs, which would have been useful in follow-up explorations. But Rábago did not exploit this opportunity for two reasons.

The first reason already had been demonstrated by the attack on the San Sabá Mission and by Parrilla's expedition to the north. Hostile Indians were in firm possession of the Plains which lay between San Sabá and New Mexico. The second reason was that Rábago was to take part in founding missions at a site too far from his Presidio, splitting his garrison and impairing its effectiveness.

More than two years later, in the fall of 1763, an attempt was made from New Mexico to take some of the sag out of the line which skirted the Great Plains. Governor Tomás Veléz Cachupín of New Mexico sent Francisco Romero and Joseph Antonio Miraval, two Indians from the old Cicuye Mission at Pecos, New Mexico, near Santa Fé, to seek a route to Presidio de San Sabá, carrying letters to its captain. Romero apparently had visited San Sabá, and perhaps had lived there. He was to guide the expedition, which included five mission Indians besides himself and Miraval. They traveled down the Pecos River. After five days four of the Indians deserted, leaving only Miraval, Romero, and Romero's brother Miguel.

The remaining three reached a Lipan village some two hundred miles from their starting point. They had been there five days when the village was attacked by Comanches, and Francisco

Romero was wounded by an arrow through the chest. Miguel went back to Pecos, New Mexico, to report, while Miraval and the wounded man remained in the Indian village three months for him to recuperate.

Three days after leaving the Lipan village, they came to a Mescalero camp among the sand dunes. They were welcomed, but soon after their arrival some wounded Indians brought word that they had been attacked by Spaniards. The excited Mescaleros planned revenge on their guests. Romero, who knew the Apache language, overheard, and he and Miraval escaped during the night.

Only two leagues from the Mescalero village, they came to a village of friendly Lipans, who furnished guides to lead them to San Sabá. After traveling ten days they came to another Lipan village at a place called Loma Pinta, where they spent the night.

After they had left the village the next morning, they were overtaken by a messenger who informed them that a party of Spaniards had come to the village. They returned to the village and met Captain Manuel Rodríguez from Presidio de la Junta de los Ríos (near present Presidio, Texas), whose mission was to punish the Apaches for raids on Spanish settlements along the Río Grande.[5]

Romero and Miraval, after traveling all this distance along the Pecos River, now went toward present Presidio, then returned to New Mexico. They never reached San Sabá, and during the life of the San Sabá Presidio no route was established between it and the settlements of New Mexico.

The line of Spanish outposts on the northern frontier still sagged in the middle. It still folded itself around the lower end of the Great Plains.

Soon after his arrival at San Sabá, Rábago y Terán had busied himself with the material improvement of the Presidio. Colonel Parrilla, having been instructed to erect buildings of timber as economically as possible, never had time to put up buildings of stone.

Rábago now instructed his men to quarry limestone to build a stockade that would last, with rooms built into the walls replacing the log cabins in which the soldiers and their families had lived. A

[5] Castañeda, *Our Catholic Heritage*, IV, 180–190.

The New Commander

blockhouse was built, and a moat was dug. Only a little more than a year after his arrival, the new commander had much progress to report to the Viceroy.

The fort, he said, now resembled a veritable castle. With completion of the stone buildings, it would be the strongest presidio on the frontier. He began to call it by a new name: Real Presidio de San Sabá. The garrison also had been improved. Rábago had found that eighteen of the men turned over to him when he assumed command were militiamen recruited for Parrilla's campaign against the Indians. They had remained to fill vacancies "temporarily." Rábago informed the Viceroy that he had replaced these men, and those who were too young or otherwise unfit for military service, with twenty new recruits from Coahuila. He also brought in more than six hundred horses, and the garrison now was up to full strength and well-mounted.

New Apache Missions

Most remarkably, Captain Rábago y Terán now became interested in saving the souls of the wily, ruthless Apaches. Says Morfi:

> Either because he desired to eradicate the perverse memory of his conduct or because he wished to make amends to religion for the damages he had occasioned as a result of his previous scandals that resulted in the ruin of the missions of San Xavier, he now applied all his energies to the conversion of the Apaches.[1]

The new commander, soon after arriving at San Sabá, had visited the ruins of the Mission Santa Cruz de San Sabá. The charred remains of this mission were an ugly scar upon the landscape. The irrigation ditch begun by the padres had never been finished. It lay empty and silent among the tall weeds. As Rábago surveyed this scene a handful of Apaches looked on from a short distance, their faces bleak and expressionless.

Of the four priests who had been assigned to San Sabá to work with the Apaches following the Mission massacre, Father Francisco Aparicio had been the only one ever to see the site. Renewal of the mission effort had awaited the outcome of Parrilla's campaign, which seems to have stalled plans still further. Father Aparicio had returned to Mission Concepción shortly after his arrival at San Sabá and had not visited the place again.

Rábago now assured the Indians that he would protect them and bring back the missionaries to minister to their needs of the spirit. Still cognizant of the rift with the padres at San Antonio, he wrote to his friend Father Jiménez at San Juan Bautista.[2]

The Apaches seemed to like Rábago, and they began to visit Real Presidio de San Sabá more frequently. Again they spoke of

---

[1] Juan Agustín Morfi, *History of Texas* (translated by C. E. Castañeda), II, 394.

[2] C. E. Castañeda, *Our Catholic Heritage*, IV, 158.

mission life. Their overtures fell on willing ears. Rábago took advantage of every opportunity to win the friendship and confidence of the Lipans, who so many times had excused themselves from their promises to take up mission life.

He sent invitations to the various chiefs, distributed many presents, and furnished military escort for the Apache buffalo hunts to protect them against their enemies, the Comanches. Yet he attempted to impress upon them that the only way they could enjoy these advantages permanently was by congregating in missions, where they could be instructed by the friars and protected by the soldiers.

The most formidable of Apache chiefs, Cabezón, came to Rábago in October, 1761, declaring that all his three thousand people were ready to be congregated in missions. Rábago sent a letter to Father Jiménez asking him to come at once. By November 4 the president of missions on the Río Grande had arrived at San Sabá.[3]

More Apache chiefs soon came to express the eagerness of their people to enter missions. The Apaches were allowed to choose the site of their own missions. Wary as they were of San Sabá following the destruction of the mission there, they chose El Río de San José (upper Nueces River) at a point near present Camp Wood, halfway between San Sabá and San Juan Bautista. San Sabá, they said, was not safe against surprise attack by their enemies.

The Indians asked to be allowed to go on a buffalo hunt to supply themselves with meat before congregating at the missions, and Rábago furnished them an escort to protect them from the Comanches. The Apaches now were closer to entering missions than they had ever been, and Father Jiménez and Rábago did not wish to let the opportunity pass.

Late in December the Apaches of Chief Cabezón returned to Presidio de San Sabá from their buffalo hunt and declared their readiness to congregate in the Valle de San José. Thirty men were ordered to accompany them to San José Valley, under command of Lieutenant Manuel Váldez. The soldiers and the Indians set out from San Sabá January 2, 1762. Rábago himself followed a few days later.

On January 16 Father Jiménez arrived, and the Mission San Lorenzo de la Santa Cruz was founded. Father Jiménez was joined

[3] *Ibid.*, pp. 158–159.

by Father Joaquín de Baños, who also was one of the original missionaries assigned to Mission Santa Cruz de San Sabá. With Father Jiménez, he had become discouraged and returned to México when the Apaches failed to congregate at that mission.

Aware that his prolonged absence from his presidio constituted negligence, Rábago prepared to return to San Sabá. A guard of twenty men under command of Lieutenant Váldez would remain to protect the new mission. As Rábago was about to leave, word came that a chief called El Turnio and his people had come to the Presidio, asking to be settled in a mission. Father Baños was left in charge of Mission San Lorenzo as both Rábago and Father Jiménez hastened to San Sabá to talk with El Turnio.

The meeting with this chief culminated in the founding of Mission Nuestra Señora de la Candelaria, named for its predecessor at San Xavier. It was located ten miles below San Lorenzo, near present Montell. Captain Rábago, in order to provide protection for the second new mission, agreed to assign an additional guard of ten men to it. Father Jiménez took charge of the establishment.[4]

The significant aspect of Rábago's part in founding the two missions without viceregal approval is that his action committed him to diminish the garrison of Presidio de San Sabá by thirty of its one hundred men in order to give the missions protection. And, forced to share the Presidio's supplies with the missions, he reduced the effectiveness of the Presidio and jeopardized the safety of its people. In effect, his lack of judgment offered an open invitation to the Indians of the north.

It was customary in founding new missions to obtain approval of the mother college—in this case the College of Querétaro—and the viceroy. Father Jiménez had taken care of the first step. The second was not so easy. Rábago, in his appointment to San Sabá, had been instructed to restore the destroyed mission there, or to found others in the vicinity. But establishing missions on a new site more than one hundred miles from the Presidio was exceeding his authority. Endless delays sometimes followed requests to found new missions, and in this case, the captain reasoned, the delays could mean the death of the project, another lost opportunity.

Father Jiménez wrote to the commissary general of the College

[4] *Ibid.*, pp. 159–167.

New Apache Missions

of Querétaro, asking for help in obtaining approval of the viceroy, the Marqués de Cruillas. Personal opposition to Rábago because of his past misdeeds, he warned, would endanger success of the enterprise. Regardless of his conduct in the past, he now was displaying the most fervent zeal for reduction of the Apaches and deserved to be supported in his earnest efforts, the padre wrote.

Rábago himself finally reported the founding of the missions to the Viceroy. But his request for official sanction met with stony silence.

Within a week after their establishment each of the two missions of El Cañon had four hundred Indians. Corn was planted, and an adobe church was built at San Lorenzo Mission. But most of the corn was consumed as roasting ears, and supplies were short. Father Jiménez foresaw the likelihood of failure because of the supply problem if official sponsorship was not granted.[5]

Rábago's involvement in the new mission project put an end to his exploration of the plains country to the north and the west. Whatever chance remained to extend the Spanish frontier, after the San Sabá massacre and Parrilla's poor showing against the northern tribes, now had been cast away.

Rábago well knew that his action in establishing the missions so far from his presidio was contrary to the wishes of the Viceroy. The Marqués de Cruillas had stressed that the forts and missions established should extend to the northwest of San Sabá, toward New Mexico, in order that the French might not take possession of this area. He informed Rábago of a report from the Tehuacana Indians that the French already had established five houses in that territory, going there under pretext of hunting buffalo.[6]

But Rábago stubbornly declined to alter his course. In founding the missions on the Nueces River instead of the San Sabá, he unwittingly had taken a big step toward determining the fate of his presidio, in fixing the pivot of Spain's northward advance in Texas. His refusal to notify the Viceroy in advance of his actions and the slowness of communication with Mexico City created a hopeless muddle. Time and time again the error of making the

---

[5] *Ibid.*, pp. 167–168.

[6] Hons C. Richards, "The Establishment of the Candelaria and San Lorenzo Missions on the Upper Nueces" (Master's Thesis), p. 29. Richards cites a letter from the viceroy, Marqués de Cruillas, to Rábago, of October 1, 1762, which this writer has been unable to locate.

San Sabá project directly responsible to the viceroy, instead of the governor of Texas or Coahuila, was proved.

While Rábago was busy making his bed of thorns, the Seven Years' War drew to a close, with implications which would vitally affect Texas. With Charles III now on the throne, Spain had joined the conflict in its final stages on the side of France. One important result of the series of events which followed was that France ceded all of Louisiana to Spain on November 3, 1762.

Thus France, whose intrusions had been so long feared in New Spain, was removed from the colonial picture. Texas, which had been a bulwark against foreign aggression, became an interior province. Because French colonists in Louisiana were reluctant to become Spanish subjects, the transfer would require seven years for completion. Yet Spain viewed the cession as a release from the burden of defending Texas against foreign encroachment. And, as always, the interest of Spain in Texas abated when the French threat seemed to abate.

Again the officials of New Spain, instead of acting, simply reacted. Instead of using the forces released by this new development to push back the frontier, they began to think of withdrawal. It was a serious mistake.

About one year after the missions of El Cañon were founded, the Viceroy wrote to the padres for a report on conditions in Valle de San José. Father Jiménez and his new assistant, Father Manuel de Cuevas, replied, taking advantage of the opportunity to point out that the most pressing need was for an adequate military guard. A presidio garrison in the vicinity of the two missions would induce the Indians already congregated to submit to mission routine and would enable the missionaries to carry their work to the other Apache tribes.

Of equal importance, said the priests, was help in obtaining supplies until the missions became self-supporting. Without such help they probably would be unable to keep the Indians in the missions; the usual grant of money made by the king for this purpose to all new missions was indispensable.[7]

Rábago also urged establishment of a presidio in Valle de San José, under his own jurisdiction. In June, 1762, the Taovayas and their northern allies had repeatedly raided the Presidio de San

[7] Castañeda, *Our Catholic Heritage*, IV, 172–174.

Sabá, killing two soldiers and seizing seventy horses. Because Rábago had split his garrison to give protection to the Nueces missions, he now was so short of men that pursuit of the Indians was out of the question.

Says Castañeda,

> Such a presidio would have afforded the new mission the desired protection, but it would have also increased considerably the expense of the royal treasury and given the commander of San Sabá not only more power and prestige but more profits as well. . . . It seems that Rábago's real interest was his own material advantage.[8]

Rábago declared in his communication to the Viceroy that establishment of the presidio on the Nueces was vital to maintenance of Presidio de San Sabá. Defense of San Sabá with a reduced garrison was impossible, he said; if a new presidio with a garrison of fifty soldiers could not be established for protection of the new missions, and San Sabá restored to full strength, it would be best to abandon the post on the San Sabá River and remove the entire garrison to Valle de San José.

The Viceroy replied October 1, 1762, giving his reasons for wanting to keep the Presidio where it was. Presidio de San Sabá and the new missions on the Nueces, he said, would facilitate communication between the provinces of Texas and New Mexico. Serving as way stations for various expeditions, they would make commercial relations between Texas and New Mexico easier, and they would keep any foreign nation from coming into the territory that lay between.[9] Yet the Viceroy did not grant the request to establish a new presidio or recognize the missions and extend them government support. His attitude toward Rábago's endeavors may have been influenced by Texas Governor Martos y Navarrete, who undoubtedly resented Rábago's refusal to place his command under Texas authority.

On March 16, 1763, the *auditor*, Don Domingo Valcárcel, issued an opinion concerning these reports. San Sabá, founded to keep watch on the Apaches, had failed in its purpose, he said, because the two new missions had been established at such a great distance from the fort. He doubted that the Apaches ever would live

[8] *Ibid.*, p. 175.
[9] The viceroy, Marqués de Cruillas to Rábago, October 1, 1762, cited by Richards, "Candelaria and San Lorenzo Missions" (Master's thesis), p. 42.

in settlements, predicted a short life for the two missions, and advocated moving Presidio de San Sabá to a less remote site. At its present location, he declared, San Sabá was useless, and the site should be abandoned.[10]

This official, like many others, failed to recognize the value of Presidio de San Sabá as a buffer against Indian attack on settlements farther south. During the lifetime of this presidio San Antonio and many of the settlements along the Río Grande were virtually free from the bloody attacks they had suffered prior to the founding of the fort, and were to suffer again soon after it was abandoned.

The Presidio, located as it was at the base of the North Central Plains, had tremendous value in this respect. With Spain no longer able to advance northward, this outpost served to hold back the Plains Indians in their southward movement. The United States Army, almost a century later, was to recognize the strategic importance of this location by placing nearby a frontier fort to serve essentially the same function.

The missions of El Cañon continued to operate without benefit of viceregal recognition or royal grant. Although Rábago did everything he could to help the missionaries to obtain the supplies they needed, his resources began to fail.

The only way to obtain food for the missions was to permit the neophytes to go on buffalo hunts, which impeded the work of the missions. The Indians took advantage of this freedom to raid the settlements in Coahuila, stealing goods and livestock.

In October, 1763, Rábago petitioned the Viceroy to have two hundred families move into the Nueces Valley. The request was not granted. The missionaries also asked for settlers for the safety of the settlement.[11]

For some eight years the mission effort on the upper Nueces was maintained without official approval or aid, at no expense to the royal treasury. But it could not continue under such a handicap forever.

More and more was Rábago caught in his own web. The Lipan Apaches took advantage of their sanctuary at the missions on the

---

[10] Valcárcel to Martínez de Soria, March 16, 1763, A.G.I., 1742–1763, Part II, Dunn Transcripts, pp. 27–30, as cited by Richards, in *ibid.*, p. 43.

[11] Richards, "Candelaria and San Lorenzo Missions," pp. 50–51.

New Apache Missions

upper Nueces. Feeling secure in the secluded canyons, with Spanish soldiers to help ward off attacks, they began to make raids on the Comanches.

After each buffalo hunt they would send the old men and the women back to the missions while the braves went into the land of the Comanches to take revenge. After striking their old enemies, they would flee for the hilly country in the region of the Frio and Nueces Rivers. For a time the Comanches would not follow for fear of ambush in the rugged country. But at last, in desperation, they did.

Morfi gives an illustration of Apache tactics which may explain why eventually the Spaniards were to wage a war of extermination on the wily Apaches:

> The Apaches would go out to rob and kill the Indians of the north, taking with them a number of hats and other things worn by our soldiers, all of which they artfully left along the way, as if by carelessness, in order to convince that the Spaniards were the perpetrators of the crimes. At the same time they would provide themselves with arrows and shoes of the kind used by their enemies and would then commit depredations near Spanish presidios and missions where it was thought the Indians of the north were responsible.[12]

Now nettled by the raiding Apaches, the Comanches began to attack the Spanish presidio on the San Sabá River anew. The Presidio was more easily accessible than the new missions to the south. The attacks on its walls seem to verify its value as a buffer. They proved also the power and mobility of the Plains Indians. Now the aggressors instead of defenders, they could attack this outpost with impunity.

The continuous state of warfare went on for years. Early in 1764 Rábago reported a severe attack on Presidio de San Sabá, asking for more arms and ammunition. The Viceroy replied that he had instructed the governor of Coahuila, Lorenzo Cancio, to fill the request. The munitions still had not arrived a full year later.

In January, 1765, a small detachment of soldiers from San Sabá went in pursuit of a deserter from the Presidio. A band of Comanches waylaid the soldiers as they were returning with the prisoner and his wife. In the skirmish in Frio River Canyon three

[12] Morfi, *History of Texas*, II, 394-395.

men and the woman were killed. A corporal escaped and fled to San Sabá with the news.

The Mission San Lorenzo was attacked twice by Indians in 1766, the Comanches having lost their fear of the hilly country. Though the Comanches were unable to carry out their plan of destroying the Mission, they continued to harass both the missions and the garrison at San Sabá. They inflicted severe losses on the Presidio early in 1767.[13]

Scouts of the northern tribes watched every movement within the Presidio and around it. Those who left the fort were either killed or captured, Rábago wrote to the Viceroy. The Indians literally covered the country, their villages extending all the way from San Sabá to the missions on the Nueces.

On January 11, 1767, Rábago recounted, Lieutenant Diego de Alles and Ensign Pedro de Sierra and three soldiers went to the river, without license, to amuse themselves. Indians, both on foot and on horseback, surrounded them and killed all five. On January 14 a squad of soldiers coming from the missions encountered a band of Indians on the road and fled for their lives. After traveling most of the night, a distance of about eight leagues, they hid in a ravine in a dense wood to elude the savages, and later made their way safely to the Presidio.

"It is certain, Most Excellent Sir [Rábago wrote], that the enemy inhabits all the country."

The year before, he continued, crops had been planted to insure provisions for the fort, but the Indians came in the night and destroyed them. It was impossible to keep horses. The fort had only enough provisions to last through March, and if help were not forthcoming the fort would be lost or the garrison would be forced to abandon it.

Rábago saw no hope for conversion of the Apaches, the reason for the Presidio in the first place, as these Indians had fled to the Río Puerco (Pecos River). He reminded the Viceroy that he had examined the Pecos, which had everything needed for several settlements—water, pasture, and good land—except wood. Perhaps efforts to convert the Apaches could succeed if the Presidio were moved to the Pecos, he suggested.[14]

[13] Castañeda, *Our Catholic Heritage*, IV, 182.
[14] Rábago to the viceroy, Marqués de Croix, January 20, 1767, A.S.F.G., 1751–1767, Vol. 20, pp. 67–70.

There is no record of the Viceroy's reply.

Not long afterward, the Comanches surprised a group of twenty-three soldiers a short distance from the Presidio and attempted to cut off their retreat. In the engagement, within sight of those in the Presidio, the Indians killed José Jiménez Sánchez and decapitated him. They killed and scalped Juan Nuncio. Rábago dared not attempt a rescue for fear of jeopardizing the women and children. The remaining twenty-one soldiers managed a narrow escape.

For two months the Presidio endured a virtual state of siege. On Good Friday, Rábago received word that a convoy of fifty men, bringing much-needed supplies and a drove of sheep, was nearing the Presidio, and sent a detail of soldiers to meet the supply detail and to give warning that the Indians were near. The soldiers were not molested as they went out and returned. The supply train appeared, and the gate opened to receive it; then the Comanches charged. The convoy of fifty men, reinforced by those of the Presidio, withstood the attack and got the supply train inside the stockade, but the sheep and the herdsmen scattered. They fell easy prey to the savages.[15]

When dawn came after an uneasy night, all was calm and peaceful. The sheep scattered by the charging Comanches the afternoon before now grazed contentedly a short distance beyond the stockade wall, apparently untended. It seemed that the Indians had gone, but the Spaniards recognized the baited trap.

When night came again, the sheep still were grazing along the riverbank. The soldiers in the Presidio waited and watched. Next morning the sheep were gone. The Indians apparently had given up.

Sometime later the Comanches attacked a band of Apaches returning from a buffalo hunt, killing or capturing thirty and driving off more than one thousand horses. The Apaches sought Rábago's help, and he and forty soldiers pursued the Comanches and engaged them in a battle, during which eight soldiers were killed and one cannon lost.[16]

Since October of the year before (1766), Rábago noted, the Comanches had made more than five separate attempts to sur-

---

[15] Castañeda, *Our Catholic Heritage*, IV, 184–185.
[16] Richards, "Candelaria and San Lorenzo Missions" (Master's thesis), p. 58; Arricivita, *Crónica*, pp. 392–393.

prise the missions of El Cañon and the Presidio de San Sabá. On three different occasions they had intercepted supply trains, and during one of these encounters they had driven off three hundred mules. In the most recent attack, they had driven off even more than that number of sheep.

Since coming to San Sabá in 1761, Rábago had spent more than twelve thousand pesos for food, clothing, and livestock, of which a large amount had never reached either the missions or the Presidio.

From fear of failure and with hope of vindicating himself, Rábago conceived a plan, which he stated in his letter to the Viceroy. He urgently requested that he be allowed to lead an expedition such as Parrilla had undertaken against the northern tribes. If he could have three hundred men for a three-month campaign, he would penetrate the very heart of the Comanches' land, and would chastise them so severely they would respect the might of Spanish arms forever.

Rábago's desperation led him to overplay his hand. To strengthen his appeal he told the Viceroy that European officers, French or English, had led the Comanches in their attacks on San Sabá during the winter. He did not realize that Louisiana technically had been a Spanish possession for four years, and that fear of foreign aggression had lost its sting.[17]

Neither the Viceroy nor his advisers bothered to reply to Rábago's appeal. There was little need to do so. Already the inspector general, the Marqués de Rubí, was on his way to Presidio de San Sabá, having been sent from Spain by King Charles III to make a general inspection of the Spanish frontier from California to Texas. As a result, it was the fears, rather than the hopes, of Rábago that were to be realized.

[17] Castañeda, *Our Catholic Heritage*, IV, 181–186. H. E. Bolton (*Texas in the Middle Eighteenth Century*, pp. 109–110) says troops were sent from San Antonio and Coahuila in 1764 and from Coahuila in 1767 to Rábago's relief. I have found no substantiation of this assistance. Especially does it seem unlikely Rábago received help from San Antonio, because of his poor relations with that settlement.

The Inspector General

It was a combination of circumstances that brought to New Spain in 1766 the king's inspector general, the Marqués de Rubí. There had been no comprehensive inspection of frontier outposts since 1730. The new king, Charles III, rightly suspected that some of the establishments had outlived their usefulness. Rumors of profiteering and other abuses by presidial commanders had reached his ears. The acquisition of Louisiana called for an investigation to determine what should be done about the new territory. The Marqués de Rubí, field marshal in His Majesty's Army, arrived in México early in February, 1766, with orders to inspect the entire frontier and report the status of each presidio, from California to East Texas.

Rubí and Nicolás de Lafora, the captain of engineers who traveled with him, covered seven thousand miles in carrying out the assignment. Their journey took three years. The inspection tour took them first into New Mexico, as far north as Santa Fé, then on to California. They returned to Monclova, Coahuila, June 15, 1767, and from there Rubí began his inspection of the province of Texas.

Rubí had explicit instructions to ascertain whether Real Presidio de San Sabá should be maintained in its present location or moved to another. From Presidio de Santa Rosa, in Coahuila, he set out for the Río Grande.

In crossing the Río Grande near present Del Rio, a Pausan Indian and two horses were drowned. The party camped at Las Moras Springs (on the present Fort Clark Guest Ranch at Brackettville) and proceeded on to the Nueces country. There the group visited the missions of El Cañon, and Lafora made a map of the missions and the surrounding country. The Candelaria Mission apparently had been abandoned because of Indian depredations sometime before. Mission San Lorenzo was tended by two missionaries, Fathers Rivera and Santiesteban, who at this time had no Indians to teach. Thirty-one soldiers from Presidio de San Sabá guarded the establishment, for which Lafora saw no purpose. He wrote in his diary:

> It merely keeps a detachment of thirty men and an officer from the Presidio of San Sabá occupied, and it maintains two useless missionaries. It has no other function than to be a provisioning point for pack trains which enter with supplies for that presidio. Its shape and bad location are shown on the map I drew of this settlement.[1]

From Valle de San José, Rubí and his party proceeded to San Sabá, crossing the Llano River below the present town of Junction. They arrived at the San Sabá River the evening of July 25. Smoke signals rose out of the hills as they traveled along Arroyo de Abuela (Las Moras Creek) toward the Presidio. Crossing the San Sabá River in shallow water, they traveled half a league downstream to reach the Presidio, where they set about gathering posts to fence in their horses. It was decided to pen the horses an hour before daylight as a precaution against thieving Indians and to turn them out after reconnaissance.

On the morning of July 29 two scouts notified the fort that they had been chased by Comanches the previous night. The same morning a sentinel reported having seen two horses running through the hills half a league distant. This incident was a false alarm, however, caused by a soldier who had pursued and lassoed a horse which had escaped from the fort. Indian signs and threats persisted during the Inspector's stay at San Sabá, but no attack occurred.[2]

During his ten-day visit Rubí made several penetrating observations. He found the garrison short of its complement of one hundred men by half a dozen, not counting the thirty assigned to guard the missions at El Cañon. The soldiers were kept at their post by debt to Rábago, who charged them exorbitant prices for food, supplies, and equipment, and they were desertion-prone. The commander maintained below the Río Grande a horse ranch from which he supplied mounts to his men at his own price. Even so, the garrison was inadequately mounted and armed,

[1] Lawrence Kinnaird (trans.), *Frontiers of New Spain*, p. 147 (translation of Nicolás de Lafora, *Presidios Internos*).
[2] *Ibid.*, pp. 150–151.

The Inspector General

having no more than one hundred horses. Five or six horses to the man was standard. The soldiers' guns were poorly cared for and not of uniform caliber. Not more than half the men had pistols. Swords, saddles, and other equipment were shabby, as were the uniforms, which consisted of blue trousers and red cloaks with silver buttons.[3]

Lafora made his own observations and recorded them in a diary. He drew a map of the area and a profile of the north wall of the Presidio, including the main buildings. He noted that the garrison, comprising one hundred men, among them five officers and a chaplain, "is an annual expense of 40,360 pesos to His Majesty and is of no advantage whatever." Lafora recorded that the location was 31°38' north latitude and 237°27' longitude, reckoned from Tenerife Meridian. He said that the defense of the Presidio included seven small cannon, four of them without trunnions, and that all the carriages were unserviceable. An extensive area around the fort had been cleared of timber, he noted, but needed to be cleared again because of a new growth of mesquite.[4]

At the conclusion of the inspection Rubí suggested that Rábago reduce the prices of various commodities. He apparently said nothing more, leaving the Presidio commander with the mistaken impression that he was well pleased with the establishment.

In a secret report to the Viceroy the Inspector General said the Presidio was without doubt the worst in the entire kingdom. Rábago, though only forty-five years old, was broken in health. The fort was poorly located between two ravines, said Rubí, one of which was formed by a small creek (Arroyo de Juan Lorenzo, present Celery Creek). The creek had heavily wooded banks and, according to Rubí, was within gunshot range of the Presidio, providing protection for the enemy to attack from a safe distance. The San Sabá River ran along the south wall of the stockade, its high bank affording protection for the enemy to crawl unnoticed along the stream to the very walls and to attack without being exposed.

In the eyes of Rubí, the moat which Rábago had so proudly constructed was poorly planned and offered practically no advan-

[3] C. E. Castañeda, *Our Catholic Heritage*, IV, 190–191.
[4] Kinnaird, *Frontiers of New Spain*, p. 151; Nicolás de Lafora, "Plano de el Presidio de San Sabá," legend of map in University of Texas Archives.

tages at all. The fort's two swivel guns were mounted in such a way that the men serving them were exposed to the fire of the enemy; the stockade was low and could be easily scaled.

If the true state of the Presidio and its garrison became known to the Comanches, declared the Inspector, this frontier outpost might be exterminated. Such a catastrophe, in his opinion, would embolden the savages and put a blemish on the prestige of Spanish arms exceeding, even, the defeat of Parrilla.[5]

It appears, from a present-day inspection of the site, that Rubí somewhat exaggerated its vulnerability. Celery Creek (Arroyo de Juan Lorenzo) is some five hundred yards from the Presidio at the closest point. An unnamed ravine to the west is closer, but still not within range of firearms of that day. It is conceivable, however, that Indians could have come down the ravine to the river and crept along its banks to reach the Presidio unseen. Lafora, in the legend of his map, calls attention to windings in the riverbank in which four to six men could hide. If the enemy had approached from across the river, according to Lafora's map he must have struggled through deep water.

But the Inspector General contended that the Presidio served no purpose. The cost of its upkeep was excessive, and he added that it offered no protection to San Antonio or to any other Spanish outpost. "It affords as much protection to the interests of His Majesty in New Spain," he declared, "as a ship anchored in mid-Atlantic would afford in preventing foreign trade with America."[6]

The Apaches had retreated beyond the Río Grande, and the two missions on the upper Nueces were a poor excuse for maintaining the Presidio, Rubí claimed. He voiced the belief that the Indians of the northern tribes were not actually enemies of the Spaniards; they merely sought destruction of the hated Apaches. But there were many things which Rubí failed to understand clearly, and this was one of them; for with or without the Apaches, the Indians of the north still constituted a serious threat, having already taken the offensive.

In Rubí's opinion, the Presidio and its stockade should be razed, the garrison discharged, and the few settlers moved to San Antonio, "the only permanent Spanish settlement in Texas."

[5] Castañeda, *Our Catholic Heritage*, IV, 190–192.
[6] *Ibid.*, p. 192.

The Inspector General

While arguing the uselessness of Presidio de San Sabá, he said its abandonment would bring the Comanches to the very walls of Presidio de San Antonio de Béjar in their raids; hence the small military detachment at Béjar should be reinforced to protect this one real Spanish outpost in Texas.[7] This is a paradox which can hardly be reconciled with the general tone of his report.

Rábago proposed to Rubí that the Presidio be moved from San Sabá. In answer Rubí enjoined Rábago to maintain the Presidio at its present site until the Viceroy decided otherwise. As the Inspector rode out of the Presidio on August 4, ten days after his arrival, Rábago thought that he and the Inspector were in accord. On August 12 he wrote three letters to the viceroy, Marqués de Croix, who had succeeded Marqués de Cruillas.

The first letter recounted his sixteen years of service as captain of three presidios on the frontier, including seven years at San Sabá, asking promotion to the rank of colonel. In the second letter he told of the inspection:

> On the fourth of the current month the Field Marshal Marqués de Rubí finished his inspection of this presidio. In obedience to the superior order of Your Excellency, I informed him of all which seems to me most appropriate to the royal service, and that this presidio should be moved and other steps taken; for should the Lipan Apaches wish to congregate in missions, there are no convenient means of obliging them, and they are thieves and assassins. Since I have experience and knowledge of the land of their most continuous habitation, it would be easy to surround them with presidios and towns, from the province of Coahuila to New Mexico, in order that they can give each other mutual aid when it is needed....
> Finally, Most Excellent Sir, do not doubt that this esteemed general gives great attention to the royal service. His great thoroughness will inform Your Excellency of all which is appropriate, the particulars of which I need not recite.[8]

In this letter Rábago seems to be referring to his previous letter to Cruillas in which he had suggested moving the Presidio to the Pecos River. In the third letter of August 12—also the date of Rubí's secret report to the Viceroy on his San Sabá inspection—Rábago asked again that he be allowed to wage a campaign

---

[7] *Ibid.*, p. 193.
[8] Rábago to the viceroy, Marqués de Croix, August 12, 1767. A.G.M., Historia, Vol. 94, Part 1, p. 130.

against the enemy Indians such as the one Parrilla had made. There is no indication that the Viceroy extended him the courtesy of a reply.

It is not surprising that Rubí's inspection led to the recommendation that Presidio de San Sabá, as well as some others, should be abandoned, and that the entire frontier should be reorganized. The abuses he found at San Sabá were but a small sampling of the undesirable conditions at the presidios all along the frontier.

A notable example was Los Adaes, the capital of the province and the residence of the governor, Angel de Martos y Navarrete, who was on leave at the time of Rubí's visit. There were sixty-one men in the garrison. Only twenty-five horses were fit for service, and only two rifles were serviceable. A few soldiers had powder horns, and they were clad, not in uniforms, but in rags, many without hat, shirt, or shoes. Until the cession of Louisiana to Spain in 1762, this presidio had been Spain's most advanced outpost on the northeast, charged with the responsibility of defending New Spain against encroachments of the French.

Governor Martos had made a profit of one thousand per cent on much of the goods sold to the soldiers, violating all regulations. Soldiers were used to look after the commander's stock ranch and to cultivate his farm.[9]

The sordid picture Rubí viewed all along the frontier gave him a clear understanding of why the presidios had failed in their purpose, of why they had been unable to repel Indian attacks and unable to protect the missions. The destruction of the Mission Santa Cruz de San Sabá was a prime example of the ineffectiveness of the presidio.

The twenty-four presidios spread across the northern frontier of New Spain had been founded haphazardly, at the dictates of misguided idealists or those with personal axes to grind. The entire northern frontier, said Rubí, should be considered as a single unit, each post an important link in a more important chain. But, as it was now, each post stood alone. There was no plan whereby one could help, or be helped by, the others.

Rubí noted that morale was extremely low on the frontier of New Spain. The chief source of discontent, he pointed out, was the practice of paying the soldiers in supplies rather than in cash.

[9] Castañeda, *Our Catholic Heritage*, IV, 238-240.

The commanders, who were the purchasing agents and distributors of supplies, were directly responsible for robbing the soldiers to the extent, in some cases, that they could not clothe themselves or their families. This practice also stood in the way of settlement; had the soldiers been paid in money, settlers would have been induced by the prospect of trade.

Once a man signed for duty at a frontier presidio, he could not get an honorable discharge except at the pleasure of the commander. The only way he could leave his post was by desertion or death.

Some of the presidio commanders became so absorbed in profiteering at the expense of their garrisons that duty was ignored altogether. They did not inspect arms and equipment to check their serviceability. At San Sabá, for example, Rubí found it necessary to suggest that a reasonable number of horses be kept within the stockade to enable the garrison to pursue the Indians when they attacked. The soldiers had to wait until horses were brought from pasture before they could follow the attackers, and then it was too late.

Lafora also contributed his part, writing in his diary a harsh indictment of the frontier commanders. The repeated depredations of the Indians, he said, were attributable to the ignorance, inexperience, and laziness of the commanders; all along the frontier, the policy seemed to be to sit quietly in the presidios following an attack, rather than mounting a force for pursuit.

The cession of Louisiana to Spain had eased the pressure on the eastern sector of the frontier, and Rubí proposed the number of frontier outposts be reduced to fifteen, along a line from the Gulf of California to the mouth of the Guadalupe River in Texas. He called for spacing the presidios forty leagues, or one hundred miles, apart. This line, he believed, was the real frontier, and by this arrangement the presidios could give real, not imagined, protection.

The missions of East Texas were to be abandoned, the capital of Texas moved from Los Adaes to San Antonio. The line of the frontier was to be moved far to the south, with San Antonio and Santa Fé left as outposts north of the line. San Sabá, said Rubí, in his final report, should either be abolished altogether or its garrison reduced to fifty men and moved to a new location near the Río Grande.

The northern frontier in Texas had been static for a number of years, unable to advance. The Rubí report signaled a retreat. It spelled the end of the mission system, for it was deemed no longer necessary to hold East Texas; the French threat had vanished with the cession of Louisiana. But the real reason for the retreat, as Webb suggests, was that the Plains Indians, whose wrath had been aroused by establishment of the San Sabá Mission for the Apaches, made it necessary. Spain was incapable of facing up to the hostile Comanches and their allies.

Why should Rubí speak of the country north of the proposed line of forts as the "imaginary frontier"? What made it imaginary? As one reads of the massacre at San Saba, of the defeat of Colonel Parrilla, of the constant raids of the Apaches on every settlement, one realizes that it was these Plains Indians who made the frontier imaginary.[10]

Rubí recommended a war of extermination on the Apaches, who had continued to raid Spanish settlements farther south while living in the missions of El Cañon. Since trouble with the Comanches had started with the Spaniards' attempt to befriend the Apaches, he blamed Apache perfidy and reasoned that if the Apaches could be removed from the scene the trouble with the Comanches would end. But Rubí, fresh from Spain, did not know the Comanches. In conclusion he said,

Once San Sabá has been evacuated then San Antonio will remain the most advanced of our frontier posts in the province of Texas. If the settlements of the *Lipanes* which now populate the banks of the Rio Grande are left on the frontier, you will have, in addition to these domestic thieves, a sure lure for raids by the Comanches and their allies of the north.[11]

The hope of settling the area between the Río Grande and the San Sabá River, said Rubí, was unfounded; in this region he had not seen a single place which he considered worthy of being settled, for most of the country was grazing land, unsuited for cultivation.

Faced with the need to occupy Alta California and Louisiana, now the buffer zones against the English, Spain could use her

---

[10] W. P. Webb, *The Great Plains*, p. 131.

[11] Hons C. Richards, "The Establishment of the Candelaria and San Lorenzo Missions" (Master's thesis), p. 67.

resources better in these areas than along "the imaginary frontier" that abutted the Great Plains, he believed.

These factors all combined to influence Rubí in reaching the conclusions presented in his report. Life still moved slowly on the frontier, and it was to be several years yet before Rubí's recommendations were implemented. But the stage for the pivot had been set.

The Pivot

The New World seethed in the backwash of the French and Indian War. Spanish attempts to take over Louisiana, ceded Spain by France in disregard of the many French subjects who lived there, culminated in open rebellion.

There was trouble, too, in the English colonies. The British Parliament, to offset the cost of the war, imposed the Stamp Act in 1765. Violent protests arose, and the stamp tax was repealed, but British prestige suffered in the colonies. Soon a colonial pamphleteer named Thomas Paine was to author a document which began, "These are the times that try men's souls."

Indeed souls were being tried on the banks of the San Sabá River in Spanish Texas. Soon after the Marqués de Rubí had departed from Real Presidio de San Sabá, its troubles began anew. With the winter of 1767 came the Comanches and their allies. On December 10 the hostile Indians caught the Presidio unaware and drove off its entire herd of cattle. The dispirited soldiers manned the stockade but made no move to pursue. The Indians taunted them to come out. Retiring to a hill overlooking the fort, they slaughtered several beeves and feasted in full view of the Spaniards.

Two days later a band of Tehuacanas rode up to the walls of the Presidio and presented a flag of truce, declaring through a Tejas Indian who served as interpreter that they were friends. Rábago ordered the men to remain at their posts and to keep the gate closed. The interpreter stated that the visitors intended to

The Pivot

harm only their enemies, the Apaches, and he asked if there were any Apaches in the fort.

On the Captain's orders, presents were distributed to the Indians, who then pitched camp against the walls of the stockade and spread out their wares to trade. No one was allowed outside the fort. Finally the Indians gave up and retired to a camp they had established a short distance away. Next morning the Indians brought buffalo meat, which they handed to the soldiers over the wall. The gate remained closed. An invitation for the soldiers to come to the camp and feast with the Indians was declined.

For a full week the Presidio went unmolested. Then on December 20, two soldiers who had gone to the River ran back to the stockade to warn of the approach of Indians. Close behind them came a band of Comanches. The Indians rushed to the stockade wall but halted suddenly when they found the guard posted and alert. They raised a flag of truce.

With the Indians was a French interpreter, who conversed in French with Pedro Miñon, an artilleryman, declaring that the Comanches were friendly and would harm only the Apaches. The Comanches asked a peace meeting with the Spaniards. While the parley was going on, a supply train came into view, and the Comanches allowed it to enter the fort.

For three days the Indians remained just outside the walls of the Presidio. The peace pipe was smoked, dances were held, and presents exchanged. On Christmas Eve, the Comanches, whose number included also some Taovayas, left in friendly spirits.

On January 2, 1768, a band of hostile Indians swept down upon the Presidio, attempting to catch the garrison by surprise and to steal the horses. The attack was repelled, and the soldiers took a captive. The prisoner mentioned that French traders were encouraging the Tehuacanas, Tonkawas, Taovayas, and Comanches to harass the Spanish presidio. The French apparently had told the Indians that there was an abundance of supplies in the fort, and that many Apaches were living with the Spaniards. Thus the series of attacks and ruses was explained, but not ended.

Twelve days later a band of Indians rose out of the river bed and took eight horses at the stockade wall. There was no pursuit.[1]

The commander of Presidio de San Sabá made frantic appeals for help. These failing, he sought permission to abandon this spot, which he had begun to think was accursed. He himself was

[1] C. E. Castañeda, *Our Catholic Heritage*, IV, 194–195.

ill, and had been for several months. His men were dissatisfied and insolent.

On February 29 Lieutenant Joaquín Orendain and three soldiers disregarded a standing order and left the fort to hunt turkeys. Hostile Indians ambushed them, and all four were tortured and killed.

Almost three months earlier Rábago had asked permission of the Viceroy to go to México for treatment of his illness. Since he had been in prison following his arrest at San Xavier, he had been afflicted with malignant sores, he explained, and these now covered his feet and legs.

During the last month an epidemic had gripped the Presidio, threatening to disable the entire garrison. At first only the women and children seemed to be affected, but soon men were ill too. The malady began with a sore mouth. The gums became inflamed and secreted pus, and the lower limbs stiffened, completely disabling the patient. Many at the Presidio died of the ailment, which was called "Mal de Loanda"—probably scurvy.[2]

The repeated Indian attacks had frayed the nerves of all those in the garrison. When the men began to grumble and manifest an insubordinate attitude, Rábago became harsh and irascible. Early in 1768 two soldiers, Juan Francisco Xavier Rodríguez and Joseph de la Pena, left the Presidio, apparently without authority, and made their way to Mexico City bearing a list of charges against their commander, which they presented to the Viceroy.

The charges accused Rábago of neglecting his duties. They claimed that food supplied the men and their families was poor and the equipment issued inadequate. The Captain never took part in campaigns; the men had been deprived of their personal liberty, and Rábago freely made love to their wives.[3]

That the food was poor is hardly open to question, in view of the illness that swept the garrison, if indeed it was scurvy. The reason for this circumstance was apparent: the Indians had been intercepting supply trains in an effort to starve the garrison out. But the soldiers, in making the complaint, were not inclined to be charitable.

Rábago was a vain and prideful man. He had a habit of acting without authority. Now, with this pressure upon him, he once

[2] *Ibid.*, pp. 196–197.

[3] Complaint signed by Juan Francisco Xavier Rodríguez and Joseph de la Pena, A.G.M., Historia, Vol. 94, Part 2, pp. 25–28.

The Pivot

again was to take precipitous action without waiting to learn the Viceroy's wishes. Truly, a haughty spirit goes before destruction, and pride before a fall.

The situation at San Sabá showed no improvement during the spring of 1768. The internal conditions of the Presidio now seemed to pose the problem, rather than harassment by hostile Indians. Yet the Indians were as responsible for the ruin of the Presidio as if they had conquered it by force of arms. They had intercepted supply trains and destroyed the crops which were planted, causing the deficient diet which resulted in scurvy. Their harassment was at least in part responsible for the mutinous attitude of the soldiers which threatened Rábago's control.

Rábago knew from experience that a new appeal to the Viceroy would be of no avail. He took matters into his own hands. He ordered the garrison of Presidio de San Sabá to abandon the post and move, with the women and children, to Mission San Lorenzo in the Valle de San José.

The transported settlement arrived at San Lorenzo June 22. On July 15 Rábago received from the Viceroy a reprimand for his conduct which had led to the charges made by his soldiers. He was warned that a second such complaint would be sufficient cause for his dismissal.[4]

Three days later, on July 18, Rábago wrote to the Viceroy that he had received His Excellency's letter of reprimand, brought from México by the soldier Rodríguez, whom the captain classed as a deserter. The soldiers' vexation was without basis, he said, as the inspection by the Marqués de Rubí verified. Rodríguez and Pena had no motive but to avoid punishment. Pena, said Rábago, had not returned with Rodríguez. He had presented no evidence of his separation, and it was said he would remain in San Luis Potosí.[5]

Under date of July 20 Rábago reported to the Viceroy that he had moved his garrison to the Valle de San José. The reasons, he said, had already been stated. Because of the hostility of the Indians, bringing in supplies had become increasingly difficult, so that now the garrison was at the point of starvation. These were contributing causes. But the final blow had been the epidemic,

[4] Rábago to the viceroy, Marqués de Croix, July 18, 1768, A.G.M., Historia, Vol. 94, Part 2, pp. 31–32; Castañeda, *Our Catholic Heritage*, IV, 197.

[5] Rábago to the Viceroy, July 18, 1768, A.G.M., Historia, Vol. 94, Part 2, pp. 31–32.

which had greatly reduced the garrison and had made the move imperative. He asked His Excellency to approve the step, which had been dictated by dire necessity, adding that the move was, of course, provisional and subject to the Viceroy's superior wishes.[6]

The Viceroy was upset at the news. A military post, he informed Rábago, should never be abandoned by its commander except when he is driven away by force of arms. The big question in his mind was whether the fortification had been destroyed, for if it had not the Presidio might be occupied by the enemy to the disadvantage of the Spaniards. He ordered Rábago to return to San Sabá at once and reoccupy the Presidio before the enemy did, and to remain there until otherwise instructed.[7]

For some reason, however, Rábago did not carry out this order. As late as March 18, 1769, he wrote to the Viceroy from Valle de San José. About this time he received from the Viceroy an order, dated February 9, which he knew to be the beginning of the end for his garrison. He was to detach twenty-one men and send them to Hugo Oconor at Presidio de San Antonio de Béjar—the same number taken from San Antonio in 1757 to found Presidio de San Luis de las Amarillas. Though the order did not say the transfer was to be permanent, Rábago had no doubt that it was.[8]

Rábago imprudently decided to employ delaying tactics. On March 18 he wrote the Viceroy that he had deferred execution of the order because Oconor, the new interim governor, was not at San Antonio, having gone to Los Adaes. But Rábago's replacement already was on his way to El Cañon.[9]

In Villa de San Fernando (probably San Fernando de Austria in Coahuila) he learned of his removal. He wrote his acknowledgment to the Viceroy on April 19. Having gone there to obtain supplies for the year, he said, he had encountered Don Manuel Antonio de Oca, who showed him His Excellency's order placing Oca in command of the presidio which had been in Rábago's charge. Rábago had acted accordingly, the change of command having taken place on April 1. Rábago set out for Mexico City to

[6] Rábago to the Viceroy, July 20, 1768, A.G.M., Historia, Vol. 94, Part 2, p. 19; Castañeda, *Our Catholic Heritage*, IV, 197-198.

[7] Viceroy to Rábago, August 19, 1768, A.G.M., Historia, Vol. 94, Part 2, p. 33; Castañeda, *Our Catholic Heritage*, IV, 198.

[8] Viceroy to Rábago, February 9, 1769, and Rábago to the Viceroy, March 18, 1769, A.G.M., Historia, Vol. 94, Part 2, pp. 59 and 60.

[9] Rábago to the Viceroy, March 18, 1769, A.G.M., Historia, Vol. 94, Part 2, p. 60.

The Pivot

make his personal report to the Viceroy, and to seek reimbursement for the personal expenditures he had made in the maintenance of Presidio de San Sabá during the nine years the fort was in his charge.[10]

From all indications, he never reached his destination. On July 5, 1769, he wrote the Viceroy from San Luis Potosí, where he had become too ill to travel further, to tell him that he would be delayed for medical treatment. Pathetically, he renewed his plea for promotion to the rank of colonel. The Viceroy replied that his request would be considered on its merits when Rábago reached the capital. But it is doubtful that he ever was able to continue his journey. This letter was his last.[11]

Little record is found regarding Captain Manuel Antonio de Oca, Rábago's successor. From correspondence of Jacobo de Ugarte y Loyola, governor of Coahuila, with the viceroy, Marqués de Croix, it appears that the new captain took the garrison from El Cañon and returned to San Sabá. He evidently remained there until early in 1770, when he again retreated to the Nueces, perhaps without authority.

Ugarte wrote to the Viceroy on April 17, 1770, that Oca and his entire company already had retired "from the abandoned Presidio de San Sabá to the place named El Cañon." He described El Cañon as useless because it had no settlements and no room for expanding.

The Coahuila governor informed the Viceroy June 1, 1771, that five soldiers of the garrison at El Cañon had filed charges (of unspecified nature) against Oca, and that he was to be brought to trial. Under date of June 8, 1771, Ugarte wrote to the Viceroy that the twenty-nine men stationed at El Cañon had been sent to San Antonio, where they were not needed, and asked that they be transferred to San Fernando de Austria. On July 21 that year, he acknowledged receipt of an order from the Viceroy, dated June 21, which called for removal of the garrison that had been stationed at El Cañon.[12]

[10] Rábago to the Viceroy, April 19, 1769, A.G.M., Historia, Vol. 94, Part 2, p. 63.

[11] Rábago to the Viceroy, July 5, 1769, and Viceroy to Rábago, July 15, 1769, A.G.M., Historia, Vol. 94, Part 2, pp. 68 and 70.

[12] Jacobo de Ugarte y Loyola to the viceroy, Marqués de Croix, April 17, 1770, June 1 and 8, 1771, and July 21, 1771, A.G.M., Provincias Internas, 1768–1792, Vol. 24, Part 1, Hackett Transcripts, pp. 57–65.

The two missions of El Cañon, long since merged into one in order to withstand Indian attacks, were abandoned about the same time. Fathers Rivera and Santiesteban were sent to missions in Sonora.

The end of Presidio de San Sabá as a frontier outpost of New Spain apparently came with a clash of wills, just as had its beginning. San Fernando de Austria and the commander of Presidio de San Antonio de Béjar, pushed by the citizens of Villa de San Fernando (San Antonio), engaged in a tug-of-war over the soldiers from San Sabá. San Antonio finally got fifty of these soldiers. The remainder of the garrison was used to found a new presidio below the Río Grande, between the presidios of San Carlos and La Bahía, in 1772, blocking the western branch of the Comanche War Trail. It was a part of the new line of defenses suggested by Rubí. Its name was San Vicente, though some continued to refer to it as San Sabá.

Those who were sent to the new presidio found they had not left all their troubles behind. Alessio Robles tells of an ambush by Indians in 1778 of a force from San Vicente, under command of Ensign José Pérez. The crosses at the graves of the twenty-two soldiers who were killed gave the place its name, "Las Cruces." [13]

In 1810 the soldiers of San Vicente were joined with presidial soldiers from Monclova, La Bahía, Agua Verde, and San Juan Bautista to march to San Luis Potosí. Under the command of

---

[13] Vito Alessio Robles, *Coahuila y Texas en la época colonial*, p. 576. Alessio Robles (*Coahuila y Texas*, p. 575) gives the location as near the border of Coahuila and Chihuahua, "one kilometer from el Río Bravo, on a mesa dominating the ford by the same name." He points out that a Colonel Langberg, in notes of his itinerary in 1851, referred to Presidio de Agua Verde as "San Vicente"; this reference gave rise to some confusion as to the location of the latter. In 1899 Robert T. Hill, an officer of the U.S. Geological Survey, made a hazardous boat trip down the canyons of the Río Grande at the Big Bend and came upon the ruins of San Vicente on leaving Mariscal Canyon. In 1916 two troops of the Eighth U.S. Cavalry, commanded by Major George T. Langhorne, crossed the San Vicente Ford to pursue the border raiders of Pancho Villa in Mexico (See Paul Horgan, *Great River*, pp. 901, 922). In 1949 a Houston attorney, Orrin H. Bonney, ran the Río Grande canyons by boat and visited the ruins, which he found "high on a mesa between San Vicente Sierra to the west and the Del Carmens to the east, accessible only by river, by horseback or by Mexican trails." Part of the ruins were serving as the sides of a goat pen, he said (Orrin H. Bonney to author, January 15, 1963).

The Pivot

Colonel Félix María Calleja, they were to put down the insurrection of Father Miguel Hidalgo, the rebel priest who started the movement to overthrow Spanish rule in México.[14]

The abandoned stone Presidio de San Sabá now stood like a hollow ghost in the middle of a vast, empty land. Its roof sagged under the weight of time. Rock squirrels and field rats played along its parapets, dislodging a stone now and then.

Despite the recommendations of the Marqués de Rubí, the stone walls and buildings had not been leveled before the presidio garrison withdrew. That remained to be done almost a century later by another generation of pioneers, badly in need of building stone with which to raise a town on the opposite bank of the San Sabá.

In 1772 King Charles III of Spain issued his decree of New Regulations pertaining to the frontiers of New Spain, implementing most of the recommendations of the Marqués de Rubí.

The decree called for leaving East Texas. Two presidios and four missions were abandoned, their people and property brought to San Antonio, the new capital of Texas.

But, more important, the decree called for the abandonment of the post on the San Sabá River, the most advanced post on the frontier. San Sabá may have been doomed, with or without the Rubí report and the ensuing royal decree, for the odds against it were heavy: the Indian depredations which cut off its supply lines and cost the lives of perhaps a hundred Spaniards; the fact that the post was directly responsible to the viceroy and the great distance and resulting lack of communication and understanding; the very nature of Felipe de Rábago y Terán; the inconstance of the Apaches; and the extreme gullibility of the Spaniards in dealing with the Indians.

The decree of 1772 hastened the end of the mission system in Texas. The Spaniards had reached the pivot point on the northern Texas Frontier.

[14] Alessio Robles, *Coahuila y Texas*, p. 578.

PART V
The Spanish Legacy

Forsaken Land

Establishment of the San Sabá Mission and Presidio had precipitated the worst kind of Indian trouble for the Spaniards. Now, as they retreated from "the imaginary frontier," they left a legacy of Indian trouble for almost all who were to come to the Edwards Plateau region for the next one hundred years. The land between the San Sabá River and the Río Grande became a battleground. From time to time the Spaniards probed the region with military expeditions, seeking to end the Indian trouble by force of arms.

These military expeditions are a continuation of the San Sabá Mission story, for the enemy the Spaniards sought to subdue was the very tribe of Indians they had sought to Christianize with the mission on the San Sabá River. In advocating total war against the Apaches, the Rubí report had touched a welcome chord. The Spaniards had exhausted their patience with these Indians, who had brought them into violent conflict with the Comanches and had continued to raid other Spanish settlements while living at the missions of El Cañon. The Apaches' behavior, to the Spaniards, was two-faced and treacherous, though the Apaches saw their actions only as what was necessary to protect their homeland, to guard their interests as best they could in a world that was fast closing in on them.

The westward movement of the English colonists had begun even before their war for independence. The Spaniards now feared the Comanches and the northern tribes would form an alliance with the English, as they previously had feared a French-Indian alliance. Having seen the error in allying themselves with the Lipan Apaches, they erroneously believed that termination of this alliance would bring lasting peace with the allied tribes of the north. The natural course, therefore, was to seek alliance with the northern tribes.

The first step in this direction fell to Athanase de Mézières, lieutenant governor of the Natchitoches district, whose jurisdiction was the Red River Valley. Attempting to conciliate the northern tribes, he made numerous trips into the Indians' country. In 1778 he visited the village of the Taovayas on the Red River, where he retrieved the two cannon abandoned by Colonel Parrilla some twenty years earlier. He took these weapons to the settlement of Bucareli on the Trinity. During this expedition he found that the Taovayas were carrying on an extensive and lucrative trade with the English. What they had to barter was stolen Spanish horses.

Plans for war on the Apaches took a setback with the accidental death of Mézières in November, 1779. Spanish officials in Coahuila and Texas, meanwhile, decided to employ the Apaches' own tactics against them, turning the Mescaleros, the Lipans, and the Apaches proper against each other. This worked well for a time, but the various Apache tribes soon made peace with each other. Their raids on Spanish settlements increased.[1]

Governor Juan de Ugalde of Coahuila, taking the field against the Apaches in 1781 and 1782, won some notable victories, but he failed to stop the Indian raids. After Bernardo de Gálvez was named viceroy of New Spain in 1785, the provinces of Texas, Coahuila, Nuevo León, and Nuevo Santander were placed under command of Ugalde. He vigorously pursued the Mescaleros and Lipans, inflicting severe losses and bringing about a reduction in their raids.

In 1789 Colonel Ugalde set out from Monclova in pursuit of the Mescaleros and the Lipans who had joined the Mescaleros in raiding settlements. Ugalde followed their trail northward, and in December he encountered the enemy on the Pedernales River in the Texas Hill Country. After a brief skirmish the Indians fled, leaving one warrior and one squaw dead and two small girls captive.

Ugalde's force pressed on to the former Presidio de San Sabá. The old fort still stood, but it now had been abandoned almost twenty years. There Ugalde made his headquarters, as he gathered in Indian allies of the northern tribes for the war against the Apaches.

The Lipans and the Mescaleros themselves had gathered quite

---

[1] C. E. Castañeda, *Our Catholic Heritage*, V, 1–7.

Forsaken Land

a force, and on December 19 Ugalde dispatched a messenger detail to San Antonio with a request for eighty-five men and a supply of ammunition. The messengers reached Presidio de San Antonio de Béjar December 21. The force requested was to set out within forty-eight hours to join Ugalde's men and two hundred Comanche allies at San Sabá to deliver a decisive blow to the large band of Lipans and Mescaleros.

For two days the blacksmith shops of Villa de San Fernando and Presidio de Béjar blazed, shoeing horses, forging swords, casting bullets. On Christmas Eve fifty-two volunteers and eleven soldiers started for San Sabá. They took the ammunition and various other supplies, including a bolt of white domestic for arm bands for the Indian allies.

A band of Lipans on its way to join the main force of Mescaleros, who were to challenge Ugalde's men, stopped at Los Almagres, near the Llano River, where a group of San Antonio citizens had gone to work the mines. The miners, believing the Indians still peaceful, welcomed them into camp. That night the five miners were murdered in their sleep.[2]

With the reinforcements from San Antonio, Ugalde marched to Arroyo de la Soledad (the Sabinal River near present Utopia), where the Lipans and the Mescaleros had pitched camp. Besides the troops from Coahuila, he had a large number of Comanches, Tehuacanas, and Wichitas (Taovayas). On January 9, 1790, Ugalde's force surprised the enemy at Soledad. The Apaches offered stout resistance for several hours, but finding themselves outnumbered they at last broke through the line of Ugalde's Indian allies. The Spaniards killed more than forty Apaches and captured a large number of women and children, as well as a sizeable herd of horses and mules.

Bolton says, "In commemoration of Ugalde's exploits, the cañon of the Nueces River became known as Cañon de Ugalde, corrupted later to Uvalde."[3]

Governor Rafael Martínez Pacheco, of Texas, reported to the Viceroy in the spring of 1790 that steady progress had been made in consolidating peace with the Indians of the north. This peaceful relationship seems to have lasted several years, despite occa-

[2] *Ibid.*, pp. 16–18.
[3] H. E. Bolton, *Texas in the Middle Eighteenth Century*, p. 127.

sional lapses. In 1793 Manuel Muñoz, the new governor of Texas, reported that marauding bands of Lipans were still active in the vicinity of La Bahía (Goliad) and that a band of Tonkawas had been thieving at San José Mission.

Early in 1795 a band of six Comanches drove off a herd of cattle from near San Juan Bautista. The Comanches were pursued to the San Sabá canyon, where the stolen cattle were recovered for return to their mission.[4]

In February, 1797, Comanches stole some three hundred cattle from Mission San Bernardo, near San Juan Bautista. A detachment of soldiers and mission Indians went in pursuit and overtook the raiders near the old San Sabá Mission, recovering most of the cattle. The San Sabá River canyon had become a favorite rendezvous for marauding bands of Comanches, who had moved in to claim the land the Spaniards had abandoned.

In May, 1798, Governor Manuel Antonio Cordéro of Coahuila sent Captain José Menchaca of Presidio de Agua Verde to San Sabá with 121 men to meet the Comanche chiefs and to demand return of stolen property. Other officials warned Governor Cordéro of the hazards of making demands against the Indians that could not be enforced, and Menchaca retired from Presidio de San Sabá without pressing the issue with the Comanche chiefs.[5]

The mission system came to an end in Texas following the decree of April 10, 1794, when secularization of the missions began. As instruments of colonization the missions, for the most part, had failed in Texas. The ten-year period normally allowed in México for the missions to become self-sustaining communities had been stretched to fifty years in Texas, and with doubtful success in most places. The missions had been a constant drain on the royal treasury. The last mission to be founded in Texas was Nuestra Señora del Refugio in 1792, near the mouth of the Guadalupe River. It is interesting to note that establishment of this mission was prompted in part by fear of intrusion in the coastal region by English or Americans, much as fear of the French had prompted the founding of earlier missions.

The reasons for failure of the mission system in Texas are manifold. Perhaps the primary reason is the nature of the Texas

[4] Castañeda, *Our Catholic Heritage*, V, 7–20.
[5] *Ibid.*, pp. 116–120.

Indians themselves, for they were a different breed from those of México. While missions succeeded with sedentary tribes, who were higher up on the cultural ladder, they were doomed to fail with the roving Plains tribes. Because of the nature of these Indians—the low level of their civilization and their nomadic way of life—it is doubtful that the mission system, even under the most astute management, ever could have become the right tool for taming this savage land. Yet it never had a chance to prove itself under such a circumstance, for the Spaniards consistently mismanaged the effort and muffed their opportunities at every turn. Much of this bungling can be laid to circumstances beyond the control of the Spaniards, for they had no guidebook to tell them that befriending the Indians of the Hasinai (Tejas) Confederacy would arouse the ire of the Apaches, or that missions for the Apaches would bring on the hostility of the Comanches. The Spaniards, learning through hard and costly experience, were not able to comprehend the meaning of this experience in time to profit from it.

Had the Spaniards confined their mission efforts to the more docile and agriculturally inclined tribes of East Texas, protecting themselves on the north and the west with stronger presidios, their chances of success might have been greater. Had they followed the Red River as they did the Río Grande, populating its banks with mission settlements, they would have been more successful at holding back the French influence over the savages. At the same time they might have found more favorable conditions for missions—for converting Indians and turning them into useful Spanish subjects.

The big mistake in the Texas mission effort may have been attempting to missionize the fierce and nomadic Lipan Apaches, who were far from being suitable material for civilized life. An Apache mission on the San Sabá River was attempted, in part, however, because of Spanish failure elsewhere. Priests and soldiers failed to get along. The soldiers molested mission converts and raped their women, an example being Felipe de Rábago at Presidio de San Xavier. Paralleling authority of priests and soldiers caused confusion of methods and purpose.

Too, missions frequently were founded under tremendous handicaps, as decisions were based on the wrong considerations. It was hard to convince the viceregal government of New Spain that a mission should be established unless there was an immediate threat of intrusion by the French. Where such threats—real, imagined, or contrived—existed was not always where a mission stood the best chance of success. This certainly was the case with the San Sabá Mission. Seldom, if ever, was a mission founded on the premise that a missionary effort might succeed in the given locality because of the type of Indians there.

Missionary zeal played a part, also. The more savage the Indians, it seems, the more the missionaries were challenged to seek to win them to Christ. Often the priests disregarded their own safety, and some sought "the crown of martyrdom," in which their lives reached fulfillment. While the missionaries heedlessly exposed themselves to dangers, the job of the presidial soldiers was to protect the religious and to keep them from being martyred. This disagreement over purpose created more conflict and confusion, as exemplified by the attack on the San Sabá Mission, where the practical-minded Parrilla was frustrated and infuriated over the friars' stubborn refusal to seek safety at the Presidio in the face of Indian threat.

For the mission system to have succeeded as an instrument of colonization, the Spaniards should have considered all these factors in advance, but, for want of empirical knowledge, they did not possess the necessary foresight. Yet the missions served a purpose. Their failure was not total. They absorbed the first shock in civilization and colonization of the raw, savage land which today is the Southwestern United States. They blazed some trails and smoothed the jagged edges of the wilderness. They planted the first seeds of culture, and thereby were responsible in part for arousing the interest of Moses Austin in bringing colonists to Texas. The mission system produced the results which caused Adams to write: "The culture of the Spaniards—notably in architecture and historical romance—has been far out of proportion to their numbers, and in these and other ways the Spanish influence still persists throughout the South and in the Far West." [6]

The missions, in Castañeda's words, were "the greatest civilizing influence in the conquest of the New World." [7]

[6] James Truslow Adams, *The Epic of America*, p. 121.

[7] Castañeda, "The Sons of Saint Francis in Texas," reprinted from *The Americas*, Vol. 1, No. 3 (October, 1945), p. 291.

A policy of appeasement toward the Texas Indians followed abandonment of the mission system. Goods which the Indians coveted were given them in the hope that such gifts would keep them from stealing and raiding settlements.

The gifts included guns and ammunition, which the Spaniards had refused to give the Lipan Apaches earlier. But it now appeared that the Indians would obtain firearms from foreign traders if the Spaniards did not provide them. The gifts went to Comanches, Tonkawas, Tehuacanas, Wichitas, and Lipan Apaches. The cost was tremendous. Even so, peace with the Comanches, whose ire had been aroused by establishment of the presidio and mission on the San Sabá River, was not lasting.

Richardson says the Comanche learned to expect gifts for keeping the peace. He learned also to look on the various settlements of white people as being different tribes, unrelated to each other. The inference is that while accepting gifts from one Spanish settlement they continued to raid others. War was the normal relationship between the two races. The Spaniards were not even able to protect those settlements within reach of the Comanches, much less to subdue the Indians themselves, as proved by the San Sabá River episode. The Comanches rather than the Spaniards had become the aggressors.[8]

In 1803 Spain, persuaded that Louisiana in the hands of France would be a lasting buffer against the aggressive Americans, receded that territory to the French, only to learn later that France had contracted its sale to the United States months before the transfer took place. The new American nation cast a long shadow over Spanish territory. Ill-defined boundaries, the continued intrusions of the filibusters into Texas, and numerous plots and schemes by American citizens or officials contributed to the hostile attitude of the Spaniards.

In 1800 the Spanish empire had an impractically extended frontier line from the army posts in the Floridas, through New Orleans, San Antonio, and other settlements in Texas, Santa Fé in New Mexico, and straggling settlements up the coast of California.

"The expansive powers of Spain [says Adams] had long since failed, and in any case it would have been impossible to settle

[8] R. N. Richardson, *The Comanche Barrier to South Plains Settlement*, p. 75.

thickly a frontier line of such endless length, edging an entire continent." [9]

Spain had been unable to cope with the Comanches. She could hardly be expected to hold back the tide of Americans.

[9] Adams, *Epic of America*, pp. 120–121.

Return to San Sabá

For many years the San Sabá Mission had been but a heap of ashes. Presidio de San Sabá was an empty shell, abandoned to the field mice and the lizards. The Spaniards who had advanced to this remote point on the frontier had turned in retreat after a dozen blood-spattered years. Yet the San Sabá story was not finished. While an aggressive element of North Americans looked hungrily on Texas and seeds of revolution germinated in México, this desolate region was penetrated by several expeditions. The old Presidio frequently served as a way station. Many times its reactivation was urged.

Some of these expeditions, which bridge the gap between Spanish and Anglo-American colonization, are of but passing interest. Others are key links between the past and the future. Generally they were prompted by three factors: Indian troubles, thirst for mineral wealth, fear of American aggression.

The first factor exemplifies the reasons that the missionary endeavor on the San Sabá River culminated in the Spanish pivot in Texas. The second shows the effect which one attempt at settlement, though unsuccessful, had in bringing permanent settlers later. The third represents the transition, the efforts of the Spaniards to hold back the ever-increasing tide of venturesome Americans who trespassed upon their territory.

It was the first factor which had brought Colonel Juan de Ugalde in 1790 and Captain José Menchaca in 1798 to the abandoned Presidio de San Sabá. Others were to come because of the second. In the meantime the third factor came into play.

Spanish officials still sought a direct route to the settlements in

New Mexico, as well as a way to keep foreign traders out of the unsettled area that lay between San Antonio and Santa Fé. In 1786 Texas Governor Domingo Cabello commissioned a French trader, Pierre Vial, to find the most direct route between these two far-flung settlements. Taking a meandering route, Vial stopped at the Taovayas village on the Red River and then visited the village of the Comanches near present Byers, Clay County, in January, 1787. He discussed with Chief Zoquiné the possibility of re-establishing the Mission and Presidio of San Sabá for the Comanches, either at the original site or on the Pedernales River. Vial promised to consult the officials in San Antonio in regard to the plan when he returned, but nothing more is heard of it.

Vial's route to Santa Fé was far from being the most direct. In 1787 José Mares traveled from Santa Fé to San Antonio, then back to Santa Fé the following year. His return trip was much shorter, but still the shortest route had not been marked.[1] The feat remained to be done by Francisco Amangual in 1808.

The stage was set for Amangual's trek by Lieutenant Zebulon Montgomery Pike of the United States Army. Under orders of the Army's chief, General James Wilkinson, Pike and his seventy-four–man crew ascended the Arkansas River, then crossed to the valley of the Río Grande. When captured by a Spanish force, Pike claimed to be unaware that he was in Spanish territory. He and his men were conducted to Chihuahua for interrogation before they were allowed to return to Louisiana.

Before his capture Pike had been the object of a search by six hundred Spanish soldiers, who covered some twelve hundred miles, a good indication of the concern he caused. It is natural, therefore, that following his expedition the Spaniards intensified their efforts to define their boundaries and to protect their frontiers. The Amangual expedition was their answer. Part of its purpose was to ascertain whether the area between San Antonio and Santa Fé was inhabited by foreigners.

Amangual's force left San Antonio March 30, 1808. From San Antonio to the old Presidio de San Sabá it laid out a route more direct than modern highways follow. Amangual estimated the distance at eighty-three leagues. He camped on the San Sabá River four and one-half leagues below the Presidio the evening of

[1] See C. E. Castañeda, *Our Catholic Heritage*, V, 150–170.

April 10, having seen many buffalo during the day's travel. Amangual wrote in his diary under date of April 11:

> This morning we set out with a patrol of ten men to reconnoiter the presidio. Upon my arrival there I found a small plaza enclosed by a wall on all sides; the wall is constructed of rock and is greatly demolished. There are signs that show there used to be bastions on each corner of the square. To the north there are ruins of a two-story house. It is evident that there was a covered road over which they went to the river to get water. The location of the presidio is to the north of and very near the banks of the river.... It is of considerable depth and affords a good view.... There are three hills of the same shape which look like a mesa. There is a sort of stairway to reach the top. There is a beautiful irrigation ditch running from east to west [sic], which it is clear was used to water a very extensive plain. From the hills to the river to the south, the land is very fertile and adaptable to all kinds of seeds.[2]

Two Comanches of Chief Cordero's *ranchería* had come to the camp, and on the following day two soldiers and an Indian were sent to report the presence of the expedition to the Chief. Later the entire force went to the *ranchería*, which is described as looking "like a city, on a beautiful plain."

A multitude of Indians on horseback, accompanied by Cordero himself, came to meet the Spaniards, who were formed into columns to receive them. Amangual noted that the Indians were smeared with *almagre*, or red ocher. After ceremonies to show friendly relations, the expedition continued on its way, accompanied by the Comanches.

At this point several pages are missing from the original manuscript, but four days later the company still traveled with Cordero's Comanches. Amangual wrote: "His [Cordero's] plan was to accompany us until we could find a large herd of buffalo in order to get meat for his *ranchería* and also for our troops."

On April 16 four men went hunting with the Indians and returned at sundown with a large amount of buffalo meat and five calves on the hoof. The following day (Easter Sunday) the company remained in camp to cure the meat and rest the horses. Mass was celebrated, the penal laws read to the troops, and a review of arms and ammunition made. Five men went on a hunt with the

[2] J. Villasana Haggard (trans.), "Francisco Amangual's Diary of the Expedition to Santa Fé," pp. 8–9.

Indians and returned at sundown, again with a supply of meat and three calves on the hoof.

On April 18 Amangual's force traveled through heavily wooded terrain. "The purpose of traveling to the west," he wrote, "was to find water." They came to a spring which the Indians said had no name, and the Spaniards named it "La Pascua," or "Easter Spring."

Further details of Amangual's expedition do not concern us. He crossed the Colorado River April 20 and reached Santa Fé June 19. His route varied somewhat on the return trip, during which he camped at the abandoned presidio on the San Sabá River, December 12, 1808. Before reaching the headwaters of the San Sabá River, he had again encountered Cordero's Comanches, on the upper Concho, and obtained permission to pass through the territory. The expedition returned to San Antonio December 23.[3]

The next two expeditions to the San Sabá Presidio were to give rise to a legend which has caused men to abandon their families, to squander fortunes, and to waste lives in a quest for easy wealth—and which appears to have been responsible for bringing German colonists to Texas. It is the legend of the Lost San Saba Mine, which still is being sought today. One may safely bet that it will never be found, for one may be fairly certain it never existed in the first place.

In 1756 Don Bernardo de Miranda discovered Los Almagres Mine, on Honey Creek in present Llano County, but never returned to work it. Both Colonel Parrilla and Captain Rábago y Terán, during the time they commanded the San Sabá Presidio, urged removal of that presidio to the Llano country to work Miranda's mine. Parrilla even went so far as to have ore samples brought from Los Almagres to his presidio on the San Sabá River, where he had a crude smelter made in order to analyze the ore. Latter-day pioneers, finding signs of this smelter, concluded a mine was located nearby.

Parrilla also sent ore samples from Los Almagres to México, hoping to convince officials of the wisdom of moving his presidio to that location. If mines existed in the San Sabá region, why were he and Rábago so eager to move to Los Almagres on the Llano?

[3] *Ibid.*

In 1810, forty years after the Presidio was abandoned, Lieutenant Juan Padilla led an expedition to Los Almagres and San Sabá, leaving in testimony thereof his name carved in the stone gatepost. One José María García reported on the expedition to Governor Manuel de Salcedo, describing the rich ore found in the mine and urging that the old Presidio be repaired and garrisoned. He failed to differentiate between the two locations of San Sabá and Los Almagres.

In 1812 Ignacio Obregón, inspector of mines, visited San Sabá and Los Almagres Mine. He collected ore samples, which assayed well, and, like García, maintained that the old Presidio de San Sabá should be reactivated. And, again like García, he failed to make it clear that the fort and the mine were some eighty-five miles apart.[4]

That nothing came of the two reports is hardly surprising. The revolution had started in México in 1810, and the Magee-Gutiérrez expedition had entered Texas in 1812. This force, known as "the Republican Army of the North," captured San Antonio early in 1813, and Governor Salcedo was put to death by the revolutionaries.

Hence no action was taken on the reports of García or Obregón.

Juan Antonio Padilla, probably the same military officer who had visited the old Presidio de San Sabá in 1810, made an official report on the province of Texas dated December 27, 1819. Padilla described the inhabitants as "barbarians and wild beasts," except for the people of San Antonio de Béjar and the Presidio of Bahía del Espíritu Santo (Goliad). Discussing the various Indian tribes, he said the hostile tribes included the Comanches, Lipans, Tonkawas, Taovayas, and Tehuacanas. The Comanches were most numerous. Perfidious and disloyal, he said, they loved their liberty and would not bear servitude: "It is certain that they are not reducible to the Catholic religion."

The increase of raids by the Comanches during the last year, said Padilla, was

... due entirely to the encouragement given them by the foreigners and certain perverse Spaniards because of their covetousness. Up to the

[4] N. H. Pierce and Nugent E. Brown (eds.), *The Free State of Menard*, pp. 34–35. The author has been unable to locate copies of the reports of García and Obregón.

year 1811 the Comanches were not so well armed, nor so warlike, nor had they penetrated into places where they are now seen. The revolution which broke out in the center of the kingdom at that time came to the ears of those Indians. . . . They took advantage of the occasion when they saw the troops with other duties and hastened to make war against the unarmed herdsmen and the peaceable settlers, robbing, killing and seizing prisoners.[5]

The Comanches now were at peace with the Lipans, who had always been their enemies, Padilla noted.

[The Lipans] unite all the vices of the Comanches with those peculiar to themselves. . . . It has not been possible to induce them to live in fixed habitation. . . . In times of peace they live on the frontiers of Coahuila, Nuevo León and Tamaulipas, pitching their camps as far as the Province of Texas.[6]

Padilla said the nation amounted to something like seven hundred of all ages and sexes.

A report prepared by the *ayuntamiento* of San Antonio about one year later, for the use of the Texas delegate to the Spanish *cortes*, called for "a respectable and well-organized campaign" against the Comanches and the Lipans "until they are exterminated or forced to an inviolable and lasting peace." On the successful conclusion of this campaign, the report said, a line of presidios should be established to guard the frontier, extending from the old Presidio de San Sabá to that of Nacogdoches. Presidios should be established at San Sabá, at San Xavier, on the Brazos, on the Tortuga, on the Trinity, and the last at Nacogdoches, on the frontier of the United States.

"It would be well for the Province of Coahuila to settle or protect—by means of one or two presidios—the unsettled or unprotected country from San Sabá to the villa of San Fernando de Agua Verde."[7]

The *ayuntamiento* made numerous other recommendations for protection and administration of the affairs of the province. But whatever action that could have resulted at this point would have been too late. The Spanish regime in Texas neared the end.

In 1821 the Spanish royalists yielded in México, and the Mexi-

[5] Eugene C. Barker (ed.), *History of Texas*, pp. 50–51.
[6] *Ibid.*, p. 51.
[7] *Ibid.*, p. 55.

can nation was born. México was in trouble over Texas almost before it was out of trouble with Spain. The Spanish government had made an agreement with Moses Austin to bring Catholic colonists into Texas from Louisiana. Stephen F. Austin and other *empresarios* brought colonists in droves in the early years of the Mexican Republic. The two cultures did not blend. The Mexican Constitution of 1824 did not allow the Americans the freedom to which they had become accustomed. México could not long hold them as subjects.

In this era another visitor came to the abandoned presidio on the San Sabá River. This inscription appeared on the stone gatepost beside the name of Padilla: "Cós 1829." This is presumed to be Martín Perfecto de Cós, brother-in-law of the Mexican dictator Santa Anna, who was to play a prominent part in goading the Texans to open rebellion. What Cós was doing at the San Sabá Presidio is not known.

After Cós came Bowie. On November 2, 1831, James Bowie, his brother, Rezin P. Bowie, and nine other men set out from San Antonio for the old Presidio de San Sabá. Some say they were seeking the Spaniards' silver mines. Others say Bowie and his men were preying upon Mexican pack trains transporting silver bullion. Still others say they were out to catch wild horses.

On November 21 the Bowie party was attacked by Tehuacana, Waco, and Caddo Indians, and a bloody battle ensued. Having been warned by Comanches that the Indians were out for their scalps, they had tried to reach the Presidio, where they could better defend themselves, but fell short by six miles, according to Rezin P. Bowie's account. They pitched camp in a grove of live oaks the evening of November 20. The Indians attacked as the Bowie party prepared to break camp next morning. Bowie's men finally drove the Indians off. One of Bowie's men, Thomas McCaslin, was killed.[8]

Legend—but nothing more than that—has it that Bowie was near his mine when the Indians attacked. There are in the Menard area two markers, some thirty miles apart, each claiming to mark the location of the battle. One of these, a historical marker erected

[8] For James Bowie's account of the expedition see Pierce and Brown, *The Free State of Menard*, pp. 39–43. For Rezin Bowie's account see J. W. Wilbarger, *Indian Depredations in Texas*, pp. 91–98, or H. Yoakum, *History of Texas*, I, 281–289.

by the State of Texas in 1936, is on the Sallee Ranch near Calf Creek in the western edge of McCulloch County. The other stands on the bank of "Silver Creek," a tributary of Dry Creek, on the ranch of B. K. Neel twelve miles northwest of Menard. It was erected by a curious pair of treasure seekers, "Princess" Wenonah and J. R. Norton, who claimed to have found the grave of Thomas McCaslin.

Norton, a retired San Antonio lawyer, and Martha Wenonah, granddaughter of a Comanche chief, spent many years and eighty thousand dollars looking for the lost mine before her death of cancer in September, 1943, and his a short time later in a stove explosion at his camp on Silver Creek. In or near the grave they believed to be McCaslin's, they found a Bowie knife and an old bridle bit, of the type used in that period to break wild horses, and an old gun barrel, reportedly of corresponding vintage. A large cross made of oil-field pipe was erected, bearing a metal plaque with this inscription:

"Here lies Thomas McCaslin who was with the James Bowie expedition and was killed November 21, 1831, in Indian fight in this thicket. Erected by M. Wenonah and J. R. Norton."

"Princess" Wenonah and Judge Norton began their search in the 1930's. Princess Wenonah, daughter of a Comanche squaw and a German immigrant, was past seventy years old at the time. She claimed to have obtained her information on "the real location" of the Bowie or Lost San Saba Mine from stories handed down by her Indian forebears, while Norton claimed to have obtained his from early-day Spanish records, both in México and Spain.[9]

Actually it appears they were following up the Dixon Expedition from San Marcos, which late in the last century traced maps obtained in México to Silver Creek. All the markers on the map were in place. They led to a pit in the bed of the creek, which opened into a water-filled cave. It appears evident their map was a hoax, perpetrated by someone clever enough to make sure it would not soon be *proved* a hoax.[10]

The colorful team of the Princess and the Judge created a veritable village on the banks of Silver Creek, in the vicinity of

[9] See Pierce and Brown, *The Free State of Menard*, pp. 43–45.
[10] See J. Frank Dobie, *Coronado's Children*, pp. 51–60.

the basin in the bed of the creek, and it is not difficult to believe they spent the eighty thousand dollars they claimed to have spent.

Having spent all her money, Princess Wenonah said she would pawn her old Indian costumes and relics—once employed by her in a career on the stage—in order to continue the search. Her fondest ambition, besides that of finding the mine, was to endow an institution for cancer research. But she died of cancer before she could do either. Judge Norton continued the search alone. A few months later his charred body was found in his cabin, where he had poured kerosene on smouldering embers and died in the resulting explosion.

The earth's surface in the vicinity of Norton's camp on Silver Creek is a veritable sieve. Holes old and new penetrate the surface strata down to an underground lake in Edwards limestone. Efforts have been made to pump out the water in order to gain entrance to the cave which many believe to be the mine opening. But these efforts have been as futile as Coronado's search for the Seven Cities of Cíbola.

Yet the legend refuses to die. The reasons seem to be the existence of the old smelter, which has been explained; silver bullets found embedded in logs along the San Sabá River near the Presidio; the mistaken belief that the Spanish settlement on the River was prompted only by the Spaniards' hunger for material riches; an inscription, "Bowie Mine, 1832," on the Presidio gatepost; and many wild stories and legends which have little, if any, foundation in fact.

Perhaps the key to the Lost San Saba Mine or Lost Bowie Mine is found in an incident in which James Bowie was involved some four years after his battle with the Indians in the vicinity of Menard. At San Antonio he mistook some bundles of hay carried by Mexican mules for bags of silver and led the so-called "Grass Fight." Then on March 6, 1836, he met his death in the Alamo— the chapel of Mission San Antonio de Valero—with approximately 180 other Texans.

The Bowie Mine, most likely, is like the "bags of silver" on the pack mules, which never existed in the first place. But the myth has played a larger part than is generally realized in the settlement of the region around Presidio de San Sabá.

The Texans, after winning their independence from México, also had Indian troubles. In 1840, following the Council House fight in San Antonio, Colonel John H. Moore raised a volunteer force in Fayette County to pursue the Comanches and to avenge a new round of raids. Moore traveled up the San Sabá River and likely reached the old Spanish presidio, for his name and the year were carved on the gatepost. He then headed north and finally engaged the Comanches on the Colorado River, where the city of Ballinger now stands, giving this tribe the most severe defeat it had suffered at the hands of the white man up to that time.

Texas land was free for the taking in this period, but the taking was not always easy. In 1842 a group of German noblemen formed themselves into a company to aid the German immigration to the "easy land" in Texas. Commissioner general of the Adelsverein (German Emigration Company) was Prince Carl von Solms-Braunfels, whose ears pricked up at rumors of rich mineral deposits discovered by the Spaniards on the San Sabá River. He found a Mexican who promised to guide him to the "rich mines," and called on the company to fill a need for fifty miners in its colony.

But fast deals—or the prince's wild enthusiasm for Spanish silver—got the company into financial trouble. A grant-concession purchased from a Frenchman, Bourgeois d'Orvanne, was already in forfeit. Solms sent good money after bad, and the company purchased, sight unseen, the Fisher-Miller Grant, between the Llano and the Colorado Rivers. This grant was more than 300 miles from the coast, more than 150 miles from the nearest settlement, and was occupied by the hostile Comanches. Time allotted for settlement of the area was running out.

Solms had selected the townsites of Carlshafen—later known as Indianola—and New Braunfels, which was located near the former site of the transplanted Mission San Francisco Xavier. After relinquishing the commissioner generalship, he engineered the appointment of his successor, Baron Ottfried Hans von Meusebach, "an accomplished student of the natural sciences." The prince hoped the mineral resources of the colony would be investigated and developed under Meusebach's directorship.[11]

Prince Solms then asked the aid of the Berlin Academy of

[11] Samuel Wood Geiser, *Naturalists of the Frontier*, p. 181.

Sciences in securing a geologist to make a survey of the Texas grant, in hope of finding the mineral deposits he mistakenly believed to have been worked by the Spaniards of San Sabá. Dr. Ferdinand von Roemer, chosen for the job, came to Texas late in 1845. Dr. Roemer was in Galveston January 4, 1846, when the steamship *Alabama* arrived from New Orleans with news that the Congress of the United States had finally approved the annexation of Texas by accepting the State Constitution.

Meusebach, who dropped his German title of nobility in favor of plain John O. Meusebach, assumed the directorship of the Adelsverein in Texas and soon learned what a sorry mess he had inherited. The company was financially insolvent; German colonists were pouring into Texas, and the company had no lands on which to settle them.

Meusebach laid out the town of Fredericksburg to take care of the stream of immigrants from Germany. The war with México, which followed annexation of Texas, made it all but impossible to obtain wagons for transporting the new arrivals from Indianola to the settlements. Hundreds died in an epidemic of dysentery and fever.

Then, late in 1846, an imposter called Dr. Schubert, or Shubbert, whom Meusebach had engaged as town physician for Fredericksburg, made an unauthorized expedition to explore the grant. Schubert dared not cross the Llano River, and returned to Fredericksburg to report that entrance into the colony was impossible because it was full of hostile Indians.[12]

Meusebach wrote later,

That report could not be allowed to go abroad unrebuked. It would have created despondency amongst the emigrants and the Company. Therefore, shortly after Schubert's return, I started with twenty men and three wagons from Fredericksburg in January, 1847, crossed the Llano River at the mouth of Beaver Creek, was met by the Comanche Chief Ketemoczy, at the place where now stands the town of Mason, and held the first council with him.[13]

---

[12] For the story of Dr. Shubbert (or Schubert) see Armin O. Huber, "Frederic Armand Strubberg, Alias Dr. Shubbert, Town-Builder, Physician and Adventurer, 1806–1889," *West Texas Historical Association Year Book*, Vol. 38 (October, 1962), pp. 37–71.

[13] John O. Meusebach, *Answers to Interrogatories*, pp. 23–24.

Roemer, who had been ill of malaria at New Braunfels, arrived in Fredericksburg just before Meusebach's departure. Because of his weakened condition, he remained at Fredericksburg and spent twelve days exploring the surrounding country. Then on February 5, Major R. S. Neighbors, government agent for Indian affairs, came with a message for Meusebach from Texas Governor J. Pinckney Henderson.

The Comanches, said Neighbors, were on the warpath. He had been sent to ask Meusebach to call off his mission to the Indians, lest they be further aroused. Their harassment of settlements at this time could seriously impede the war with México. Major Neighbors and his Delaware Indian interpreter had instructions, in the event Meusebach would not change his plans, to accompany him on the visit to the Comanches. But Meusebach already was well on his way to meet the Comanche chiefs.

Roemer now was feeling stronger, and he wanted to see more of the Indians. He joined Neighbors as he hurried to overtake Meusebach, who had departed ten days earlier. They left Fredericksburg February 7, following the tracks left by Meusebach's wagons. On February 10 Neighbors and Roemer overtook the Meusebach party camped in a bend on the San Sabá River, where it already had been accorded a royal reception by the Comanches.

The following morning the council with the Indians, begun several days previously, was continued. The Delaware chief, Jim Shaw, served as interpreter. Meusebach told the Comanche chiefs that he had come peacefully with his people to view the land and to greet them as friends, and that they would be received as friends when visiting the cities of his people.

The principal chiefs were absent, however, and could not be gathered in for several weeks. It was agreed that Meusebach would meet again with the Indians at the next full moon, when the other chiefs would be present. Meusebach wished to explore as much of the grant as possible in the meantime. He particularly wanted to explore the San Sabá River in the vicinity of the old Spanish fort. He engaged Major Neighbors and the Delaware interpreter for the trip, sending most of his company, with the wagons, back to Fredericksburg. Dr. Roemer went along as Meusebach's guest.

"It was our intention from the very beginning to visit this fort," Roemer says, "since there was a persistent rumor among

Return to San Sabá

the Texas settlers that the Spaniards had worked some silver mines in the vicinity of the fort."[14]

Not even Neighbors or the Indian Jim Shaw had penetrated so far into Comanche country. According to Roemer's account, seventeen men made the trip. Included were Meusebach's servant named Schmitz, five young German military men in Meusebach's employ, Neighbors and an American companion, Jim Shaw and another Delaware Indian, two Mexican muleteers, and three Shawnee Indians who had been engaged by Meusebach as hunters.

As they progressed up the valley, Roemer took note of the wide level plain that spread out from the San Sabá River, and the tender green grass that covered it. The flat river bottom spread out more than a mile from one side to the other and extended several miles along both sides of the deep stream of crystal clear water, he noted. On February 18, the expedition had traveled six miles from its camp of the night before when it came upon the old Presidio.

Peering ahead through the mesquite trees, members of the Meusebach expedition blinked with incredulity. There, in the middle of this trackless wilderness, far from the abode of civilized man, stood a structure of old masonry. Though they had heard of the old Spanish fort in this vicinity, they had not expected such an impressive structure. Pressing to the walls, the explorers peered through an opening in the masonry into an inner courtyard. Here they decided to pitch their tents and explore further.

The old fort, Roemer says, lay close to the river on the north bank, which rose some twenty feet above the water. The fort now consisted of a crumbling stockade wall, 5 or 6 feet high, forming an almost square rectangle. In some places the masonry walls rose 15 to 20 feet. The shorter wall of the stockade, along the riverbank, measured 300 feet, the longer ones 360 feet.

Some fifty rooms abutted the inner side of the stockade walls, each room 18 feet deep and opening into the courtyard. In the

---

[14] Oswald Mueller (trans.), *Roemer's Texas*, p. 247. The portion of Roemer's narration dealing with his visit to Presidio de San Sabá is given also by Adèle B. Looscan, "The Old Fort on the San Saba River as Seen by Dr. Ferdinand Roemer in 1847," *Southwestern Historical Quarterly*, Vol. 5, No. 2 (October, 1901), pp. 137–141.

northwest corner of the compound stood a main building, with seven rooms and a small courtyard. Walls of the main building were fairly well preserved as high as the upper crossbeams.

Above this northwest corner rose a large round tower for defense. Smaller towers projected from the other three corners. The main entrance to the fort opened on the west side, and a smaller gate opened on the side next to the River. The stones of the walls were held together by earth, but Roemer observed that mortar had been used in the walls of the main building. While the structure was similar to the buildings of the Spanish missions at San Antonio, he wrote in his book, there was no church—"or [it] was very small and insignificant."

He noted specifically that there was no indication that land around the fort had ever been cultivated, and that there was no trace of an aqueduct for irrigation. (The aqueduct and fields, located on the opposite bank of the River, had been observed by Amangual and were noted by settlers who came a dozen years later, however.)

Even after his return to civilized Texas, Roemer was unable to learn much about the fort. In Texas, it seems, there was little more than legend concerning it. But he had concluded that the establishment on the San Sabá River was not a mission at all— "perhaps nothing more than a strong point for guarding the San Saba valley."

Though Roemer could only venture a guess, it had been seventy-seven years at that time since the garrison of Presidio de San Sabá had abandoned the once-important post for the last time. But he observed the large mesquite trees and the Opuntia cacti, "as tall as a man," growing inside the courtyard and the casemates. He concluded that for many generations no human being had inhabited the place.

On the walls of the main entrance were carved the names of some who had visited during that century. He recorded the names and dates: Padilla, 1810; Cós, 1829; Bowie, 1829; Moore, 1840.

The Bowie inscription now reads:
BOWIE
MINE
1832

Mrs. H. H. Wheless of Menard recently produced a photograph taken in 1895 by Noah H. Rose, showing how it has been altered.

The word "Mine," which does not appear in the photograph, has been superimposed over the 1829 date, abetting the Bowie Mine myth. The date 1832 is unrelated.

On the day after the Meusebach expedition came upon the long-abandoned presidio, Dr. Roemer set about exploring the surrounding country. On the opposite side of the River, he and his companions ascended a steep bluff, "about one hundred fifty feet high." From this summit they could see for miles around.

Roemer had heard the tales of rich silver mines in the San Sabá River country. Some of the Texans with whom he had talked said the fort was established for the sole purpose of protecting a mine in the vicinity. One of his main reasons for making the trip, he says, was to determine the grounds for the mine legend. He examined the profile of exposed rock strata in the high bluff from which he viewed the countryside. While he observed an abundance of marine fossils, he saw no sign of a formation which would yield precious metals. If such mineral ores were to be found in this region, he said, it would have to be in the metamorphic transitional rocks farther down the San Sabá River, or in the granite rocks between the San Sabá and the Llano, not in the vicinity of the fort.

The moon waxed full, and the band of explorers came again to the Comanche camp on the lower San Sabá, twenty-five miles above its confluence with the Colorado. The following day Meusebach made his treaty proposals to the principal chiefs. He asked the Comanches to permit the Germans to establish a settlement on the Llano and to survey the valley of the San Sabá. In return for the concessions, the Comanches would receive presents valued at three thousand dollars. Next day the chiefs accepted the treaty.

Dr. Roemer returned to Germany to publish an account of his eighteen months in Texas. His description of Presidio de San Sabá served as a guide for rebuilding part of the old fort in 1936.

After serving first on the faculty of the University of Bonn, Dr. Roemer was called to a professorship at the University of Breslau, in East Prussia, in 1855. He remained there until his death in 1891.

In the years which followed the visit of Meusebach and Roemer to the old Real Presidio de San Sabá, many new settlements were founded within the Fisher-Miller Grant. Two years later wagons were rolling up the San Sabá Valley, where the first settlers almost a century earlier had met failure.

The annexation of Texas in 1845 produced war between the United States and México. The treaty of Guadalupe Hidalgo at the end of the war settled the boundaries between Texas and México, as well as other boundaries between México and the United States. As a condition of the treaty, the United States agreed to keep the Plains Indians from raiding across the border —an agreement easy to make but difficult to keep.

Then gold was discovered in California in 1848, touching off a scramble by the United States Army to find trails to take those afflicted with gold lust across the continent. On orders of Major General W. J. Worth, in charge of the San Antonio district, Captain William Henry Chase Whiting set out from San Antonio February 12, 1849, to find a suitable trail across the unexplored wastes of West Texas. Whiting's party moved up through the new German settlement of Fredericksburg, then the extreme outpost in Texas, and on north to the San Sabá River.

"They paused long enough on the San Saba [writes Haley] to view and speculate on the old Spanish mission and fort near present Menard. From here they kept west along a Comanche trail to the headwaters of the San Saba, March 1, 1849." [15]

On reaching El Paso, Whiting's party returned by a more southerly route, which came to be called the Lower Road. The other—north to the San Sabá River and out through the Concho country—became the Upper Road, which was the better.

Trails first opened by the Spaniards of the Mission and the Presidio of San Sabá now were used to take the Anglo-Americans' wagons west toward California gold and ultimate fulfillment of "Manifest Destiny."

In the fall of 1849 Captain Whiting began an official inspection of the Texas frontier. He then made recommendations for increased garrisons and additional forts. In view of the growing traffic through the San Sabá and Concho country, he urged reinvestment of the old Spanish presidio near present Menard. He suggested other posts along the Comanche war trails, to stop the Comanches, Kiowas, and Apaches from raiding into México.

[15] J. Evetts Haley, *Fort Concho and the Texas Frontier*, pp. 24–25.

As a result of Whiting's suggestions, Forts Belknap, Phantom Hill, Mason, and Clark were established along the frontier. Instead of rebuilding the old Spanish presidio on the San Sabá, the Army placed Fort McKavett on that river twenty-one miles upstream.[16]

These outposts, and others built in the years following, had the multiple purpose of trying to keep the marauding Plains Indians out of México, in accord with the treaty of Guadalupe Hidalgo, of protecting the emigrant trains in their westward movement, and of making the frontier safe for settlement. Fort McKavett, established March 13, 1852, like Presidio de San Luis de las Amarillas, founded ninety-five years earlier, was to serve as a buffer against Indian depredations to the south.

In the early 1860's a number of families who had come to the raw new land made homes within the walls of the old Presidio de San Sabá, which they mistakenly called "the mission." The roof was gone from the old fort's buildings, but the settlers cut poles, placed them across the top of the masonry walls for rafters, and stretched a wagon sheet over them to turn the weather. Babies were born in these bizarre surroundings to at least two families in 1863 and 1864. Families living in the Presidio during this period became linked by marriage, and their descendants inhabit the area today.

Across the River a mile or so downstream, meanwhile, a man named Tull Smith built the first house on the present townsite of Menard in 1864, thus shaping the final destiny of the old Spanish fort.[17]

The end of the Civil War a year later brought more people. As settlements grew up around favorite springs, the Comanches became increasingly resentful. Some of the settlers, to escape the Indians, sought refuge from time to time inside the walls of the Presidio. The William Graham family, for example, harbored there in December, 1869, during an Indian scare. A daughter was born to this family in the fort on Christmas Day.

[16] *Ibid.*, pp. 54–55.

[17] Information gathered by the author in personal interviews with several persons indicates that Isaac W. Cox, 1862, may have been the first Anglo settler to inhabit the Presidio. Others included the families of Peter Robertson, Ace Ellis, and Adam Bradford. Information on the first house built in Menard is from W. C. Godfrey, in a personal interview with the writer, in August, 1962.

During the 1870's the Presidio compound served to pen cattle, as drovers gathered trail herds of wild Longhorns—Spanish cattle—to be driven north to the railheads or west to Indian reservations, where there was a market.

In 1879 one Otto Kordzik opened up the old Spanish irrigation ditch. Through the ditch he channeled water from the river to turn his grist mill.[18]

No matter how dismal the Spaniards' failure on the San Sabá River, they had left a legacy for the permanent settlers who came later.

Now the old fort served one last purpose. Its stones were used to build a town. The inside walls which formed the soldiers' quarters came down first, as a courthouse and jail and a schoolhouse were built. The outside walls were left to pen cattle. Then, as the Longhorn vanished and trail driving went the way of the unfenced range, the outside walls came down too. A saloon, fences, and residences were built from the ready supply of stone. Some of the stones quarried by the Spaniards still may be seen in the walls of business buildings along the town's main street.

And if those stones could talk . . . .

[18] Nancy Jane Graham, easement granted Otto Kordzik, November 17, 1879, Records of Menard County, Vol. C, p. 26.

Bibliography

I. PUBLISHED WORKS

Books

Adams, James Truslow. *The Epic of America*. Little Brown and Company, Boston, 1931.
Alessio Robles, Vito. *Coahuila y Texas en la época colonial*. Editorial Cultura, México, 1938.
Arricivita, Juan Domingo. *Crónica seráfica y apostólica del Colegio de propaganda fide de la Santa Cruz de Querétaro en la Nueva España, segunda parte*. F. de Zúñiga y Ontiveros, México, 1792.
Bancroft, Hubert Howe. *The Works of Bancroft*. XV. A. L. Bancroft & Company, San Francisco, 1889.
Barker, Eugene C. (ed.). *History of Texas*. The Southwest Press, Dallas, 1929.
Bolton, Herbert Eugene. *Texas in the Middle Eighteenth Century*. University of California Press, Berkeley, 1915. University of California Publications in History, III.
Brown, Nugent E., and N. H. Pierce (eds.). *The Free State of Menard*. The Menard News Press, Menard, Texas, 1946.
Castañeda, Carlos Eduardo (trans.). Juan Agustín Morfi's *History of Texas, 1673–1779*. Vol. II. Quivira Society Publications, VI, Albuquerque, 1935.
———. *Our Catholic Heritage in Texas*. Vols. III, IV, and V. Von Boeckmann-Jones Company, Austin, 1938, 1939, 1942.
Croix, Teodoro de. *Teodoro de Croix and the Northern Frontier of New Spain, 1776–1783*. Translated and edited by A. B. Thomas. Oklahoma University Press, Norman, 1941.
Dobie, J. Frank. *Coronado's Children*. Grosset & Dunlap, New York, 1930.
Fulmore, Z. T. *The History and Geography of Texas as Told in County Names*. The Steck Company, Austin, 1935.
Geiser, Samuel Wood. *Naturalists of the Frontier*. Southern Methodist University Press, Dallas, 1937.
Hackett, C. W., and Charmion Shelby (trans.). *Pichardo's Treatise on the Limits of Louisiana and Texas*. Vol. II. University of Texas Press, Austin, 1934.
Haley, J. Evetts. *Fort Concho and the Texas Frontier*. San Angelo Standard-Times, San Angelo, Texas, 1952.
Hildrup, J. S. *The Missions of California and the Old Southwest*. A. C. McClurg Company, Chicago, 1914.
Horgan, Paul. *Great River: The Rio Grande in North American History*. Holt, Rinehart and Winston, New York, 1954.

Hunter, J. W. *Rise and Fall of Mission San Saba*. Menard, Texas, 1905; reprinted by *The Frontier Times*, Bandera, Texas, 1935.
Kinnaird, Lawrence (trans.). *Frontiers of New Spain* (Nicolás de Lafora, *Presidios Internos*). Quivira Society Publications, Berkeley, 1957.
Lafora, Nicolás de. *Presidios internos (Relación del viaje que hizo a los presidios situados en la frontera de la América septentrional, perteneciente al Rey de España, 1766–1768)*. Editorial Pedro Robredo, México, 1939. Translated by Lawrence Kinnaird as *Frontiers of New Spain*. Quivira Society Publications, Berkeley, 1957.
Morfi, Juan Agustín. *History of Texas, 1673–1779* (translated and annotated by Carlos E. Castañeda). Vol. II. Quivira Society Publications, VI, Albuquerque, 1935.
Mueller, Oswald (trans.). *Roemer's Texas* (translation of Dr. Ferdinand von Roemer, *Texas*, Bonn, Germany, 1849). Standard Printing Company, San Antonio, 1935.
Nathan, Paul D. (trans.), and Lesley Byrd Simpson (ed.). *The San Saba Papers (A Documentary Account of the Founding and Destruction of San Saba Mission)*. John Howell Books, San Francisco, 1959.
Newcomb, W. W., Jr. *The Indians of Texas: From Prehistoric to Modern Times*. University of Texas Press, Austin, 1961.
Pierce, N. H., and Nugent E. Brown (eds.). *The Free State of Menard*. The Menard News Press, Menard, Texas, 1946.
Richardson, Rupert Norval. *The Comanche Barrier to South Plains Settlement*. The Arthur H. Clark Company, Glendale, California, 1933.
Roemer, Dr. Ferdinand von. *Texas, with Particular Reference to German Immigration and the Physical Appearance of the Country*. Bonn, Germany, 1849 (translated by Oswald Mueller as *Roemer's Texas*). Standard Printing Company, San Antonio, 1935.
Simpson, Lesley Byrd (ed.), and Paul D. Nathan (trans.). *The San Saba Papers (A Documentary Account of the Founding and Destruction of San Saba Mission)*. John Howell Books, San Francisco, 1959.
Shelby, Charmion, and C. W. Hackett (trans.). *Pichardo's Treatise on the Limits of Louisiana and Texas*. Vol. II. University of Texas Press, Austin, 1934.
Thomas, A. B. (ed. and trans.). *Teodoro de Croix and the Northern Frontier of New Spain, 1776–1783*. Oklahoma University Press, Norman, 1941.
Thrall, Homer S. *A Pictorial History of Texas*. N. D. Thompson & Company, St. Louis, 1879.
Webb, Walter Prescott. *The Great Plains*. Grosset & Dunlap, by arrangement with Ginn and Company, New York, 1931.

Wilbarger, J. W. *Indian Depredations in Texas.* The Steck Company, Austin, 1935.
Yoakum, H. *History of Texas: From Its First Settlement in 1685 to Its Annexation by the United States in 1846.* The Steck Company, Austin, 1935.

Articles

Allen, Henry Easton, "The Parrilla Expedition to the Red River in 1759," *Southwestern Historical Quarterly*, Vol. 43, No. 1 (July, 1939), pp. 53–71.
Bolton, Herbert Eugene, "The Founding of the Missions on the San Gabriel River, 1745–1749," *Southwestern Historical Quarterly*, Vol. 17, No. 4 (April, 1914), pp. 323–379.
Bonilla, Antonio, "A brief compendium of the history of Texas, 1772" (an annotated translation by Elizabeth H. West), *Southwestern Historical Quarterly*, Vol. 8, No. 1 (July, 1904), pp. 3–78.
Castañeda, Carlos Eduardo, "The Sons of St. Francis in Texas," reprint from *The Americas*, Vol. 1, No. 3 (October, 1945), pp. 289–302, in Main San Antonio Library.
Dunn, William Edward, "The Apache Mission on the San Saba River: Its Founding and Failure," *Southwestern Historical Quarterly*, Vol. 17, No. 4 (April, 1914), pp. 379–414.
————, "Apache Relations in Texas, 1718–1750," *Southwestern Historical Quarterly*, Vol. 14, No. 3 (January, 1911), pp. 198–274.
————, "Missionary Activity among the Eastern Apaches Previous to the Founding of the San Saba Mission," *Southwestern Historical Quarterly*, Vol. 15, No. 3 (January, 1912), pp. 186–200.
Huber, Armin O., "Frederic Armand Strubberg, Alias Dr. Shubbert, Town-Builder, Physician and Adventurer, 1806–1899," *West Texas Historical Association Year Book*, Vol. 38 (October, 1962), pp. 37–71.
Looscan, Adèle B., "The Old Fort on the San Saba River as Seen by Dr. Ferdinand Roemer in 1847," *Southwestern Historical Quarterly*, Vol. 5, No. 2 (October, 1901), pp. 137–141.
West, Elizabeth H. (trans.), "A brief compendium of the history of Texas, 1772" (translation of Bonilla), *Southwestern Historical Quarterly*, Vol. 8, No. 1 (July, 1904), pp. 3–78.
Williams, J. W., "New Conclusions on the Route of Mendoza, 1683–84," *West Texas Historical Association Year Book*, Vol. 38 (October, 1962), pp. 111–134.

Pamphlets

Flores de Lemus, Isabel. *Un Gloria de Cortegana: el mártir, Fray Alonso Giraldo de Terreros.* Pamphlet printed in Spain, provided by

Doña María Jesús Castilla de Terreros, Cortegana, Huelva, Spain, in possession of Perry Hartgraves, Menard, Texas.

Meusebach, John O. *Answers to Interrogatories in Case No. 396*, MARY C. PASCHAL, ET. AL., *vs.* THEODORE EVANS, *District Court of McCulloch County, Texas, November Term, 1893*. Issued in pamphlet form, Austin, 1894 (Texas State Library).

II. MANUSCRIPT SOURCES

Letters and Reports

Amarillas, Marqués de las, Viceroy. Letters. Archivo del Marqués de San Francisco, University of Texas Library.

Croix, Marqués de, Viceroy. Letters. Vol. 94, Part 2, Archivo General de la Nación México, Historia, University of Texas Library.

Dolores y Viana, Father Mariano Francisco de los. Letters. Archivo del Marqués de San Francisco, University of Texas Library.

Marfil, Jacinto. Letters. Archivo del Marqués de San Francisco, University of Texas Library.

Molina, Father Miguel de. "Informe de Fray Miguel de Molina." Archivo del Marqués de San Francisco, University of Texas Library.

———. Letters. Archivo de Marqués de San Francisco, University of Texas Library.

Parrilla, Diego Ortiz. Letters. Vol. 84, Vol. 95, Archivo General de la Nación México, Historia, University of Texas Library; Archivo del Marqués de San Francisco, University of Texas Library.

———. Reports ("Carta Consultiva," "Consulta del Coronel Diego Ortiz Parrilla," and "Testimonio de Parrilla"). Dunn Transcripts, 1759–1761, Archivo General de Indies, Audiencia de México, 92–6–22, University of Texas Library.

Rábago y Terán, Felipe de. Letters. Vol. 94, Part 1, Part 2, Archivo General de la Nación México, Historia, University of Texas Library; Vol. 20, Archivo San Francisco el Grande, 1751–1767, University of Texas Library.

Rodríguez, Juan Francisco Xavier, and Joseph de la Pena. Report to Viceroy. Vol. 94, Part 2, Archivo General de la Nación México, Historia, University of Texas Library.

Santísima Trinidad, Father Francisco de la. "Libranzas y cartas." Archivo del Marqués de San Francisco, University of Texas Library.

Terreros, Father Alonso Giraldo. Letters. Archivo del Marqués de San Francisco, University of Texas Library.

Terreros, Don Pedro Romero de. "Borradores de cartas." Archivo del Marqués de San Francisco, University of Texas Library.

Ugarte y Loyola, Jacobo de. Letters. Archivo General de la Nación

México, Provincias Internas, Hackett Transcripts, 1768–1792, Vol. 24, Part I, University of Texas Library.

Ynstrucción que debera observar el Coronel Dn. Diego Ortiz Parrilla. Vol. 95, Archivo General de la Nación México, Historia, University of Texas Library.

County Records

Graham, Mrs. Nancy Jane. Easement granted to Otto Kondzick. Vol. C, Records of Menard County, Menard County Clerk's Office, Menard, Texas.

Diary

Haggard, J. Villasana (trans.). "Francisco Amangual's Diary of the Expedition to Santa Fé." Bexar Archives, University of Texas Library.

Map

Lafora, Nicolás de. "Plano de el Presidio de San Sabá." Plan, map, and legend in University of Texas Archives.

Thesis

Richards, Hons Coleman. "The Establishment of the Candelaria and San Lorenzo Missions on the Upper Nueces." Master's thesis, University of Texas, August, 1936.

Index

Adams, James Truslow: 192, 193–194
Adelsverien: 204, 205
Agua Verde, Presidio de: as "San Vincente," 182 n.; and Hidalgo insurrection, 182–183; mentioned, 190
Aguayo, Marqués de San Miguel: 93, 138
Alabama, the : 205
Alles, Diego de: 164
Almagres. SEE Los Almagres
Almanza regiment: 38
Alonso, Friar. SEE Terreros, Father Alonso Giraldo de
Alta California: as buffer zone, 174–175
Amangual, Francisco: expedition of, to Santa Fé, 196–198; on San Sabá presidio, 196–197; mentioned, 208
Amarillas, Marqués de las: and San Sabá plan, 37, 41; presidio named for, 37; and San Sabá garrison, 37, 58–59; and Terreros mission plan, 40, 41; Parrilla's communications to, 45, 88, 103, 136; and continuance of San Sabá, 61–62; Father Terreros' letter to, 67; appeal for reinforcements to, 92; Apache mission support, 98; and Parrilla's San Sabá proposals, 107; requests information on Apaches, 108; approves Indian campaign, 110; replacement of, 137; mentioned, 116, 119
Americans: as threat to Spanish, 190, 195–196; penetration of, into Texas, 195; as colonists, under Mexican Republic, 201. SEE ALSO United States; U.S. Army
Andrés (Sayopín Indian): and Rábago affair, 34, 150
Andrés, Father Juan: at San Sabá, 43
Apachería: 25, 27
Apaches: weapons of, 15; and Father Vergara, 18; and silver deposits, 28; Barrios on, 21; illness among, 55; and use of Spanish, 57, 132; living habits of, 58; Father Terreros on, 67; Father Aparicio on, 97; federations of, 102; Parrilla on, 105, 107, 135; and Felipe Rábago, 149, 156–157; and San Sabá massacre, 77, 82, 91; in Parrilla's Indian campaign, 118, 121, 123–124, 123 n., 125, 127, 134, 135; mentioned, 61, 97, 137, 154
—, attacks of, on Spanish: in settlements, 3, 10, 12, 154, 174, 185, 187; at San Antonio, 12, 15, 18, 19; at Mexican mission, 23; at San Xavier missions, 32; in Coahuila, 162; reasons for, 187; in Mexico, 210; ambush by, feared, 94
—, missions for: Santa Ana's program for, 19; proposed plans for, 20; study of proposals for, 21; Apaches' conduct, while waiting for, 20–21; reasons for requesting, 23–24; in Mexico, 23; promises of, to join, 25, 26, 55, 58, 63, 108–109, 157; leave mission areas, 35, 57, 63, 164, 170; financial support of, 41; source of missionaries for, 41; and San Sabá site, 21–22; and Apaches at San Sabá, 55, 57, 63, 70; joining of missions by, 104, 132, 134–135; interest in mission life, 156–157; and El Cañon missions, 157, 158, 160; and suitability of Apaches for missionizing, 191
—, Spanish policy toward: military campaigns against, 5, 12–15, 129, 188–189; alliance with, 19, 21, 31, 87, 191; peace with, 10, 15, 18, 27; fear of French-Apache alliance, 113; pacification of, urged, 141; abandonment of, urged, 141; Spanish protest of, 142, 157; and proposed Almagres presidio, 142; and abandonment of San Sabá, 151; war on, recommended, 174
—, and other tribes: as enemies, 11–12; and conflict with Comanches, 11, 103, 163, 165; and mission Indians, 31; and attack by Tejas,

220 Index

55; and northern expedition of, 57; and fear of Comanches, 107–108; and attack by northern tribes, 109; and attack by Tonkawas, 108; sought by Tehuacanas in presidio, 176–177; sought in mission by Comanches, 177. SEE ALSO Apachería; Comanches; Lipans

Aparicio, Father Francisco: and San Marcos missions, 35, 97; at San Xavier missions, 96–97; and San Sabá project, 96–97; at San Sabá Mission, 94, 96–97, 98, 156; mentioned, 35

Aranda, Father Miguel de: 25–26, 35

Aranda, Marqués de: 93
Arcayos, Father Tomás: 123
Arkansas River: 22, 196
Army, U.S. SEE U.S. Army
Arroyo de Abuela: 168
Arroyo de Juan Lorenzo: 169, 170
Arroyo de la Soledad: 189
Arucha (soldier): wife of, 33–34
Austin, Moses: and colonization of Texas, 192, 201
Austin, Stephen F.: brings colonists to Texas, 201
Ayala, Lázaro de: in San Sabá massacre, 77, 87; mentioned, 70

Bahamas: 5
Bahía del Espíritu Santo, Presidio de: sites of, 30; and San Sabá relief, 92; and Hidalgo insurrection, 182–183; and Lipans, 190; Padilla on, 199; mentioned, 143, 182
Ballinger, Texas: 7, 118, 204
Bancroft, H. H.: 57
Bandera Pass: 12, 15
Baños, Father Joaquin de: as San Sabá missionary, 43; complains of San Sabá project, 59–60; and return to Querétaro, 59; at San José mission, 158
Barrios y Jáuregui, Jacinto de: on Apaches, 21; opposes San Sabá plan, 26, 36–37; and Miranda expedition, 27, 28; relations of, with French, 37, 111–114 *passim*; and San Sabá jurisdiction, 38; and defense of San Antonio, 91; appeal to, for forces, 115; on French among Indians, 140; on Rábago, 149

Barrio y Espriella, Pedro del: 32, 33
Beaver Creek: 205
Berlin Academy of Sciences: 204–205
Bidais: 69, 73, 102
Bienville, Sieur de: 9, 22
Blancpain, Joseph: 111, 112
Bolton, H. E.: 189
Bonilla, Antonio: on Bustillo attack, 15; on San Sabá fatalities, 88 n.; on Parrilla's retreat, 127
Bonn, University of: 209
Bonney, Orrin H.: on San Vicente location, 182 n.
Bowie, James: in San Sabá region, 201, 203; and Bowie Mine legend, 201, 203; in "Grass Fight," 203; at the Alamo, 203; and San Sabá Presidio inscription, 208
Bowie, Rezin P.: in San Sabá region, 201
Bowie battle: 201–202
Bowie Mine. SEE San Sabá Mine, legend of
Brackettville, Texas: 167
Bradford, Adam, family of: 211 n.
Brazos River: 111, 119, 200
Breslau, University of: 209
Bruyère, Fabre de la: 22
Bucareli settlement: 188
Bustillo y Ceballos, Juan Antonio: expedition of, against Apaches, 13–15; discovers San Sabá river, 13
Byers, Texas: 196

Cabello, Domingo: 196
Cabezón (Apache chief): 157
Caddos: attack Bowie Party, 201
Cadena, Ascensio: in San Sabá massacre, 73, 75, 82, 88 n.; mentioned, 70
Calahorra y Sáenz, Father Joseph de: warns of Indian attack, 110, 114–115; on English in New World, 140; and Indians' peace overtures, 140–141; urges missions for northern tribes, 141
Calf Creek: 202

Index

California: and Rubí's inspection tour, 167; and Spanish frontier line, 173, 193; gold in, and Texas, 210; mentioned, 166
Camp Wood, Texas: 157
Canary Islands: 12
Cancio, Lorenzo: 163
Candelaria Mission (El Cañon). SEE Nuestra Señora de la Candelaria, Mission (El Cañon)
Candelaria Mission (San Xavier). SEE Nuestra Señora de la Candelaria, Mission (San Xavier)
Cañon de Ugalde: 189
Capadocia (Asia Minor): 13 n.
Carbajal, Nicolás: 34
Carlshafen: as Solms townsite, 204
Casablanca (Apache chief): 55
Castelo, Don Domingo: 124
Casteñeda, C. E.: on F. Rábago's misconduct, 31; on San Sabá Mission guard, 70 n.; on witnesses of Santiesteban's fate, 87 n.; on San Sabá Mission fatalities, 88 n.; on Indian policy changes, 141; on Parrilla's removal, 138; on San José presidio, 161; on influence of missions, 192
Cavelier, René Robert: 6
Ceballos, Juan José: and Rábago affair, 33, 34, 96, 148, 149
Celery Creek: 169, 170
Cerro del Almagre: ore samples from, 27–28; Miranda on mines of, 28. SEE ALSO Los Almagres Mine
Chaguacanes: 125
Chaguesas. SEE Iscanis
Chapuis (from Fort Chartes): and Illinois–New Mexico trade route, 23
Charcas (place): 124
Charles III: and Pedro Terreros' title, 41; and inspection of frontier, 166, 167; frontier decree of, 183; mentioned, 138, 160
Chihuahua: 151, 196
Chirinos, Luis: in San Sabá massacre, 80, 88
Cicuye Mission: 153
Civil War: and San Sabá settlement, 211
Clay County, Texas: 196

Clear Fork: 119, 130
Coahuila: Apache mission in, 23; Rábago in, 34; and San Sabá Presidio, 107, 151, 166 n.; Indian raids in, 162; Lipans in, 200; mentioned, 118, 149, 180, 188, 200
—, governor of: Rábago as, 26; and aid to San Sabá, 93, 163; and Indian campaign council, 107; and campaign against Apaches, 129; and San Sabá jurisdiction, 159. SEE ALSO Cordéro, Manuel Antonio
Coco Indians: and Rábago affair, 34
Colegio de la Santa Cruz de Querétaro: establishment of, 8, 12; Terreros prepares at, 39; guardian of, 40, 57; missionaries selected from, 41; San Sabá missionaries from, 43; San Sabá as mission of, 59; and approval for missions, 158–159; mentioned, 33, 98
Colegio de San Fernando de Méjico: founding of, 8; San Sabá missionaries from, 43; selection of missionaries from, 47; mentioned, 8, 65
Colombo, Christoforo: 5
Colorado: 11
Colorado River: attack of Apaches on, 55; and Parrilla's campaign route, 118; Comanche defeat at, 204; mentioned, 7, 28, 151, 198
Columbus, Christopher: 5
Comanches: Mallet brothers on, 22; and San Sabá garrison, 26; success of federation of, 102; and settlement of Plains, 102; and Spanish expansion, 132, 151; and San Sabá Presidio, 170; Rubí's understanding of, 174; as agressors, 193; Vial at village of, 196; accompany Amagual expedition, 197, 198; as hostile tribe, 199; Padilla on, 199–200; warn Bowie party, 201; on Fisher-Miller grant, 204; councils of, with Meusebach, 206, 209; and San Sabá settlement, 211; mentioned, 28, 55, 150
— and Apaches: relations of, with Lipans, 10; press on, 11, 18, 24; Apaches' fear of, 19, 21, 107–108;

and Apaches' motives, 37; Apache revenge on, 55; attacks on, 109, 153–154, 163; as Spanish allies against, 189
— and the French: treaty with, 22–23, 112; alliance with, 23, 113; and harassment of Spanish, 177
—, attacks of, on Spanish: 102–103, 114, 190, 193; in San Sabá, 73, 92, 163–166 *passim*, 171, 176; in San Antonio, 171; in Mexico, 210
— and Spanish Indian policy: Comanche peace offer, 117; campaigns against, 109, 121, 125, 131, 200, 204; Spanish-Apache alliance, 174, 187, 191; Spanish-Comanche alliance, 187–188; of appeasement, 193. SEE ALSO Comanche War Trail; Indians
Comanche War Trail: 182, 210
Come Caballos: 45
Come Nopales: 45
Concepción Mission: 9, 25, 98, 156
Concho country: 210
Concho River: exploration of, 151; mentioned, 48, 77, 118
Conde de Santa María de Regla. SEE Terreros, Pedro Romero de
Cordéro, Manuel Antonio: 190
Cordero (Comanche chief): and Amangual expedition, 197
Coronado, Francisco Vásquez de: 5–6, 7, 28, 131
Cortegana, Huelva, Spain: 39
Cortés, Hernán: defeat at landing of, 123, 129; mentioned, 5, 6
Cortinas, Juan: 95, 115
Cós, Martin Perfecto de: at San Sabá Presidio, 201, 208
Cox, Isaac W.: 211 n.
Croix, Marqués de: Rubí's San Sabá report to, 169–171; letters from Rábago to, 171; and charges against Rábago, 178; reprimands Rábago, 179; and San Sabá garrison, 180, 181; on San Sabá Presidio abandonment, 180
Cruillas, Marqués de: replaces Amarillas, 137; relieves Parrilla of command, 137–138; regime of, 138; Parrilla on frontier to, 138–143; lack of action of, 141; and Rábago appointment, 148, 149; mission plan of, 159; and El Cañon missions sanction, 159; and San José valley report, 160; on Rábago's requests, 161; and munitions request, 162; and Indian campaign request, 166; mentioned, 147, 171
Cuba: 38
Cuevas, Father Manuel de: 160

Delaware Indians: 206, 207
del Río, Domingo: 111–112
Del Rio, Texas: 167
de Rubí, Marqués. SEE Rubí, Marqués de
de Soto, Hernando: in Texas, 6
de Vaca, Cabeza: 5
Dixon Expedition: and mine map, 202
Dolores y Viana, Father Mariano de los: mission plan of, 20, 21; in Apachería expedition, 25; attitude of, toward Apaches, 20–21, 109; advocates San Xavier missions, 32; and San Xavier presidio removal, 33; and Guadalupe missions, 35, 44; and Father Terreros, 44–45, 46; and El Chico, 55; on Indian campaign council, 110; and Rábago's appointment, 148–149; on Parrilla's Indian campaign, 126, 127; mentioned, 23, 26, 58, 64, 65
—, and San Sabá: report of massacre of, 91; Apaches sent to observe, 91; reinforcements for, 91–92, 93; Father Aparicio sent to, 97; reestablishment of, 98
d'Orvanne, Bourgeois: 204
Dry Creek: 202
Dunn, W. E.: on T. Urrutia's expedition, 16; on Coahuila mission failure, 23; on Rábago's San Sabá report, 27; on French and San Sabá Presidio, 37; on San Sabá Mission guard, 70 n.; on Parrilla's campaign, 129; on campaign against Apaches, 129

Eagle Pass, Texas: 9
"Easter Spring": 198
East Prussia: 209

Index

East Texas: expeditions to, 6, 9; French threat in, 8–9, 173; abandonment of, 183; missionizing of Indians of, 191; mentioned, 167. SEE ALSO East Texas missions

East Texas missions: first, founding and abandonment of, 8; second, difference from first, 9; objectives of, and Indians, 9; withdrawal of, to San Antonio, 9–10, 12, 30, 183; abandonment of, 9–10, 173, 183

Eca y Músquiz, Joseph: and San Antonio reinforcement, 93; mentioned, 61, 65, 67, 106, 108, 128

Edwards Plateau region: 7, 187

El Cañon missions: and San Sabá project, 30; site of, 157; approval for, 158–159; and San Sabá garrison, 158, 181; consequences of, 159; supply problem at, 159, 160, 162; report on conditions of, 160; function of, 161; maintenance of, 162; official recognition of, 162; attacks on, 165–166; Rubí's inspection of, 167; activity of Apaches of, 174, 187; abandonment of, 182; mentioned, 180. SEE ALSO Nuestra Señora de la Candelaria, Mission, (El Cañon); San Lorenzo de la Santa Cruz, Mission

El Chico (Lipan chief): 55

Ellis, Ace, family of: 211 n.

El Paso area: 7, 210

El Río de San José: 157

El Río San Sabá de las Nueces. SEE San Sabá River

El Turnio (Apache chief): 158

English, the: ambitions of, in New World, 5; Sea Dogs, raid of, 6; on Eastern seaboard, 6; in King George's War, 19; and San Sabá site, 22; as threat to French, 112; and Spanish expansion, 132; in French and Spanish territory, 140; and Comanche attacks, 166; buffer zones against, 174–175; trouble in colonies of, 176; alliance of, with Indians, 187; trade of, with Taovayas, 188; and last Spanish mission, 190; mentioned, 38. SEE ALSO French and Indian War

Espinosa, Francisco: 124

Espíritu Santo presidio. SEE Bahía del Espíritu Santo, Presidio de

expeditions (against Indians). SEE Indians, campaign against

expeditions (exploratory). SEE exploration (expeditions)

exploration expeditions: Mendoza, Edwards Plateau region, 7; Mallet brothers, to Santa Fé, 22; Galván, of Apachería, 25–26; Pedro Rábago, of San Sabá, 26–27; Miranda, of Llano region, 27–28; Parrilla, San Sabá region, 43, 53; Guzmán, of Los Almagres, 106; Ruíz, to Trinity settlements, 111; Felipe Rábago, of west of Menard, 151–153; Romero, to San Sabá, 153–154; Pike, 196; Amagual, to Santa Fé, 196, 198; Vial, to Santa Fé, 196; Padilla, of Los Almagres and San Sabá, 199; Bowie, of San Sabá, 201; Meusebach, of Fisher-Miller Grant, 206–207; Whiting, of West Texas trails, 210

Fayette County, Texas: 204

Ferdinand VI: 62, 110, 148

Fisher-Miller Grant: location of, 204; purchased by Adelsverein, 204; Schubert on, 205; Meusebach's exploration of, 206–208; settlements within, 209–210

Flores, Friar Sebastián: 35

Flores, Joseph Antonio: and Indian attack, 68; and San Sabá massacre, 80, 81, 83 and n., 87, 101; on Comanche hostility, 102

Florida: 6, 193

Florido River: SEE Concho River

Fort Belknap: 211

Fort Chartres: 23

Fort Clark: 210

Fort Clark Guest Ranch (Brackettville): 167

Fort Griffin: 119

Fort Mason: 210

Fort McKavett: as buffer, 211

Fort Phantom Hill: 210

Fort Saint Louis: fate of, 8; effect of, on Spanish, 111; mentioned, 30, 130

Franciscan order: training of missionaries by, 8
Franciscan priests: propose Apache mission, 12
Fredericksburg, Texas: 205, 206, 210
French, the: claims of, in North America, 6; penetration of, into Spanish territory, 6–7, 111–112; movement of, up Red River, 18; in King George's War, 19; Missouri River post of, 22; Illinois–New Mexico trade route of, 23; in New World colonization, 112; mentioned, 5, 159
— and Indians: and firearms, 11, 105, 132; trade between, 31; treaties of, 112; and San Sabá massacre, 112, 113–114; in Red River battle, 130–132; alliance between, 136; activities among, 139–140; and Comanche attacks, 166; as Comanche interpreters, 177; encourage Spanish harassment, 177. SEE ALSO French and Indian War
— and the Spanish: French threat and Spanish missions, 7, 9, 18, 22, 30, 111, 113, 174, 191–192; attack on Spanish, 9–10; and Spanish presidio, 37; Barrios trades with French, 111; French embargo on corn, 112; Spanish grievances against French, 112; French mistrust of Spanish, 113; Spanish attitude toward French, 114; and Spanish expansion, 132; and Louisiana, 160, 193. SEE ALSO French and Indian War
French and Indian War: effect of, on Spanish, 29; and French in Southwest, 112; English success in, 140; mentioned, 176
Frio River Canyon: 163–164

Gallardo (soldier): 127
Galván, Juan: and Apachería exploration, 25–26; trail of, and later expeditions, 26, 50; on San Sabá area, 27; at San Xavier mission, 32–33; recommends San Sabá site, 32, 53; and San Sabá massacre, 81–82, 86, 87, 91, 93; and petition to Parrilla, 95; mentioned, 36, 65, 69
Galván expedition: 25–26
Galveston, Texas: 205
Gálvez, Bernardo de: 188
Ganzábal, Father Juan José de: murder of, 34, 96, 148, 150
García, Father Joseph: 98, 110
García, Joaquín: and San Sabá massacre, 80, 88
García, José: and San Sabá massacre, 77, 87; mentioned, 70
García, José María: 199
Garza, Ildefonso de la: 124
Garza Falcón, Blas María de la: 44
Garza Falcón, Elías de la: 124
Garza Falcón, Miguel de la: 34
German immigrants: and San Sabá mine legend, 198, 204; company to aid, 204; and Fredericksburg, 205; and Comanche treaty, 209
Goliad, Texas: 30
governor. SEE Coahuila; Nuevo Léon; Texas; Veléz Cachupín, Tomás
Graham, Wm., family of: 211
Great Plains: settlement of, and Comanches, 102–103; and Spanish expansion, 132
Guadalupe Hidalgo, treaty of: 210, 211
Guadalupe missions: mission proposed, 20; establishment of, 35, 190; temporary mission, 44; financial support for, 44, 48; San Sabá soldiers at, 70; soldiers from, at San Sabá, 93; attack on, feared, 94; Father Aparicio at, 97; abandonment of, 97. SEE ALSO Nuestra Señora del Refugio, Mission; San Xavier de Horcastis, Mission
Guadalupe River: settlement on, 91; moving of San Sabá Mission to, 97; Apaches move to, 105; moving of San Sabá Presidio to, 106–107; and line of outposts, 173; mentioned, 28. SEE ALSO Guadalupe missions
Guadalupe River settlement: ordered to San Antonio, 91
Guerra y Hacienda, Junta de. SEE Junta de Guerra y Hacienda

Index

Gulf of California: 173
Gulf of Mexico: French colony on, 8
Gutiérrez, Enrique: and San Sabá massacre, 77, 87; mentioned, 70
Gutiérrez, José: and San Sabá massacre, 79
Gutiérrez, Juan Antonio: and San Sabá massacre, 76, 79, 82, 84, 87–88; mentioned, 70
—, wife of: 72–73, 82
Gutiérrez, Vicente: and San Sabá massacre, 82; mentioned, 70
Guzmán, José de: 106

Haley, J. Evetts: 210
Hasinai Confederacy: Spanish alliance with, 191. SEE ALSO Tejas Indians
Henderson, J. Pinckney: 206
Hidalgo, Father Francisco: urges Apache missions, 3, 12; death of, 3, 18; mentioned, 13, 38
Hidalgo, Father Miguel: 183
Hierbipiames: 127–128
Hill, Robert T.: 182 n.
Hinojoso, Joseph: 126
Holy Cross Ford: 26, 54
Honey Creek: 27–28
Houston County, Texas: mission in, 8
Hudson's Bay: 6

Ignacio (Indian): 82
Illinois: 23, 140
Indianola, Texas: 204, 205
Indians: of Mexico, 6, 191; revolt of, in New Mexico, 7; number of, and East Texas missions, 9; intertribal enmities among, 10; cultural changes among, 10–11; and acquisition of horses, 10–12, 112, 132; weapons of, 11, 101–102, 112, 132; and Spanish pivot, 22, 174; increased capabilities of, 95, 136, 163; and Spanish-Apache alliance, 97; alliances among, 136; and English, 140; and Rábago's expedition, 153; Plains, movement of, 162; attacks of, on San Sabá Presidio, 162, 164, 168, 176–178; and San Sabá Presidio ruin, 179; and failure of mission system, 190–191; Plains, nature of, 191; tribes of, Padilla on, 199; raids of, and Hidalgo treaty, 210, 211. SEE ALSO Apaches; Bidais; Chaguacanes; Coco Indians; Comanches; Come Caballos; Come Nopales; Delaware Indians; English, the; French, the; Hasinai Confederacy; Hierbipiames; Iscanis; Jumanos; Karankawa Indians; Kiowas; Lipans; Mescaleros; Natagés (Natajés); Nasonis; Norteños; Parrilla, Diego Ortiz; Pelones; Pima rebellion; Pueblo Indians; Rábago y Terán, Felipe; San Sabá massacre; Shawnee Indians; Spanish; Tancagues; Taovayas; Tehuacana; Tejas Indians; Tlaxcalteca; Tonkawas; Waco Indians; Wichitas; Yacaeles; Yojuane
—, campaign against: Bustillo's, against Apaches, 13–15; Urrutias', against Apaches, 15, 16, 18; proposed, 105–106, 127–128, 166, 200; Ugalde's, against Apaches, 188–189; Moore's, against Comanches, 204. SEE ALSO Parrilla, Indian campaign of
—, mission: harassment of, by Apaches, 12; in raid on Apaches, 13; Parrilla requests force of, 91–92; harassment of, by soldiers, 54; in Parrilla campaign, 121, 123. SEE ALSO Apaches; Tejas Indians; Tlaxcalteca; San Sabá massacre; San Xavier mission
—, northern tribes of: and Spanish-Apache alliance, 24; alliance among, 57, 113, 114; attacks by, rumored, 63, 68, 114–115; hostile activity of, 108, 160–169; knowledge of plans against, 117; Parrilla on intentions of, 103–104; number of, 105; weapons of, 105; horses of, 105; attack of, on San Sabá Presidio, 108, 160–161; attack of, on Apaches, 109; foreign influence on, 135–136; mission among, advocated, 141; extension of villages of, 164; Rubí on intentions of, 170; Spanish alliance with, 187–189; peace with, 189–190

Ipandes. SEE Lipans
Irion County, Texas: 151
Iscanis: 109, 114, 125

Jiménez, Father Diego: and San Sabá, 43, 59–60; and return to Mexico, 59; and Rábago's conduct, 149–150; and El Cañon missions, 157–158, 158–159, 160; mentioned, 126, 156
Jumanos: ask for mission, 7; treaty of, with French, 22–23, 112. SEE ALSO Wichitas
Junction, Texas: 7, 168
Junta de Guerra y Hacienda: and San Sabá plan, 36, 37; recommends Indian campaign, 110. SEE ALSO viceregal government
Junta de los Ríos, Presidio de la: 154; Rodríguez from, 154

Kansas: 132
Karankawa Indians: 8
Ketemoczy (Comanche chief): 205
King George's War: 19
Kiowas: 210
Kordzik, Otto: 212

La Bahía Presidio: SEE Bahía del Espíritu Santo, Presidio de
Lafora, Nicolás de: accompanies Rubí, 167; and El Cañon missions map, 167; on San Lorenzo mission guard, 168; on San Sabá Presidio, 169; and San Sabá Presidio map, 169, 170; on frontier commanders, 173
Laguna, Marqués de la: 7, 8, 9
Langberg, Colonel: 182
Langhorne, Geo. T.: 182 n.
"La Pascua": 198
Lara, Father Francisco de: at San Sabá Presidio, 44, 65; mentioned, 66
La Salle, Sieur de: 6, 8, 130
"Las Cruces": 182 and n.
Las Moras Creek: 168
Las Moras Spring: 167
Las Nueces: 13. SEE ALSO San Sabá River
La Viscaína mine: 40
Leal, Juan: and San Sabá massacre, 72–73, 78, 82; mentioned, 70

Le Blanc, Cesar: and San Sabá spoils, 113, 114; warns of Indian attack, 114
Le Moyne, Jean Baptiste. SEE Bienville, Sieur de
León, Alonso de: 8
Lipans: Spanish attack on, 16; promises of, to enter missions, 45, 55; on arrival of missionaries, 53; character of, 135; Romero expedition among, 153–154; and intertribal conflict, 188; Ugalde's campaign against, 188–189; murder of miners by, 189; as marauders in La Bahía, 190; gifts of munitions to, 193; Padilla on, 199–200; campaign against, proposed, 200; mentioned, 57. SEE ALSO Apaches
Llano Estacado: 63, 153
Llano River: presidio on, proposed, 142; removal of San Sabá garrison to, 59; mentioned, 50, 168, 189, 205. SEE ALSO Llano Estacado; Llano River region
Llano River region: and San Clemente mission, 7; exploration of, 25, 26, 27–28; and Los Almagres Mine, 27–28, 106, 198; German settlement in, 209
Loma Pinta: 154
López, Father José: 26, 35
López, Father Nicolás: 7
Los Adaes, Presidio de: establishment of, 10; as Texas capital, 10, 38, 173; and line of Spanish outposts, 19, 31, 153; and San Sabá relief, 92; conditions at, 172; mentioned, 114, 139, 180
Los Almagres: presidio at, and Miranda, 28; exploration of, by Parrilla, 106 and n.; settlement of, 141; murder of miners at, 189. SEE ALSO Los Almagres Mine
Los Almagres Mine: discovery of, 27–28, 59, 133, 198; effects of Miranda's report on, 28; legend of, and settlement, 28; presidios near, proposed, 59, 142, 198, 199; Padilla expedition to, 199; Obregón visits, 199. SEE ALSO Miranda, Bernardo de; San Sabá Mine
Louisiana: Spanish mission in, 9; Spanish frontier west of, 132; as

buffer zone, 174–175; rebellion against Spanish in, 176; receded to French, 193; sale of, to U.S., 193; Catholic colonists from, 201; mentioned, 113, 196
— as cession to Spain: 160, 172, 174; and frontier, 167; effect of, on eastern frontier, 173. SEE ALSO Natchitoches, Louisiana

Magee-Guttiérrez expedition: 199
Mallet brothers: 22, 112
Mares, José: and San Antonio–Santa Fé route, 196
Marfil, Jacinto: 61–62
Mariscal Canyon: 182 n.
Martos y Navarrete, Angel de: and San Sabá relief, 92–93, 116; requests increased force, 92–93; and Rábago, 147, 161; abuses of, 172
Massanet, Father Damian: 8
Mayeyes. SEE Tonkawas
Mazapíl, Mexico: 28
McCamey, Texas: 151
McCaslin, Thomas: 201, 202
McCullogh County, Texas: 202
Menard, Texas: settlement in, 211; mentioned, 15, 26, 50, 83 n., 151, 201–202, 203
Menard County, Texas: 13
Menchaca, José: 190, 195
Mendoza, Juan Domínguez de: mission established by, 7; argument of, for mission, 7; and San Sabá River, 13
Mescaleros: Romero expedition among, 154; and intertribal conflict, 188; Ugalde campaign against, 188–189; mentioned, 45. SEE ALSO Apaches
Meusebach, Baron Ottfried Hans von: and Adelsverein, 204; on Schubert's report, 205; lays out Fredericksburg, 205; exploration of San Sabá River by, 206–207; and Comanches, 206, 209; exploration party of, 207
Meusebach, John O. SEE Meusebach, Baron Ottfried Hans von
Mexican Constitution of 1824: 201
Mexican Republic: birth of, 200–201

México: attack on settlements of, 12; Comanches in, 102–103; missions in, 190; revolution in, 195, 199, 200–201; mentioned, 34, 39, 41, 149, 167, 198. SEE ALSO Coahuila, Chihuahua, Mexico City, Mexican Constitution of 1824; Mexican Republic; Viceregal government
Mexico City: 7, 24, 40, 61, 62, 65, 71, 93, 106, 148, 178, 180–181
Mézières, Athanase de: 188
Milam County, Texas: 30
Miñon, Pedro: 177
Miranda, Bernardo de: 27–28, 133, 142
— and Los Almagres Mine: discovery of, 27–28, 59, 198; report on, 28–29; development of, 28, 41; and presidio command, 28
Miraval, Joseph Antonio: in Romero expedition, 153–154
mission Indians. SEE Indians, mission
missions: first Texas, 7; colleges, founding of, 8; Apache, proposals for, 12; Father Terreros' plan for, 40; Apache, terms of payment for, 40; description of, 42; purpose of, 42; and religious-military conflicts, 46, 142, 143, 191, 192; end of, in Texas, 174, 183, 190; expense of, 190; accomplishments of, 192; reasons for failure of, 189–192; Apache, 191; and zeal of missionaries, 192. SEE ALSO Apaches; East Texas missions; El Cañon missions; Guadalupe missions; Nuestra Señora del Espíritu Santo de Zúñiga, Mission; Nuestra Señora de la Candelaria, Mission (El Cañon); Nuestra Señora de la Candelaria, Mission (San Xavier); Nuestra Señora de la Purísima Concepción, Mission; Nuestra Señora de la Luz del Orcoquisac, Mission; Nuestra Señora de los Dolores, Mission; Nuestra Señora del Refugio, Mission; San Antonio, missions of; San Antonio de Valero, Mission; San Clemente, Mission; San Francisco de los Neches, Mission; San

Francisco de los Tejas, Mission; San Francisco Xavier de Horcasitas, Mission; San Ildefonso, Mission; San José de Aguayo, Mission; San José de los Nazonis, Mission; San Lorenzo, Mission (Coahuila); San Lorenzo de la Santa Cruz, Mission; San Miguel de Linares, Mission; San Sabá Mission; Santísimo Nombre de Maria, Mission; San Xavier missions

Mississippi Valley: French claim, 6

Missouri River: French traders' post on, 22

Molina, Father Miguel de: arrival of, at San Sabá, 65, 68; on San Sabá situation, 65; on Mission security measures, 70; in San Sabá massacre, 73, 75, 77, 78, 82–83, 86; on San Sabá massacre, 84 n., 103; sent to San Antonio, 95; on converting Apaches, 104

Monclova, Coahuila: 150, 167, 188; soldiers from, and Hidalgo insurrection, 182–183

Moneo, Santiago: 124

Montell, Texas: 158

Moore, John H.: 204, 208

Morfi, Juan Agustín: on Apaches, 24, 156, 163; on French in battle, 131; on Rábago, 156

Muñoz, Manuel: on Indian raids, 190

Nacogdoches, Texas: presidio at, proposed, 200; mentioned, 91, 114, 140

Nasonis: 113

Natagés: Spanish attack on, 16; mentioned, 45

Natajés: at San Sabá, 58

Natchitoches, La.: French settlement at, 9, 37; French at, and Blancpain affair, 112; mentioned, 111, 113, 139

Natchitoches district: 188

Nathan, Paul D.: 70 n.

National Pawn Shop (of Mexico): 41

Neel, B. K.: marker on ranch of, 202

Neighbors, R. S.: and Meusebach, 206

New Braunfels, Texas: mission near, 35, 44, 204; townsite selected by Solms, 204

Newcomb, W. W., Jr.: 131–132

New Mexico: settlement in, 6, 7, 10; Indian revolt in, 7; introduction of horses in, 11; and trade with French, 22; routes to, 23, 103, 151, 195–196; Comanches in, 102; route to San Sabá from, 153; and mission and fort locations, 153, 159, 161; mentioned, 26, 167, 151, 193

New Orleans, La.: and English intentions, 140; and Spanish frontier lines, 193; mentioned, 9, 22, 111–112, 205

Nocona, Texas: 120

Norteños: 91, 105

Norton, J. R.: 202, 202–203

Nueces missions. SEE El Cañon missions

Nueces River: 163, 181, 189. SEE ALSO El Cañon missions

Nueces Valley: 162

Nuestra Señora de Guadalupe de Zacatecas (College of): 8

Nuestra Señora de la Candelaria, Mission (El Cañon): location of, 158; force at, 158; abandonment of, 167. SEE ALSO El Cañon missions

Nuestra Señora de la Candelaria, Mission (San Xavier): establishment of, 32; Cocos flee from, 34; mentioned, 33. SEE ALSO San Xavier missions

Nuestra Señora del Espíritu Santo de Zúñiga, Mission: sites of, 30

Nuestra Señora de la Luz del Orcoquisac, Mission: establishment of, 112

Nuestra Señora de la Purísima Concepción, Mission: 9, 25, 98, 156

Nuestra Señora de los Dolores, Mission: founding of, 9

Nuestra Señora del Refugio, Mission: founding of, 190

Nueva Vizcaya. SEE Chihuahua

Nuevo León: governor of, 93, 115; mentioned, 188, 200

Nuevo Santander: 107, 188

Nuncio, Juan: 165

Index

Obregón, Ignacio: 199
Oca, Manuel Antonio de: 180, 181
Oconor, Hugo: 180
Ogeda, Tomás de: 69
Oñate, Juan de: 11
Orendain, Joaquín: 178
Ortuza, Juan Angel de: 126
Oyarzán, Angel de: 124

Pacheco, Rafael Martínez: 189
Pachuca, Mexico: 40, 61
Padilla, Friar Juan: 7
Padilla, Juan Antonio: 199, 199–200, 208
Padilla, Luis: 69
Paine, Thomas: 176
Painted Rocks, the: 118
Paint Rock, Texas: 118
Palou, Father Francisco: 98
Parliament (British): 176
Parras, Father Pedro de: 98
Parrilla, Diego Ortiz: appointed San Xavier commander, 37; background of, 38; character of, 38; change of attitude of, 58; and Los Almagres mine, 59, 106, 142, 198; cattle of, 63; and conference with Viceroy, 65, 66–68, 136–137; pleas of, for reinforcements, 116; and petition to move presidio, 95–96; and frontier situation, 95, 135–136, 138–143; and soldiers for San Antonio, 134; on French and Indians, 136, 139–140; appointed Coahuila governor, 137–138; on English in Spanish territory, 140; evaluation of conclusions of, 143; protests Rábago appointment, 148; mentioned, 43, 46, 54, 56, 61, 68, 86, 114, 115, 130, 150, 154, 188
—, Indian campaign of: 38, 98, 166, 172; Parrilla appointed leader of, 107; orders for, 108, 116; time for start of, 109–110; cost of, 110, 137; approval for, 110; and preparation for attack, 115; delays in, 116–117; force of, 118, 122, 134, 136; and continuation of, 118–119; Apaches in, 118, 121, 123–124, 123 n.; and attack on Tonkawa camp, 119; and Indians' trap for Spanish, 120, 126; Indians' weapons in, 120, 121; battle at Taovayas village, 120–122, 123, 125–126 and 126 n., 130–132; desertions in force in, 121–127 *passim*, 123 n.; Spanish retreat in, 121, 122, 127; and weather, 122; Spanish casualties in, 123–124, 123 n.; Indian losses in, 124; valor in battle in, 124; troop movements after battle in, 124–125; Parrilla's wounds in, 125; prisoners taken in, 125; and council of officers, 127–128; Parrilla's report on, 128, 133; distance traveled by force, 128; as defeat, 129, 170, 174; significance of, 129–130, 132, 137; Parrilla's attitude after, 133
— and Indians: relations with, 43; on Apaches, 45; proposals of, concerning, 105–106; on northern tribes, 105; on Apaches and missions, 134–135; understanding of, of Apaches, 135; on their peace overtures, 140–141; on pacification of Apaches, 141
— and missionaries: relations with, 43; in Father Dolores' faction, 45; conflict between, 38–39, 46, 105, 142, 192; missionary-military *junta*, 142–143
— and San Sabá, establishing of: transfer of San Xavier garrison, 38, 43, 44; authority to recruit, 43; instructions for, 43; inspection of sites, 43, 44, 53, 56; delays, 45, 48; San Sabá group, 49; route to San Sabá, 50; return to San Antonio, 49–50
— and San Sabá massacre: warning to Father Terreros, 69; mission protection, 70–71; Indians demand note, 76; messenger sent, 79; preparation for attack, 80–81, 85–86; scene described, 87; wounded soldiers, 88; help sent for, 90; supplies sent for, 95; accounts of, gathered, 95, 101–102; understanding of, 103–104, 132; and blame for, 104–105
— and San Sabá project: failure of, 39; misgivings on, 45–46; understanding of, 45–46; abandonment of, 53–54, 58–59; proposals on,

104, 105–107; continuance of Presidio, 136, 142
Paso de la Santa Cruz: 26, 54
Pecos, New Mexico: 153
Pecos, Texas: 151
Pecos River: Indians of, 7; and French threat, 112; exploration of, 151; and Romero expedition, 153; and San Sabá Presidio, 164, 171; Apaches flee to, 164
Pedernales River: mission on, proposed, 20; exploration of region of, 25, 26; Indian attacks on, 68–69 and 69 n., 75, 188; San Sabá project on, 196; mentioned, 50
Pelaes, Father Santiago: 123
Pelones: 45. SEE ALSO Apaches
Pena, Joseph de la: 178, 179
Pérez, José: and Indian ambush, 182
Pérez, Xavier: 126
Pike, Zebulon Montgomery: 196
Pima rebellion: 38–39
Pinilla, Father Miguel: 33–34, 48
Plains of Abraham, Battle of: 130
Platte River: Mallet brothers at, 22
Presidio, Texas: 154
presidios: cooperation of, with missions, 42; purpose of, 42; attacks on, feared, 92, 93; inadequacy of, 130, 136, 172; conditions in, 172–173; abandonment of, proposed, 172; proposed line of, 200. SEE ALSO Agua Verde, Presidio de; Bahía de Espíritu Santo, Presidio; Los Adaes, Presidio de; Reyno, Presidio del; Río Grande, Presidio del; San Agustín de Ahumada, Presidio de; San Carlos Presidio; Santa Ana de Camargo, Presidio de; San Antonio de Béjar, Presidio de; San Luis de Amarillas, Presidio de; Santa Rosa del Sacramento, Presidio del; San Vincente presidio; San Xavier de Gigedo, Presidio de
Puebla, Mexico: 38
Pueblo Indians: 11
"Puerto de Baluartes": 26, 53

Quebec, Canada: won by British: 130, 140

Querétaro, College of. SEE Colegio de la Santa Cruz de Querétaro

Rábago y Terán, Felipe: relations of, with missionaries, 148, 150, 191; Barrios's appraisal of, 149; route of, to San Sabá, 50; exploratory expedition of, 151–153, 159; visits San Sabá Mission site, 156; illness of, 169, 177–178; death of, 181; mentioned, 35, 38, 166, 178
— and El Cañon missions: founding of, 157, 158; guard for, 158; approval for, 158, 159; explorations, 153, 159; and San José Presidio, 160, 161; settlers for, 162
— and Indians: conversion of Apaches, 156, 164; missions, 156–157; protection of Apaches, 156, 157, 165; attacks, 161–166 passim; offensive campaign, 166, 171–172
— at San Xavier, misconduct of: 31, 33–34, 96, 148; removal of, 31; reinstatement of, 31, 137–138, 147–148; results of, 31; investigation of, 34, 148
— and San Sabá Presidio: appointment, 31, 137–138, 147–148; errors, 143; ineffectiveness, 147; San Sabá jurisdiction, 147; Presidio funds, 148; Father Jiménez' advice, 150; conditions, 150–151; maintenance, 151, 171; improvement of, 154–155; El Cañon missions, 158, 160–161; Indian attacks, 161–166 passim; munitions, 163; transfer, 164, 171, 177, 179–180, 198; Rubí's inspection, 168, 169, 171; soldiers' charges, 178; removal of Rábago, 180
—, relations of, with viceroy: letter to, 164, 166, 171; requests promotion, 171, 181; and journey to Mexico City, 178; and viceroy's reprimand, 179
Rábago y Terán, Pedro de: expedition of, 26–27; report of, on San Sabá, 27; supports San Sabá project, 27, 32, 36; recommends San Sabá site, 27, 32, 53; transfers San Xavier missions, 34–35; death of, 37; mentioned, 29, 50, 54
Ramón, Diego: 71

Index

Reagan County, Texas: 151
Red River: French settlement on, 9, 18, 37; Parrilla-Indian battle on, 120, 127, 129, 130; missionizing on, 191; mentioned, 113, 188, 196
"Republican Army of the North": 199
Revilla Gigedo, Conde de: and Santa Ana petition, 18, 19, 20; and Father Dolores' mission plan, 21, 22; and San Sabá plan, 36; mentioned, 37
Reyes, Nicolás de los: 82, 84
Reyno, Presidio del: 124
Richardson, R. N.: 193
Río Cadodacho. SEE Red River
Río de las Chanas. SEE Llano River
Río Florido. SEE Concho River
Río Grande, Presidio del: and San Sabá relief, 92; soldiers of, and Hidalgo insurrection, 182–183; mentioned, 44, 124, 128, 143
Río Grande missions: 23, 39, 157
Río Grande River: and Rubí's presidio plan, 173, 182; missionizing on, 191; mentioned, 7, 8, 12, 19, 21, 43, 167, 182 n.
Río Grande settlements: 9; and line of outposts, 19, 153; and Indian attacks, 154, 162. SEE ALSO San Juan Bautista settlement
Río Puerco. SEE Pecos River
Rivera, Father: 167–168, 182
Rivera, Pedro de: 82, 90, 93
Robeline, La.: 10
Robertson, Peter, family of: 211 n.
Robles, Alessio: 182 n.
Rockdale, Texas: 30
Rodríguez, Juan Francisco Xavier: and Rábago, 178, 179
Rodríguez, Manuel: 124, 128, 150, 154
Roemer, Ferdinand von: and survey of Texas, 205; and Meusebach party, 206; on San Sabá Presidio, 206–208, 209; and San Sabá mine, 206–207, 209; after return to Germany, 209
Romero, Francisco: 153–154
Romero, Miguel: 153–154
Rubí, Marqués de: orders of, 167; inspection tour route of, 167; on San Sabá Presidio, 168–169, 170; on El Cañon missions, 170; report of, to viceroy, 169–171; mentioned, 138, 166, 176
——, recommendations of: 143; to Rábago, 169; on San Sabá Presidio, 170–171, 183; presidio plan of, 172, 173–174; war against Apaches as, 174, 187; implementation of, 183
Ruiz, Marcos: 111
Russians: 132

Sabine River: 9, 19
Sacramento, Coahuila: 148
Sacramento, Presidio del. SEE Santa Rosa del Sacramento, Presidio de
Saint Denis, Louis Juchereau de: 9
Saint Quentin (French trader): 113
Saint Sabbás: 13 and n.
Salamanca, University of: 40
Salcedo, Manuel de: 199
Sallee Ranch: 202
Saltillo, Mexico: 43, 44
San Agustín de Ahumada, Presidio de: establishment of, 112
San Antonio: Apache raids on, 3, 12, 15; beginning of, 9; as capital of Texas, 10, 173, 183; survival of, as settlement, 12; and trade with Apaches, 18, 21; and Spanish frontier line, 19, 153, 173, 193; and San Marcos missions, 35; and San Sabá jurisdiction, 38; San Xavier garrison moved to, 44; Apaches invited to, 45; San Sabá group at, 45, 49; El Chico visits, 55; San Sabá supplies from, 68, 95, 116; and San Sabá massacre, 82, 91; Indian attack on, rumored, 91, 110, 114–115; council of, and Parrilla's campaign, 106, 107, 108, 109–110; epidemic in, 137; as permanent settlement, 170; and San Sabá as buffer, 170; moving San Sabá settlers to, 170; East Texas settlements transferred to, 183; taken by Magee-Gutiérrez force, 199; mentioned, 16, 25, 26, 27, 28, 33, 34, 43, 44, 50, 128, 133, 140, 180, 196, 200, 204
——, missions of: purpose of, 9; missionaries of, 15; and Father Santa Ana, 20; Apaches at, 21, 58; and

Parrilla campaign, 110, 118; mentioned, 148–149. SEE ALSO East Texas missions; San Antonio de Béjar, Presidio de; San Antonio de Valero, Mission; San Antonio River; San Fernando de Béjar, Villa de

San Antonio de Béjar, Presidio de: founding of, 9; effect of Apache mission on, 19; moving garrison of, proposed, 20; and San Sabá garrison, 36, 37, 38; reinforcement of, 92, 93, 115, 134, 171; and San Sabá as buffer, 162; San Sabá soldiers transfer to, 180, 181; and San Sabá reinforcement, 166 n.; men and munitions from, for Ugalde, 189; Padilla on people of, 199; mentioned, 12, 15, 16, 18, 25, 69, 93, 143, 189. SEE ALSO San Antonio

San Antonio de Valero, Mission: founding of, 9, 10; mentioned, 20, 203. SEE ALSO San Antonio

San Antonio River: 9, 30

San Augustine, Texas: 9

San Bernardo, Mission: 190

San Carlos Presidio: 182

Sánchez, José Jiménez: 165

San Clemente, Mission: establishment of, 7

San Fernando, College of. SEE Colegio de San Fernando de Méjico

San Fernando de Agua Verde, villa of: 200

San Fernando de Austria, Villa de: transfer of soldiers to, 181; mentioned, 23, 150, 180

San Fernando de Béjar, Villa de: council of, 20, 20–21; supports Apache mission plan, 27; mentioned, 10, 189. SEE ALSO San Antonio

San Francisco de los Neches, Mission: establishment of, 9

San Francisco de los Tejas, Mission: founding and abandonment of, 8; mentioned, 9

San Francisco Xavier de Horcasitas, Mission: establishment of, 35; reestablished on Guadalupe, 35; mentioned, 204. SEE ALSO Guadalupe missions; San Xavier missions

San Gabriel missions. SEE San Xavier missions

San Gabriel River. SEE San Xavier River

San Ildefonso, Mission: establishment of, 32. SEE ALSO San Xavier missions

San José, Valle de: Apaches promise to congregate in, 157; presidio at, urged, 160, 161; mission San Lorenzo in, 179; mentioned, 180. SEE ALSO El Cañon missions

San José de Aguayo, Mission: establishment of, 10. SEE ALSO San Antonio

San José de los Nazonis, Mission: founding of, 9. SEE ALSO East Texas missions

San José missions. SEE El Cañon missions

San Juan Bautista, presidio of. SEE Río Grande, Presidio del

San Juan Bautista settlement: French trader at, 9; and line of Spanish outposts, 19, 31, 153; and mission sites, 40, 157; mentioned, 39, 43, 126, 149, 156, 190. SEE ALSO Río Grande settlements

San Juan Capistrano: 95

San Lorenzo, Mission (Coahuila): fate of, 23; and Father Terreros, 23, 40

San Lorenzo de la Santa Cruz, Mission: founding of, 157–158; attacks on, 164; conditions at, 167–168; guard at, 168; presidio settlement moved to, 179. SEE ALSO El Cañon missions

San Luis de las Amarillas, Presidio de. SEE San Sabá Presidio

San Luis Potosí: and Hidalgo insurrection, 182–183; Rábago's death in, 181; mentioned, 124, 179

San Marcos, Texas: 35

San Marcos River: and San Xavier Mission and Presidio: 30, 33, 35, 44, 95; San Sabá group at, 48; and San Sabá Mission and Presidio, 97, 106–107; Apaches move to, 105; mentioned, 43, 55, 56

Index

San Miguel de Linares, Mission: founding of, 9; attack at, 9–10

San Saba, Texas: 16 n.

San Saba County: 16 n.

San Sabá de la Santa Cruz, Mission. SEE San Sabá Mission

San Sabá massacre: factors contributing to, 11; and rumor of attack, 68; warning of attack, 72; missionaries refuse to leave Mission, 69–70; guard at Mission, 70 and n.; activities before attack, 72; inaction to Indian threat, 75; and appeasement attempts, 76–77; survivors of, in Church, 78; defensive action during, 78; messenger sent to Presidio, 79; survivors escape from Mission, 82; survivors report, in San Antonio, 82–83; viewing of scene of, 87–88 and n.; condition of mission after, 87–88 and n.; fatalities in, 77, 88 and n.; significance of, 101, 132; and future missionary efforts, 102; effects of, 102; Parrilla's reasons for, 105; French influence in, 112; spoils from, 113, 119, 125; and religious-military conflict, 192; mentioned, 159, 174

—, Indians in: stampede of horses by, 68; and tribes attacking, 69, 73, 102; and mission Indians, 70, 80, 82, 90; declaration of peace by, 73; ford crossed by, 73 n.; weapons of, 75, 79, 104, 132; and gifts for, 75; plunder by, 76, 78; leave for Presidio, 76; take note to Parrilla, 76, 77 and n.; burning of Mission, 77–78; attack of scouting party, 80; number attacking, 80, 101, 104, 132; baiting of soldiers by, 81, 85, 86; number killed, 84 and n.; withdrawal of, from Presidio, 86; reasons for success of, 101–102

— and Presidio garrison: location of soldiers, 70–71; and scouting mission, 80, 81, 82; size of, at attack, 81, 85; and warning supply train, 81; and messengers to San Antonio, 82, 90; reported under attack, 83; reinforcement of, 86, 90, 93; preparations of, for defense, 87; anxiety of inhabitants after, 90; conditions at, after attack, 93–94. SEE ALSO Parrilla, Diego Ortiz; Santiesteban, Father José de; Terreros, Father Alonso Giraldo de

San Sabá Mine, legend of: and San Sabá mineral deposits, 19, 26, 27, 106 and n.; and settlement, 27, 29, 203; and Parrilla smelter, 106 n.; existence of, 198; and Norton and Wenonah, 202–203; basis for, 203; exploration of, 203; and Solms-Braunfels, 204–205; and Meusebach's party, 206–207; and Roemer, 209. SEE ALSO Los Almagres Mine

San Sabá Mission: and Father Hidalgo, 3; establishment of, 5, 6, 113, 157; and French threat, 6, 113, 192; expeditions influencing founding of, 12–13; and expeditions against Apaches, 16; correct name of, 16 n.; and Father Santa Ana, 17; Father Terreros as head of, 39; factions in San Sabá group, 48–49, 54; building of, 54; Apache promises to join, 58; officials' attitude toward, 61–62; weather at, 64; number of persons at, 70; location of cemetery of, 89; re-establishment of, 98, 134–135; 196; effect of Parrilla campaign on, 110

—, failure of: and Rábago, 31; and Parrilla, 39; reasons for, 53, 61, 183

—, missionaries of: 43–44, 65; attitude toward Apaches, 53; and Parrilla, 53–54; despondency of, 55–56, 57; remaining, 59, 60; ask return to Mexico, 59; factionalism among, 60; appointed after massacre, 98, 156

—, site of: reasons for, 6, 21–22, 54; and San Clemente site, 7; selection of, 43; inspection of, 47, 54; effect of, 54; mentioned, 19, 23, 28, 149. SEE ALSO Apaches; Terreros, Father Alonso Giraldo de; San Sabá massacre; San Sabá Presidio; San Sabá project

San Sabá Presidio: and French threat, 6–7, 113; name of, 16 n.;

and Father Santa Ana, 17; and Los Almagres Mine, 28; appointment of commander plan, 49; construction of, 54, 169–170; life of persons at, 64; reinforcement of, 90–93 *passim*, 92 and n., 115, 116, 116 n., 128, 136, 155, 171; effects of weather at, 91; and continuation of, 107, 136, 141–142; Indian attacks on, 110, 114–116 *passim*, 160–161, 164, 165–166, 176–177; as largest presidio, 130; fortifications of, 131; importance of, 151; as Real Presidio de San Sabá, 155; function of, 161; as buffer, 162, 163, 170, 171, 211; Rubí's instructions concerning, 167; number at, 169; expense of, 169; location of, 169, 170; physical destruction of, 170, 183, 212; and abandonment of, 172, 182, 183; morale at, 177, 178; epidemic at, 178, 179–180; as San Vincente Presidio, 182 and n.; supply problem at, 183; cultivation at, 208

— after abandonment: as Ugalde headquarters, 188; Menchaca at, 190; and expeditions into Texas, 193; and Amangual expedition, 196–198 *passim*; re-establishment of, proposed, 199, 200, 210; Cós at, 201; Bowie at, 201; inscription on gatepost of, 203; Moore at, 204; description of, 207–208; Muesebach party at, 207–208; Whiting party at, 207–208; rebuilding of, 209–211; settlers use of, 211–212, 211 n.

—, conditions at: after massacre attack, 93–94; after attack on livestock, 116; upon Rábago's arrival, 150–151; and Rubí's inspection of, 168–169; in 1768, 178, 179

—, garrison of: sources of, 37, 38; instructions for recruiting, 38; desertion from, 105, 168; in Parrilla campaign force, 118; and soldiers' duties, 150–151; and El Cañon missions, 158, 168, 181; transferred to San Antonio and San Vincente, 182

—, transfer of: to Llano River, proposed, 59, 198; soldiers petition for, 95–96; to San Marcos River, proposed, 106–107; to Guadalupe River, proposed, 106–107; to San José valley, proposed, 161; advocated, 162, 171; to San Lorenzo Mission, 179; men of, to San Antonio, 182; men of, to San Vincente, 182. SEE ALSO Rábago y Terán, Felipe; Rubí, Marqués de; Parrilla, Diego Ortiz; San Sabá massacre; San Sabá Mission; San Sabá project

San Sabá project: significance of, 22; Father Arnada's plan for, 26; Father Dolores' plan for, 26, 41, 45; and San Antonio Presidio, 26; San Fernando villagers support, 27; approval for, 35; referred to Junta, 37; and jurisdiction question, 38, 147, 153, 159–160, 183; Terreros' plan for, 41, 65–66; abandonment of, 53–54, 55; continuation of, 61–62; Parrilla's plan for, 65–66; original objectives of, 103; Rubí's suggestions for, 173; precipitates Indian trouble, 187. SEE ALSO San Sabá Mission; San Sabá Presidio

San Sabá region: settlement of, 27, 29, 203, 204–206, 209–210, 211–212; Parrilla expedition to, 47, 50; location of, and New Mexico, 153–154. SEE ALSO expeditions (to explore); San Sabá Mine, legend of; San Sabá River

San Sabá River: discovery of, 5, 13; Bustillo expedition at, 13; name of, 13 and n.; and T. Urrutia expedition, 16; and J. Urrutia, 15; as mission site, 21–22, 25, 54; and Rábago expedition, 26; and San Xavier garrison, 43; inspection of, 48, 49–50, 168; Canyon, and Comanche rendezvous, 190; Amangual camp on, 196–197; and Muesebach-Comanche council, 206; mentioned, 8, 13, 18, 53. SEE ALSO San Sabá Mine, legend of

Santa Ana, Father Benito Fernández: opposes J. Urrutia's expedition, 15; attitude of, toward Apaches, 15–16, 17; and San Sabá Mission and Presidio, 17; Indian

Index

policy of, 18, 19–20; advocates exploration, 19; mission plan of, 20; supports San Sabá plan, 26; advocates San Xavier Mission, 32; mentioned, 23

Santa Ana de Cumargo, Presidio de: 44

Santa Anna, Antonio López de: 201

Santa Brígida Mine: 40

Santa Cruz de San Sabá Mission. SEE San Sabá Mission

Santa Fé, New Mexico: Mallet brothers at, 22; French penetration to, 112; location of, as outpost, 173; and Spanish frontier line, 193; routes to, 196; reached by Amangual, 198; mentioned, 11, 23, 153, 167

Santa Rosa del Sacramento, Presidio de: and San Sabá relief, 92; Rábago's misconduct at, 34, 149; mentioned, 70, 106, 167

Santiesteban, Father: at San Lorenzo Mission, 167–168; transfer of, 182

Santiesteban, Father José de: as San Sabá missionary, 43, 60, 65; in San Sabá massacre, 72, 73, 77, 86–87 and n., 88, 98

Santísimo Nombre de María, Mission: building of, abandonment of, 8

Santos, José de los: and San Sabá massacre, 82, 84; mentioned, 70

San Vicente Presidio: location of, 182 and n.; ambush at, 182; visitors at ruins of, 182 n.; garrison of, and Hidalgo insurrection, 182–183

San Xavier de Gigedo, Presidio de: Felipe Rábago at, 26, 27, 31, 33–34, 148; garrison of, transferred to San Sabá, 30, 35, 36, 37, 38; authorization for, 33; removal of, to San Marcos, 35; and soldiers' conditions at San Marcos, 44. SEE ALSO San Xavier missions; San Xavier project

San Xavier missions: location of, 13; establishment of, 32; attacks on, 32; and Galván, 32–33; and Barrios, 32, 33; and Rábago affair, 31, 33–34, 137; suffering in, 33, 34; transfer of, to San Marcos, 35, 97; and move to San Sabá, 35; transfer of property of, 37, 38, 41, 65, 94; mentioned, 21, 25, 40, 96–97, 148–149

—, missionaries of: dispute of, with Barrios, 32; and Galván, 32–33; and Rábago, 32–34; request to be recalled, 33

—, Indians of: and San Sabá attack, 31, 69, 75; soldiers' treatment of, 32, 33; and Rábago affair, 34; relocation of, 44. SEE ALSO Guadalupe missions; San Francisco Xavier de Horcasitas, Mission; San Ildefonso, Mission; San Xavier de Gigedo, Presidio de; San Xavier project; San Xavier River

San Xavier project: decline of, 27; relationship of, to San Sabá, 30–31; dissolution of, 32. SEE ALSO San Xavier de Gigedo, Presidio de; San Xavier missions

San Xavier River: Bustillo expedition reaches, 13; missions founded on, 30; Tonkawa on, 32; presidio at, proposed, 200

Sayopín nation: 34

Schleicher County, Texas: 151

Schmitz (Meusebach's servant): 207

Schubert (Dr.): 205

Serra, Father Junipero: 98

Seven Years War: implications of, for Texas, 160

Shackelford County, Texas: 119

Shaw, Jim: 206

Shawnee Indians: 207

Sierra, Pedro de: 164

Silva, Father Francisco Xavier: 21

Silver Creek: 202

Simpson, Lesley Byrd: on military-religious conflict, 46, 142; description of San Sabá Presidio by, 54; on San Sabá Mission guard, 70 n.; on overlapping authorities, 94; and Parrilla retreat, 127

Sinaloa: Parrilla as governor of, 38–39

Smith, Tull: and Menard, Texas, 211

Solms-Braunfels, Prince Carl von: and miners colony settlement, 204-205
Sonora: Parrilla in, 38-39, 46, 105, 106
Sordo, Francisco el: 126
Spanish, the: period of glory of, 5; decline of, 6; wealth from New World, 6; towns of, 1574, 6; population of, in North America, 1574, 6; line of settlement of, 19; gullibility of, 53, 183; attitude of, toward Americans, 193; and Pike's expedition, 196. SEE ALSO explorations (expeditions); presidios; viceregal government
—, and, the French: French trade, 23; Natchitoches settlement, 37; check on, 112; mistrust of French, 114; fear of French, 130, 132; allies in Seven Years War, 160; cession of Louisiana, 193. SEE ALSO French, the
—, frontier expansion of: northwest of San Antonio, 19; and San Sabá site, 22; and cost of Texas colonization, 31-32; place of missions in, 42; and Apache's northern expedition, 57; factors in failure of, 61; reasons for end of, 101-102; effects of Apache alliance on, 102; and Indian hostility, 132, 174; and new frontier situation, 136; line of, and Great Plains, 151; and line of outposts, 154; and El Cañon missions, 159; and withdrawal policy, 160, 174, 183, 187; reasons for abandonment of, 174; and frontier inspection, 167; and frontier line, 173, 174-175, 193-194
—, Indian policy of: retaliation, 3; relations with Indians, 6; early missionary activity, 10; effects of, 10; and naïveté in Indian affairs, 11; treatment of Apache captives, 12, 15; change in, urged, 15, 18, 141; of Father Santa Ana, 18; of Father Vergara, 18; attitude toward Apaches, 23; alliance with Apaches, 31, 34, 97, 102, 133; purpose of missions, 42; peaceful relations with Indians, 47; responsibility for Indians' power, 132; Indians' peace overtures, 140-141; alliance with northern tribes, 187-188; attempt in conciliation, 188, 193. SEE ALSO Apaches; Comanches; missions
Spanish Armada: defeat of, 6
Stamp Act: 176

Tancagues: attack by, 69. SEE ALSO Tonkawas
Taos: 23
Taovayas: Spanish campaign against, 109; and attack on Spanish, 113-114; and San Sabá Presidio raid, 160-161; French encourage harassment by, 160-161; and trade with English, 188; Vial among, 196; mentioned, 125 n., 134, 140, 177, 199
— and Parrilla attack: 120-122; fortifications of, 120, 125, 131. SEE ALSO Red River, Parrilla, Wichitas
Tehuacanas: and campaign against northern tribes, 109, 113; and attacks on Spanish, 113, 115; and San Sabá spoils, 113; in Taovayas village battle, 121; report French establishments, 159; peace offer of, 176-177; French encourage harassment by, 177; in battle against Apaches, 189; Spanish gifts to, 193; as hostile tribe, 199; attack Bowie party, 201
Tejas Indians: mission settlement among, 8; and Spanish-Apache alliance, 10; and Bustillo expedition, 13; and the Apaches, 55; and San Sabá attack, 73, 102; and attack of settlements, 115; mentioned, 77, 176. SEE ALSO Hasinai Confederacy
Terreros, Father Alonso Giraldo de: founds Coahuila mission, 23, 40; background of, 39-40; mission plan of, 40; and Guadalupe mission support, 44-45; faction of, with Father Trinidad, 45; concern of, with costs, 47, 48; on San Marcos move, 48; and Father Dolores' patent, 64-65; mentioned, 16 n., 41, 54, 61

— and Parrilla: clash with, 39; and Parrilla's delay, 47; on Parrilla's inspection, 56; attitude toward, 58
— and San Sabá: accepts directorship of, 40; on Apaches at, 47, 67; misgiving of, concerning, 47–48; requests laborers for, 47; attitude of, toward, 56; on situation at, 56, 57, 66–67; remains at, 59, 60, 65; on his suffering at, 64; plan of, for, 65, 67; on livestock at, 66; on his intentions concerning, 66; his obsession with death at, 66; on leaving mission, 69–70; and massacre at, 72, 73, 75, 76, 77, 87, 88, 98
Terreros, Pedro Romero de: background of, 40–41; philanthropy of, 41; receives title, 41; request to, for laborers, 49; reward from King for, 62; mentioned, 44, 62–63, 88, 103, 108
— and Apache missions, sponsorship of: mission plan of, 40; financial agreement for, 41, 98; and Guadalupe mission, 44; concern for expense to, 47, 48, 60, 63
Texas: French penetration of, 6–7; capital of, 10, 38, 173, 183; and San Sabá jurisdiction, 38, 147, 159; Comanches in, 102–103; and Louisiana cession, 160; inspection of outposts of, 167; and Spanish frontier line, 193; expeditions into, 193; colonizing in, 201, 204–205; Indian troubles of, 204; independence of, from Mexico, 204; annexation of, 205, 210; and war with Mexico, and Comanches, 206; Indian raids on Mexican boundary of, 210; and search for trails across, 210; mentioned, 151, 188, 201–202. SEE ALSO East Texas; West Texas
—, governor of: and San Sabá assistance, 93; and Indian campaign council, 107. SEE ALSO Barrios y Jauregui, Jacinto de; Barrio y Espriella, Pedro del; Bustillo y Cabellos, Juan Antonio; Cabello, Domingo; Henderson, J. Pinckney; Martos y Navarrete, Angel de; Muñoz, Manuel; Oconor,

Hugo; Pacheco, Rafael Martínez; Salcedo, Manuel de
Tlaxcalteca: as instructors of neophytes, 43; in San Sabá group, 48, 49; at San Sabá Mission, 70 n.
Tom Green County, Texas: 151
Tonkawas: and attack of Spanish, 73, 102, 114, 190; and Comanches, 103; ambush of Apaches by, 108; Spanish campaigns against, 109, 127–128; French encourage harassment by, 177; Spanish gifts to, 193; mentioned, 130, 199
— and Parrilla attack: 119; and location of Wichitas, 120; as prisoners, 124, 137. SEE ALSO Yojuanes
Tortuga River: 200
treaty of Guadalupe Hidalgo: 210, 211
Trinidad, Father Santísima: on Parrilla, 48–49, 58; and factions, 45, 48–49; on visit of Apaches, 57–58; remains at San Sabá, 60; mentioned, 44, 65
Trinity River: French settlement on, 111; mission and presidio on, 112; presidio on, proposed, 200; mentioned, 32, 188
Trujillo, Joseph: and San Sabá massacre, 82, 90, 93

Ugalde, Juan de: campaign of, against Apaches, 188–189; at San Sabá Presidio, 195
Ugarte y Loyola, Jacobo de: 181
United States: effect of, on Spanish territory, 193–194; and war with Mexico, 210; and Mexican boundary raids, 210. SEE ALSO Americans; U.S. Army
U.S. Army: fort of, near San Sabá, 162; searches for trails, 210; purposes of outposts of, 211; mentioned, 196
University of Bonn: 209
University of Breslau: 209
University of Salamanca: 40
Upton County, Texas: 151
Uraga, Carlos de: and San Sabá attack, 68–69
Urrutia, José de: expedition of, against Apaches, 15, 18

Urrutia, Toribio de: expedition of, against Apaches, 16; and Apache captives, 16, 19; and peace treaty with Apaches, 19; investigation of Apache behavior by, 21; on number of Apaches, 27
— and San Sabá attack: reports to, on, 83, 91; and aid to Presidio, 90, 91, 92, 94; assumes Presidio fallen, 92; on foreign influence in, 92
Uvalde, Texas: origin of name of, 189

Valcárcel, Domingo: on aid to Texas missions, 93; on San Sabá project, 161–162
Valdés, Joaquín: in San Sabá massacre, 82
Váldez, Manuel: and Rábago, 149; mentioned, 157, 158
Valle de San José. SEE San José, Valle de
Varela, Father Benito: searches for Indians, 54–55; returns to Querétaro, 59
Vásquez, Joseph: and San Sabá massacre, 80 and n., 82, 83–84 and n., 88
Veléz Cachupín, Tomás: on French among Indians, 140; and route to San Sabá, 153
Vera Cruz: Parrilla in garrison of, 38
Vergara, Father Gabriel: in Bustillo expedition, 13; Indian policy of, 13, 15, 18
Vial, Pierre: and route to New Mexico, 196; and reconstruction of San Sabá, 196
viceregal government: and Apache mission decision, 21; orders exploration of Apachería, 25; and San Sabá plan, 35–38; and continuation of San Sabá project, 61–62, 97–98; on Urrutia's appeal for help, 93; on Parrilla's proposals, 107; approves Indian campaign, 107; reaction of, after Parrilla defeat, 130; inaction of, under Cruillas, 141; on Rábago's campaign request, 166. SEE ALSO Spanish, the; viceroy
viceroy. SEE Amarillas, Marqués de las; Croix, Marqués de; Cruillas, Marqués de; Laguna, Marqués de la; Gálvez, Bernardo de; Revilla Gigedo, Conde de
Villa, Pancho: 182 n.
Villa de Guerro, Coahuila: 9
Villa de San Fernando de Austria. SEE San Fernando de Austria, Villa de
Villa de San Fernando de Béjar. SEE San Fernando de Béjar, Villa de
Villareal, Andrés de: and San Sabá massacre, 76, 79, 82, 88 n.; mentioned, 70

Waco Indians: attack Bowie party, 201
Ward County, Texas: 151
Watling's Island: 5
Webb, Walter Prescott: on Indians and Spanish expansion, 103, 132, 174; on Rábago exploration, 151
Weches, Texas: 8
Wenonah, Martha ("Princess"): and McCaslin grave, 202; and search for lost mine, 202–203
West Texas: search for trail across, 210
Whiting, Wm. Henry Chase: 210
Wichitas: and Apaches, 11–12, 24, 189; Spanish campaign against, 109; and French, 112, 131–132; and attack on Spanish, 114, 115; subtribe of, 125 n.; and Spanish expansion, 132. SEE ALSO Iscanis, Jumanos, Taovayos
Wilkinson, James: 196
Worth, W. J.: 210
Wyoming: 11

Yaceales: and Parrilla campaign, 121
Yojuanes: attack by, 69; lead Spanish into trap, 126. SEE ALSO Tonkawa
Yreugas, Francisco: report of, on Indians, 68; and San Sabá massacre, 86, 87, 88; mentioned, 95
Yucatán: 8

Zacatecas mines: 149
Zoquiné (Comanche chief): and re-establishment of San Sabá, 196

www.ingramcontent.com/pod-product-compliance
Lightning Source LLC
Chambersburg PA
CBHW031241290426
44109CB00012B/384